The Maternal is Political

NANCY PELOSI

BENAZIR BHUTTO

MARION WINIK

BARBARA KINGSOLVER

REBECCA WALKER

GAYLE BRANDEIS

ANNE LAMOTT

SUSIE BRIGHT

CINDY SHEEHAN

ANNA QUINDLEN

Women Writers at the Intersection of Motherhood & Social Change

edited by **SHARI MACDONALD STRONG**

with a foreword by **KRISTIN ROWE-FINKBEINER**

THE MATERNAL IS POLITICAL

The Maternal is Political

Women Writers
at the Intersection
of Motherhood
and Social Change

EDITED BY SHARI MACDONALD STRONG

SEAL PRESS

The Maternal is Political
Women Writers at the Intersection of Motherhood and Social Change

Copyright © 2008 by Shari MacDonald Strong

Published by
Seal Press
A Member of Perseus Books Group
1700 Fourth Street
Berkeley, California

Library of Congress Cataloging-in-Publication Data

The maternal is political : women writers at the intersection of motherhood and social change / edited by Shari MacDonald Strong.

    p. cm.

  ISBN-13: 978-1-58005-243-6

  ISBN-10: 1-58005-243-6

1. Motherhood--History. 2. Motherhood--Political aspects. 3. Social action. 4. Women and literature. 5. Motherhood in literature. I. Strong, Shari MacDonald.

  HQ759.M3732 2008

  306.874'3--dc22

              2008005310

Cover design by Kate Bassart, Union Pageworks
Interior design by Megan Cooney
Printed in the United States of America
Distributed by Publishers Group West

For my children, of course.

CONTENTS

TEACH

ACT

The hand that rocks the cradle
Is the hand that rules the world.

—*William Ross Wallace*

FOREWORD

by Kristin Rowe-Finkbeiner

IN THIS TIME OF DIVIDE-AND-CONQUER politics, I can say with absolute certainty that we all have one thing in common: mothers. And that one thing in common has some work to do: work we must do together.

It's time to start talking. It's time to start sharing. Stories. Hardships. Successes. Dreams. There are patterns in our stories, in our lives, and those patterns tell a tale of continued inequality for women in the United States. Yes, even though it's commonly assumed that the fight for equality is over and women won, this is far from the truth in the United States—and it's farthest from the truth with motherhood.

Most Americans are not aware that there is profound bias against mothers in hiring and wages (one study found that women without children make 90 cents to a man's dollar, mothers make 73 cents to a man's dollar, and single mothers make the least, at about 60 cents to a dollar). Even fewer know that the majority of other countries have significantly better family-friendly policies and programs than we do—policies that are taken as a given and are shown to decrease the maternal wage hit.

For example, there are only four countries in the world that don't offer some form of paid leave for new mothers: Swaziland, Liberia, Papua New Guinea, and the United States. We are the only industrialized nation without some form of universal healthcare (and even though we spend more per capita than any other nation on healthcare, we have some of the worst health outcomes, ranking a low thirty-seventh of all nations in childhood mortality, according to the World Health Organization). And, of the top twenty economies, we are the only country without a guaranteed minimum of paid sick days. We are far behind.

But watch out. We mothers pack a powerful (and largely untapped) political punch—particularly when we work together. A full 82 percent of American women have children by the time they are forty-four years old, and women make up 54 percent of the voting electorate. And we all do need to work together because the fact that the United States is woefully behind the rest of the world with respect to family-friendly policies and programs has dramatic implications, and not just for mothers. The repercussions of this are far reaching for women, for children, for families, and for our nation:

- A full quarter of families with children under six years old live in poverty.
- More than nine million children are without any health-care coverage at all.
- Forty thousand kindergartners are home alone each day after school.
- Having a baby is a leading cause of "poverty spells" in our country—a time when income dips below what's needed for basic living expenses, like food and rent.

These economic impacts are also intertwined with a motherhood wage penalty, in the form of a very tall maternal wall. Right now, even though 58 percent of current college graduates are women, that maternal wall is standing in the way of women's ever getting to the glass ceiling. Motherhood is a time when many women first fully experience the barriers that impede their economic security and options for leadership roles.

In fact, a 2007 article in the *American Journal of Sociology* reported that mothers are 79 percent less likely to be hired than non-mothers with equal resumes and job experiences. Mothers also face steep wage hits. A Cornell University study recently found that mothers were offered $11,000 per year *lower* starting pay than nonmothers with the same resume for highly paid jobs, while fathers were offered $6,000 *more* in starting pay. This study also found that mothers were treated more harshly for fewer late days than nonmothers.

These statistics begin to explain why so many women and children are living in poverty, and why so few women are in leadership positions. But we can solve this. Countries with family-friendly policies in place—like paid family leave and subsidized childcare—don't have wage gaps as wide as we do in America. We know exactly how to fix this problem.

The central issue here is that times have changed and women, mothers, have entered the workforce in record numbers. Women are in the workforce to stay, but our policies and our programs haven't caught up with modern realities.

There are relatively new statistical trends being played out each day with modern families: In more than half of all couples with children, both are now in the workforce, and three-quarters of mothers are currently in the labor force.

It's harder and harder for families to live on one income—in fact, families with one full-time parent are seven times more likely to live in poverty than those with two parents in the labor force. This is quite different than even a generation ago, when far fewer women were employed and far more families had a full-time parent.

It's time to catch up. It's time to break down the maternal wall to help women and families by passing policies like paid family leave, healthcare for all, access to affordable childcare, paid sick days, fair wages, and flexible work options.

The first step is consciousness raising, between and among women, that the issues we face are shared. That when this many people are having the same problem at the same time, we have a societal structural problem that needs to be fixed, and not an epidemic of personal failings, as is commonly reported in the media.

Sharing stories helps lift the stigma of dealing with these issues by uncovering the truth that a personal issue is truly a shared issue with a path toward a solution. Bringing the stories of real modern mothers out in the open between women, and to the media, expands the dialogue and empowers women to move toward the personal becoming the political. Because, after all, the personal truly is the political when those issues—those same stories—are shared by the majority of women in our nation.

Our challenge is that the time when women become mothers and face harsh economic discrimination is often the busiest in their lives, leaving little time for advocacy, story sharing, or public engagement. This makes story sharing all the more important. Through story sharing, mothers in the United States learn that the issues they face aren't their "fault," as is commonly positioned in the media, but rather is a result of our nation's not stepping up to the plate with a structure of family support, as most other nations have done. Not only is that the right thing to do, but children are quite literally the economic engine of our future, so it is also the smart thing to do economically.

So turn the page; read on for the essays and stories of change, of life, and of dreams. Watch the personal become political as the stories form a pattern of shared need. Then take the next step and work for a peaceful revolution of the way we support families in America.

Kristin Rowe-Finkbeiner
Author of The Motherhood Manifesto,
co-founder of MomsRising.org

INTRODUCTION

by Shari MacDonald Strong

AS A TEENAGE GIRL GROWING UP in the '80s, I was a *Family Ties/* Alex Keaton–type Republican. In the 1990s, I struck out for more neutral territory as an Independent. By 2001, I was a card-carrying Democrat with Green-leaning tendencies. These days, I'm something greater than all these put together.

I am a Mother.

By "greater," I don't mean "better" in a condescending, you'd-understand-if-you-had-children sort of way. I mean that since becoming a parent, I've tapped into something more primal, more global, more far-reaching and intuitive, than a political loyalty. Yes, I (usually) identify with a particular party, but I'll back any politician, any bill or measure, that I believe to be in the best interests of the children. My kids. Iraqi kids. Sudanese kids. Your kids. There was a time when I let other people decide the issues and tell me what to support, who to put my faith in, how to live my life. Not anymore—not by a long shot. Today I'm a woman with a mind of her own. A new revolutionary, if you will. You may be one, too.

Call us members of the Mothering Party.

In the summer of 1992, I was working as an advertising manager at an organization with deep conservative roots. At the time, I didn't yet realize that I was a progressive; I just knew that I was different from the other people at my workplace—and the novelty of that realization amused me. Around the time I started getting strongly worded memos from coworkers, intimating how all good citizens would cast their ballots in the upcoming election, I announced that I would be voting for Ross Perot.

"What?" They gaped at me as if I'd suggested John Hinckley as a write-in candidate. "WHAT?"

Ha! I snickered. I didn't really care whom I voted for. The guy with the big pitcher ears was as good a candidate as any—and even if I didn't vote for him, what fun there was in watching people's faces when I told them that I would! What was it to me? I knew nothing about politics, really. I doubted that my vote would make a difference either way. I'd voted for the first time when I was eighteen, passionately—and easily two-thirds of the measures I supported went the opposite way; it took weeks to get past the frustration and disappointment. By the 1992 election, I had already decided that one vote—*my* vote—didn't matter.

I was twenty-five years old at the time. I was still underestimating my power as a voter.

I was still underestimating my power as a woman.

I wasn't alone. Eight years later (and, presumably, with the benefit of eight more years of collective political and social enlightenment), close to nineteen million young women between the ages of eighteen and twenty-four neglected to vote in the 2000 presidential election.

Considering that U.S. women have been legally voting since 1920, it's astonishing that (a) more women aren't voting, and (b) more weight isn't given to women's priorities. Of particular note is society's failure to take seriously the voices of mothers: those of us who arguably care most about the children who hold this country's future in their hands.

There are, of course, exceptions to this oversight. In the United States, the 1992 and 1996 presidential elections launched the high-level wooing of middle- to upper-class "soccer moms." In the months leading up to the 2004 elections, much was made of the power wielded by an emerging, vaguely defined voting group known as "security moms." The problem is that the "security mom" moniker is an artificial construct, invented by marketers intending to label, influence, and claim a particular segment of the general population— one whose members may or may not have aligned with a particular voting pattern before being told that they should. Moreover, those numbers are representative only to the degree that so-called "security moms" cast their ballots as predicted.

If one defines "security" as children's well-being and survival, then I too am a "security mom." I don't own a gun, don't believe in preemptive war. Still, nothing matters more to me than my children's welfare. I long for leaders who will do everything possible to keep my children safe (and in the process not make them more of a target than they were before). In short, I care deeply about security, just as I care deeply about poverty, healthcare, and education. I care about the economic welfare of women and children. I care about peace, and about fair trade policies and practices; about how we're treating the planet and how we're treating each other. I believe our government has the responsibility to provide medical care to all children, period. Clearly, this issue of *safety* is multilayered, complex, and multifaceted; it isn't simply a matter of national security. I'm fairly certain there are other "security moms" out there who agree. *Poof.* Goodbye, "security mom" construct. *Poof.* Goodbye, vote predictability. It's hard for the media to take seriously a "group" whose behaviors they can't predict—or turn into soundbites.

The truth is, "security moms" and "soccer moms" are just labels. The proof is in the pudding, as they say, and damn if moms don't know from pudding. The media can call us what they want. Or they can ignore us altogether. But they can't silence us. They can't disempower us. Nor can they *em*power us. That's something we have to do for ourselves—both in and outside of the voting booth—and we've got the best reason on the planet to do it: those demanding, delicious little people who call us Mom. As in "Mommy, where's the milk?" "Mama, can you come wipe my bottom?" As in "Mom, why do I have to register for the draft?" and "Momma, will I be able to go to college someday?" When it comes to ensuring our children's safety, well-being, future—"Mom" is the bottom line.

For centuries, women have been fighting to claim our voices and digging deep for the courage to use them. There's never been a more critical time, or a more vital reason, to speak, to act, to move forward. The group Mothers Acting Up says it best: "Let us whisper this to each other, sing it out in the streets, yell it from our rooftops, declare it in our houses of government: we will protect our children with our personal and political strength, wherever they live on earth!"

Why?

Because we're mothers.

Shortly before the 2004 elections, syndicated columnist Michelle Malkin quoted conservative activist Kay R. Daly as saying: "Hell hath no fury like a momma protecting her babies." We mothers can and do disagree with one another—at the playground, at our playgroups, at our kids' schools—about what that looks like in practice. But God forbid that we forget we're in this together, that the future of the children who grew in our collective wombs now rests, largely, in our collective hands.

Elections come. Elections go. With each one come the inevitable bumper stickers: VOTE REPUBLICAN. VOTE DEMOCRAT. I'm looking for one that reflects where I'm really at, whose instructions—if followed—would make a measurable difference in this world. Would bring us that much closer to those Miss America goals of ending global hunger and achieving world peace: for ourselves and for our children. Say it with me. Better yet, let's *do* it together, and let's urge everyone we know—regardless of gender, parent or child-free—to do the same:

Vote Mother.

In *The F Word: Feminism in Jeopardy,* Kristin Rowe-Finkbeiner says of those who were qualified to vote in the year 2000: "Too few of these young women vote." That's nineteen million votes left uncast—by a group that (interestingly enough) will be, very soon, our next generation of mothers. A demographic that consisted not so long ago of—well . . . *us.*

Not only do too few young women vote, but one could also argue that too few mothers vote. (In light of our collective power, anything less than a 100 percent turnout by the more than eighty million moms in the United States, for example, could rightly be called too few.) But, of course, the problem is bigger than that. The problem is not just a failure to vote. It's also our hesitation (frequently inspired—it's true—by exhaustion) to stand up, speak out, and rock the boat even as we're rocking the cradle. It's our failure to recognize, celebrate, and effectively seize the vast power inherent in the mothering role: power that we wield whenever we shop, whenever we speak, whenever we choose to take (or not to take) a stand.

I realize I'm opening a can of worms. Mothers carry a heavy enough burden without being told we need to do more in the political realm. Some days, it's all we can do just to survive. If that's where you're at—well, bless you. You're not alone. When the house is a veritable disaster zone, when you're trying to burp the baby and stock the cupboards and find time to pay the bills and pick up one kid from a playdate before driving across town to the other one's band concert—really, who's got the time to worry about immigration and national healthcare and fluorocarbons and Gitmo and the future of *Roe v. Wade?* Some days, it's just easier to block it all out, to curl up with a pint of Ben & Jerry's (or it would be if someone else in your house hadn't gotten to it first), and curl up to watch *American Idol* while hoping somebody else will step up and fix things.

Except no one else has stepped up. *No one else is going to do it.* If we truly want to leave our children a world that's worth living in, we moms are going to have to fix it ourselves. I'm reminded of a documentary I saw several years ago about female leaders in developing countries. One woman from a war-torn nation said something to the effect of: "If women were the ones who came to the table to negotiate peace, none of us would leave until an agreement had been reached—because we know that women and children are the ones who will suffer the consequences if we don't."

One woman alone can't do everything—can't stop the war, for example. We learned this by watching Cindy Sheehan, the activist mother who set up camp outside of George W. Bush's Crawford, Texas, ranch in an attempt to force him to meet with her to discuss her soldier son's death in Iraq. Though Cindy triggered a powerful surge in the peace movement, she couldn't end the war. But could any administration stand up to *all* the mothers? Could we turn things around, could the trajectory of our nation shift, if all the mothers looked around us and said: Enough!

In the 1960s, Martin Luther King Jr. had a dream. Later, John Lennon had a dream. We all have dreams, and here is mine: that one day, all mothers will use our political power and voices not the way that the media and patriarchy and our husbands, pastors, fathers, and political leaders direct, but rather as we're led by our personal wisdom, our deepest intuition, our maternal instincts. I dream of a day when the image of a woman with child in tow is the first one that comes to mind when people hear the word "activist." I envision a country in which voters' primary concerns revolve not around oil and money, but around the issues facing families and children. I imagine what it will be like when the most active political groups in the world are not those obsessed with winning a war, but those determined to win the peace. I picture a day when the driving force behind politics in my country is not power or money, but maternal love.

How many years will pass before people will be saying, "It's been only ____ years since mothers forced the country to adopt a stronger healthcare policy, since moms put the brakes on U.S. empire building, since our country made the protection of children internationally an integral part of every facet of foreign policy"? Truth is, mothers have been influencing politics and effecting social change since the beginning of time—we just rarely get credit for it. Not that we care about credit. We all just want to make sure that our kids are okay.

And there's hope that mothers are truly waking up, that somehow we'll find a way to do it. Back when the new millennium dawned, I was the last person anyone would have thought would organize a project of this sort. Seven years ago, I was so apolitical, I didn't even vote. I didn't know what district I lived in, who my representatives were. I didn't know a thing about the issues—and I didn't care. *Even if I did care,* I thought, *my involvement wouldn't make a difference anyway.*

Then I became a mother. And if my life as a mother of three children has taught me one thing, it's that *there is no more powerful political act than mothering.* There is no greater reason *than my children* for me to become politically involved, and there is no more important work to put my efforts to than those things that will make this world a better, safer place for my kids.

How will changes like this come about? There are as many answers to that question as there are mothers, but as I dialogued with the women who contributed to this volume, several themes consistently emerged. Books like this one are part of this movement of change, as is your reading of it—because the fires of change so often spark first in the mind and in the heart. Change begins with what we think, what we believe. Change also comes about through what we teach: the values we pass on, the sense of responsibility we instill, the passion for a better world with which we infuse our children (the next generation) and one another. And finally, change is about how we act: what we do, how we love. How we live.

Belief. Teachings. Action. These are the things that make up who we are—as mothers, as women, as political beings. Every word we say, every step we take, every breath we draw, is political when you get right down to it. It's like the old '60s saying: "The personal is political." So is the maternal. It's a good thing, too. As mothers, we know how to love the messy, the confused, the heartbroken, the hopeless, and the stubborn parts of our children, right along with the intelligent and the strong, the courageous and the wise, the powerful and the beautiful. It's the kind of love that, as the Beatles sang, the world needs now: love, sweet love. A mother's love.

Exactly the kind that you and I know how to give.

BELIEVE

Do not believe in anything simply because you have heard it. Do not believe in anything simply because it is spoken and rumored by many. Do not believe in anything simply because it is found written in your religious books. Do not believe in anything merely on the authority of your teachers and elders. Do not believe in traditions because they have been handed down for many genera-tions. But after observation and analysis, when you find that anything agrees with reason and is conducive to the good and benefit of one and all, then accept it and live up to it.

—*Buddha*

Motherhood Made Me Do It
Or, How I Became an Activist

by Judith Stadtman Tucker

I HAVE A CONFESSION TO MAKE: I used to read fiction. New writers, contemporary novels, mysteries, modern classics—I loved them all. It's not an exaggeration to say that fiction reading was the great passion of my youth. I always had a book with me—even at parties. I've read fiction indoors and out, on planes, trains, cars, buses, subways, and ferries. I've read fiction sitting, standing, lying down, and in movie theaters, waiting for the house lights to dim.

(It's also true that I once had a penchant for wearing black and hanging out in punkish nightclubs. But that's a story for another time.)

If someone had taken me aside fifteen years ago and predicted that one day I would stop reading fiction and would instead surround myself with volumes sporting titles like *Mothers Who Kill Their Children* and *Rethinking Family: Some Feminist Questions,* I'm sure I would have responded with a quizzical look—you know, the one that says: *Obviously, you are out of your mind.*

But here I am, smack in the middle of my life, living in a comfortable house in a pleasant New England town with an agreeable husband and two reasonably well-adjusted kids, plus a growing collection of books about motherhood, feminism, changing families, and the politics of care in the United States. Moreover, I'm the founder and editor of a well-trafficked website calling for social and economic justice for mothers and others who provide the indispensable work of caregiving in our society. I have a pretty good idea of how all this transpired. But when I actually stop and think about it, I'm still surprised by the turn of events. Because before I became a mother, I wasn't much of an activist, or even much of a feminist.

DHARMA

I'm always reluctant to make sweeping generalizations about the psychology of motherhood, but I think it's safe to say that the process of becoming a mother can alter a woman. Some changes may be superficial and transitory; others are more lasting. Sometimes the process of becoming a mother works into the deepest cavities of the self and fundamentally transforms a woman's worldview. In my case, becoming a mother heightened my sensitivity to the asymmetrical distribution of power in our society, and to how disastrous that unfairness is for women and families.

I suppose there was a kind of chain reaction that took place, some sort of alchemy between the intricacies of my personal history and the anguish and outrage I felt when I was utterly unprepared for the realities of new motherhood. Before I debuted in my maternal role, I thought I could easily handle whatever challenges motherhood brought my way. As a first-time mother at age thirty-six, I wasn't exactly a spring chicken; I had faith in my abilities as a capable and competent adult. And, of course, I was well informed—I'd read the recommended pregnancy and childbirth books. But I soon discovered that—unlike the passive, sterilized versions of motherhood dished up in the *What to Expect* series and other baby bibles—real-life mothering is culturally complicated and emotionally messy. It puts the kibosh on the neo-liberal fairytale of individualistic autonomy and calls for a completely different spin on the concepts of self-sufficiency and moral agency. But mostly, motherhood was, for me, a raging torrent of conflicting feelings and desires, and it hit me like a ton of bricks.

Once I recovered from the initial shock of my disillusionment and brushed off the debris of my shattered self-image, I started to look around. Was it really *fair* that my husband's day-to-day life looked pretty much the same as it did before we were parents, while mine looked so much different? After several years of an ideally egalitarian and intensely intimate partnership, why were we starting to look suspiciously like Ozzie and Harriet? Was it really *fair* that taking sixteen weeks of unpaid family leave left us financially strapped? Was it really *fair* that just when my fussy newborn was starting to develop a cheerful demeanor, I had to hand him off to a paid sitter and head back to work? Was it *fair* that even though my own options for parental leave were less than ideal, there were other new mothers who couldn't take any time off work at all? Why did the most talented women at my place of employment disappear shortly after the birth of their first or second child? How did it come to pass that all the rising stars at that firm were male—and of those who were dads, nearly all had stay-at-home wives? Why was it so much harder for mothers to have a good job and raise a family than it was for the fathers I knew?

I didn't have the answers then. And I didn't know I'd just discovered my calling—my dharma.

WAKE-UP CALL

I've never aspired to a conventional career, which makes me something of an outlier among the fashionable young people I worked and socialized with during my fiction-reading phase. Nevertheless, I enjoyed the creative aspects of my job and fell unreflectively into the "overwork culture" of the late 1980s. During the peak years of my fertility, the possibility that I might one day consider myself motherhood material rarely crossed my mind. I even went through a stage— a rather prolonged stage, as it happens—when I thought babies were repulsive and avoided the company of young children. But sure enough, as I approached my mid-thirties, I decided I wanted a baby of my own. When I finally connected with a man I was eager to share my life with (a process that involved more false starts than I care to admit), we went about the business of procreation with the kind of reckless enthusiasm that betrays an alarming excess of naiveté. But soon we had a baby boy—a very nice one—and went home to remake our happy couple into a family. I suppose the rest is history.

Actually, a few other things happened along the way that led me to question the definition of productive labor, the organization of work, and the way motherhood and fatherhood are packaged in our society. Shortly after my son's first birthday, we moved from our home in Washington, D.C.—a location where decent bookstores and quality childcare are relatively easy to find—to a small town in southeastern Pennsylvania with no bookstores, limited public amenities for families with young children, and few acceptable childcare options. In one fell swoop, our family life became defined by my husband's job and career goals, and almost entirely dependent on his paycheck.

I was not exactly thrilled with my new status as a "trailing" spouse. The wives of my husband's coworkers—who soon became my new social circle—had a Stepfordesque quality I found unnerving. And, much to my dismay, it started rubbing off on me. I took to baking bread several times a week—partly because I missed the tasty baguettes from the artisan bakeries in D.C., but mainly because I needed the distraction. The isolation and limited mobility of early motherhood, financial pressures, my husband's frequent business travel, the endless rounds of ear and respiratory infections my son brought home from the daycare center (and, when he turned two, his yearlong campaign against toilet training), the challenges of meeting my project deadlines given all of the above, the culture shock of living in a community where 70 percent of registered voters were Republicans, and three early miscarriages in the space of eighteen months—this was not what I had in mind when I pictured the joys of marriage and motherhood. This sucked.

In short, I was miserable. But, given my tendency to overthink everything, I was also intellectually curious about why my life was going so badly, and why my expectations had been so far off the mark. So much of what made my situation intolerable—and the subtle forces that seemed to shape the lives and opportunities of other mothers I knew—was related to antiquated values and social arrangements that split paid work and family work into separate, gendered spheres. For example, my husband's employers took great pride in the company's family-friendly culture. As it turned out, their notion of "family-friendly" was installing a secondhand diaper-changing table in the men's restroom and organizing children's holiday parties. The chief executives—all married men with young families—were candid about their preference for hiring and promoting married men with young families for key positions. But fathers were also expected to travel—to Europe and Asia, sometimes for weeks at a stretch, often on short notice. And mothers were expected to pick up the slack at home.

Those of us who were disgruntled about the perpetual absence of our parenting partners were urged to put on a happy face and make the best of it. Complaining—which I excelled at—was frowned upon among the wives as being "unsupportive." Not coincidentally, during the three years my husband worked for this outfit, only a handful of women were ever employed in decision-making positions, and no women with young children at home were hired for jobs requiring travel. Although I couldn't quite put my finger on it at the time, a deadly combination of lack of practical support for the work of child rearing, gender bias, and pressure to conform to the "ideal worker" norm in my husband's workplace was pushing me to the brink. Something, I concluded, had to change.

Eventually, my husband received an attractive job offer in New Hampshire, and we abandoned the Pennsylvania experiment with few regrets. And after giving birth to another healthy son, I started looking for a different kind of book to read.

¡VIVA LA REVOLUCIÓN!

My husband and I rented a DVD of *The Motorcycle Diaries* a while back, and while the film's romantic account of Che Guevara's awakening as a revolutionary diverges from real events, I was sympathetic to the narrative. Once young Ernesto Guevara begins to see injustice, he sees it everywhere. By the end of the movie, you know he has his heart set on overthrowing the system. His fate is sealed.

So there I was—a white, middle-aged, middle-class woman, lying awake in my cozy bed in my comfortable house, beloved husband by my side, kids sleeping safe and warm in a room down the hall. And I'm thinking: *Old Che and I have something in common.* Once you see injustice, you start to see it everywhere. And once you start to see injustice everywhere—once you take the awareness of its prevalence and corrosive power into your heart—you can't stop thinking about what it would take to put things right. Unlike Che, I'm not a big fan of violent revolt. If middle-class mothers decided to get together and destroy the symbols of our oppression, what would we blow up? Our microwaves? Our minivans?

The motherhood problem is not a figment of our imagination. Nor is it the product of the "choices" women make about education, work, and family formation. In fact, feminist thinkers and social scientists have been documenting the causes and effects of the motherhood problem for over thirty years. They point out that the problem is embedded in stale ideas about the essential qualities of men and women, and in myths about what children need. It's fortified by cultural norms and laws, and by the way we think and talk about the boundaries of public and personal responsibility in advanced societies. It's tucked snugly into our core institutions—like marriage, and workplaces, and our public-school system, to name just a few. And it's entrenched in an economic model that has historically privileged men and relied on women's altruism for sustainability and growth, but that fails to recognize caregiving as a primary—and mandatory— human activity in civilized societies.

In fact, the motherhood problem is woven so seamlessly into the fabric of contemporary society that it's extremely difficult to tease out. And because the disproportionate hardships and vulnerabilities that beset mothers and other caregivers in the United States—from unconscionably high maternal- and infant-mortality rates to job discrimination against workers with family responsibilities—are ultimately traceable to the inequitable distribution of social power in America and the self-interested actions of those who want to protect the status quo, the motherhood problem will be exceptionally hard to dismantle.

But once you learn to see it, you start to see it everywhere.

My fate is sealed.

THE JOURNEY

As the story goes, Che's radicalization was the outcome of an epic journey.

I'm much more of a homebody. When I travel, I like clean sheets, warm showers, and regular meals. Not to mention the fact that when my growing comprehension of the motherhood problem aroused my inner activist from her slumber, I had two small children to look after and a spouse I was quite fond of. While an epic journey wasn't out of the question, it seemed ill-advised. So I started reading books and reports about motherhood and family policy, and later started sharing what I learned with anyone who would listen. Eventually, I decided to create a web-based clearinghouse for all the information I was gathering as a resource for mothers and others who crave social change. In April 2003 I published the first edition of the Mothers Movement Online, and the whole thing snowballed from there.

Once in a while, I'll be prattling away about women, work, and family, and the value of unpaid caregiving—or lawmakers' pathetic response to the need for more and better support for maternal employment in the United States—and someone will ask me: How did you get involved in all this? And honestly, I'm at a loss for words. "All this"—the conceptual and strategic work of building a social movement—is completely new to me. I have no special qualifications for it—no advanced degree in women's studies, no track record as a theorist or policy expert or grassroots organizer, and not all that much experience as a writer. All I can say is that the complexities of my own lived experience of motherhood led me to this work, the work of social change. And now it's the only kind of work that makes sense to me.

LABOR AND DELIVERY

The immediate task at hand is how to move ideas into action. We've defined the motherhood problem pretty well. We know what it looks like in women's lives, and for the most part, we know which policy solutions are called for. The momentum for change is growing. So how do we breathe life into the mothers' movement?

There is no great mystery about what goes into effective organizing. Vision and impassioned leadership are only a small part of social activism (some people argue that vision and leadership are the most important elements, but I'm not convinced). Successful organizing takes many forms but almost always requires funding, strategic planning, outreach, communication, coordination, and cultivating supportive relationships with other individuals and organizations with compatible goals. This is the long, unglamorous slog of making social change. It doesn't have the immediacy of donating clothing and supplies to the local homeless shelter, or volunteering to answer phones for a domestic-violence hotline, or putting together a fund-raising event to help families displaced by natural disasters. Effective organizing is not always fast or easy, but meaningful progress is impossible without it.

Another aspect of successful social movements is consciousness raising. Consciousness raising is how social activists get the message out and engage individual supporters where they live. With mothers' issues, this can be tricky. Since motherhood is such an ideologically loaded topic, it's easy for open discussions to veer off track. At the same time, consciousness raising works only when people have an opportunity to connect their personal stories to the big picture. But once we get women (and men) talking about the motherhood problem and what to do about it in their own communities, we need to connect nascent activists with savvy organizers who can mobilize their commitment to change without exploiting their goodwill or wasting their time. This is not an insurmountable task. We have many inexpensive yet highly sophisticated communication tools at our disposal. We have a selection of good models. Expert knowledge is available. We just need the right resources—and enough people with the dedication and know-how to make it happen.

Then again, the mothers' movement isn't about me or my grand plan—I'm just a channel, an incubator. This revolution is about *us*— as women and mothers—and the future of our sons and daughters and the welfare of America's workers and families. It's about laying the legislative groundwork for a caring society—the next New Deal. Above all, it's about social justice, shared prosperity, and fulfilling the promise of democracy. But if we want a mothers' movement, we have to do the work. We have to give birth to it.

THE PROSPECT OF HUMAN SALVATION

Well, perhaps I do have a flair for zealotry. Dr. Martin Luther King Jr. once wrote that "human salvation lies in the hands of the creatively maladjusted." All right—I'm creative. And I'm definitely maladjusted. But I don't know about the human salvation part—that's a pretty tall order. Just thinking about it makes my hands sweat.

My younger son recently informed me that he wants to have a job like mine when he grows up. I was slightly taken aback, since the last time we had this conversation he wanted to be a rockstar—not just any kind of rockstar, mind you, but an emo rockstar.

"So you want to be a women's rights activist?" I asked (I thought I'd better double-check).

"No," he said, "I want to work to make the world a better place. Dad said that's what you do."

So we've been talking about this off and on, and we've agreed there are many different ways people can work to make the world a better place. Even rockstars can work to make the world a better place (but I'm not so sure about the emo thing).

So here I am, in my comfy house in a lovely little town with my genial husband and two great kids, a whole bunch of books, my WOMEN'S WORK COUNTS! posters, a high-speed Internet connection, and a large, friendly housecat who likes to bug me while I'm working. In other words, there is nothing remarkable about me at all. I'm just another mother. And I'm working to make the world a better place, because it's the only thing that makes sense to me.

Alien

by Sarah Masterson

Mamita, Mamita
de mi corazón,
te quiero mucho,
con todo mi amor.

    —my bilingual daughter's morning song

YOU'D HAVE THOUGHT that coming of age in a border state might have afforded me some distinct and certain viewpoint—one way or the other—on the politics of the border. But as a white middle-class girl growing up in the affluent, homogenous sprawl of Dallas in the 1970s and '80s, I had a genuine encounter with an immigrant about as often as I worked the coal mines or saw snow.

Which is to say, never.

Even later, as a student at the University of Texas at Austin—a multicultural hotbed where I came to think of myself as a feminist and a progressive—the politics of the border remained mostly an abstraction, a faint blip on my otherwise blossoming social and political consciousness.

Still later, when my husband and I lived and worked for a short time in a small, conservative South Texas town with a significant Mexican American population—even as I began to recognize firsthand the deep conflict over immigration and multiculturalism—never did I feel fully entitled to a definite political opinion. What could a white girl from the suburbs really have to say?

Eventually Noah and I had a baby and moved to Washington, D.C., for a job. There, by divine providence or dumb luck, we found

Mimi (not her real name) before the boxes were even unpacked. And there, separated by four thousand miles from her own daughter, Mimi began to love mine.

She's leaving Bolivia for the first time in her twenty-seven years. Freshly divorced from the abuser she'd once adored, Mimi is burying her face in three-year-old Adrianna's dark curls and breathing in deeply for the last time. Her daughter will stay behind with Mimi's own aging parents. Mimi has accepted the paradox of abandoning her child in order to feed and clothe and educate her child. She wants more choices—any choices—for Adrianna. And choices are few in Bolivia, the poorest country in South America—second only to Haiti as the most impoverished place in the Americas and the Caribbean.

Mimi arrived in Washington, D.C., on the tail end of an immigration wave that brought Bolivians from all walks of life—business owners, service workers, artists, teachers—to this area starting in the mid-1980s. But some ambitions are closer to the bone. She came as a mother, and she stays because she is a mother—though she hasn't buried her face in Adrianna's dark curls for more than a decade, and may not for years more to come.

It's for Adrianna that Mimi stays, long after her visa has expired. It's for Adrianna that Mimi helps to mother the babies of professional women who will never face the choices she has faced. Women, like me, who need Mimi as much as she needs us.

My daughter is now three years old—the same age Adrianna was when Mimi said goodbye. (It makes my heart squeeze tight just to think.)

We have no family here in Washington. It is Mimi who, when I cannot be there, feeds my child and cleans her face and fusses over the minutia of her daily bowel habits. It is Mimi who holds her hand to cross the street, wipes her tears, and endures her histrionics. It is

Mimi who rocks her to sleep, calms her fears, and swings her high in the air. It is Mimi who indulges her, sneaking an illicit *dulce* to Ava when she begs, and it is Mimi who watches vigilantly for any *emergencia*. It's Mimi who is named in Ava's prayers each night, and Mimi who has instilled in her the joy of a good belly laugh, the abandon of dancing the salsa, the knowledge of how to ride the bus across town, the thrilling terror of a new adventure. It's Mimi who shows Ava how to be strong and kind and brave, who buries her face in my little girl's dark hair and breathes in deeply just like I do—like someone in love. And it's she who comes to my door on Mother's Day, just to bring me the gift of *saltanas* and cake, who holds my face in both hands and kisses my cheeks before she turns to go.

It was Mimi who taught my child to pledge allegiance to the United States of America, one nation, under God, indivisible, with liberty and justice for all. It's Mimi who rehearsed with Ava the name of our president, the colors of our flag, the day of our independence—and she beams with pride when the lesson is performed. As I have watched this illegal alien, this outsider, pore over her own federal tax return; heard of her efforts to work with the police in her neighborhood to get safety messages to her Spanish-speaking neighbors; watched her encounter every problem like a good American, simply figuring out how to fix it or get around it, I've come to know who she really is and why she's really here. In her trembling voice, when she speaks to her own mother and daughter on a long-distance line—in the way she stands a bit taller when she speaks of her Bolivia, her home—I've recognized Mimi as myself, as every mother.

For Adrianna, Mimi rents out the one bedroom in her small apartment, creating for herself a makeshift sleeping space draped with a single white sheet across the living area. For Adrianna, Mimi resists the urge to make the visit home to Bolivia that would assuredly turn out to be a one-way ticket. For Adrianna's sake, Mimi lives in the shadows of a place where she doesn't fully belong, suspended surreally and indefinitely between two worlds—neither of which fully belongs to her now. For Adrianna's schooling, for her blue jeans, for her *quinceañera* party, which Mimi herself could not attend.

There are a thousand ways in which this woman defies the fables we're fed by the pundits and the fearmongers. There are a thousand small moments in which Mimi's very American sensibility has caught me by surprise, and a thousand ways in which this woman makes the privileges of my middle-class Americanness possible. Mimi has no idea, I'm certain, that the moral of her story is how big the chasm can be between what is legal and what is moral—between what is authorized and what is right.

It is Mimi who weeps at the small gift of flowers from our garden on her birthday, who continues to live in the shadows, too fearful of deportation to pursue legal residency. My daughter knows nothing about naturalization or documentation. But she is beginning to understand that something is wrong with this picture. She's starting to notice the disconnects, to ask: "Why can't Mimi go home?" "When can Mimi see Adrianna again?" "Why is Mimi sad for Christmas?"

I would like to be able to answer my daughter's questions. I would like to have an answer that is acceptable, that helps us sleep at night. I would like to be able to help secure a documented, legal status for Mimi without putting her in jeopardy in the process. I would like to be able to see Mimi go home to Bolivia for a visit with her family and be able to return to the working life that is supporting her daughter. Better yet, I would like to see Mimi be able to return to her home and make a viable existence for herself and her dependents—or to care for her loved ones here. I'd like to worry less about what the future holds for Mimi if we can't afford her, or if we outgrow the need for full-time childcare. I'd like not to think about what it would mean for my daughter to lose this woman she has no memory of ever having lived without. Because Mimi is not just an employee. She is my mother. She is me.

Only because my life coincidentally intersected with a Bolivian mother's do I know that demographic data on spreadsheets sheds little light on immigration to the United States and will never solve our problems. Only because Mimi has mothered me and mine, only because the necessities of her life have collided with the necessities of my own, do I understand why, for the sake of her daughter's future, no wall, no fence, no law, no army could ever keep her out. Only when I saw myself in Mimi's dark and resilient eyes could I know how and why my government is getting it all wrong.

Because I am a mother, I am entitled to speak about any politics that separate people from their children. I am entitled to state, loud and clear, that until my country's policies respond in a real way to the roots of persistent injustice and suffering around the world, no border patrol or red ink will protect us from the ghosts of the Third World. I am entitled to take the political very, very personally.

If my Spanish were up to the subtleties of the task, I would explain to Mimi—whose homeland has survived more coups d'etat during its history than any nation on earth—that she has unwittingly fanned the flames of my very American political gumption. It's because of her that I speak up—with confidence—when I encounter ignorance-laden banter about immigrants on the playground or at the neighborhood potluck. It's because of her that I pay attention to controversial immigration policies in my local community, as well as at the national level, and vote accordingly. And it's because of Mimi that I will proudly attend—and take my children to—any public demonstration that advocates for justice and human dignity. It's something to do with that fire in the belly that can make patriots and protesters out of white girls from the suburbs.

Mom, Interrupted: Toward a Politics of Maternal Mental Health

by Marrit Ingman

"I HAVE TO SEE EVERYTHING," the nurse said. "That means your pants, too."

She noted my tattoos, my bruises, and everything else I'd brought into the hospital on my body, a baseline against any further signs of self-injury.

"And look," I said, eager to comply. "Here's the scar from my caesarean."

She approved. "You can barely see it. The doctor did a good job."

"Yes," I agreed, "she did." I tucked away my stretch marks and my faint pink line.

The nurse folded my chart closed. "We're ready to go up," she declared, and escorted me to the elevator.

On the fifth floor of Seton Shoal Creek, the elevator is exit only. From the outside the doors open with an orderly's key, or if activated by a button at the nurses' station. But I didn't know that yet. All I knew was that there was nowhere to go, that things weren't right, that neither dying nor running away was an option, and so I was here, on the fifth floor, exiting the exit-only elevator with a linebacker-size clinical assistant named Mike at my back. Mike was friendly enough, but when I balked at the dayroom—where patients in pajamas and slipper-socks worked thousand-piece jigsaw puzzles and made colored pictures with motley broken crayons from a coffee can—he shook his head, arms folded. *You ain't leaving.*

Apparently my HMO had agreed to pay.

I'd already surrendered the drawstring in my pants, the laces in my shoes, everything that could poke or strangle. Toothless, I would remain on suicide watch until I was pronounced past self-harm. Until then, Mike kept me in his sight, peering at me from an unobtrusive distance while I ate my supper tray and sat in group.

"First thing you've got to do is get one of these," a young woman said. She was awaiting her discharge orders and was full of advice for the newcomer. "One of these yellow bracelets. That means you can go down to the cafeteria for meals and go outside for fresh-air break."

"Fresh-air break," I repeated.

"Yeah. You get to go out to the patio for fifteen minutes. You can't smoke, of course. But it helps."

"Okay."

"Do you have your diagnosis yet?"

I shrugged. I didn't know what I was, except that I took medication after medication for whatever was wrong with me and still never stopped crying. I'd gone from incapacitating depressions to rages I suppressed with anything within reach. Two nights ago I'd drunk a bottle of wine while cooking supper and found myself facedown in the yard, snarling at anyone who approached—my husband, my son, my cat. I'd told them to "shut the fuck up and leave me alone," to "put a goddamn sock in it," to "quit ruining my life." I spent an hour crawling on my hands and knees looking for my glasses, which were someplace in the grass I hadn't mowed.

"Do you do drugs?" she asked.

"Sometimes," I said.

"Work the program, and it'll get better," she said.

I was not the only mother on the ward. Julie, a bipolar with paranoid features, had two children whom she'd lost custody of— because, she said, of her diagnosis. She managed a Domino's Pizza.

Eerily serene Mandy, who'd overdosed on her Seroquel in a semi-serious attempt, had been brought in by her hippie husband, who made note of my Biscuit Brothers T-shirt. Sure enough, they had a two-year-old daughter, and Mandy wanted to get better for her. Melissa, who was my roommate, had a son, but he had been in a car accident with her. She'd watched him die and had been depressed ever since. She was an addict, too, but had quit shooting heroin because, she said, it was unladylike and too unsafe. And Yvette, who had hipped me to fresh-air break and told me to work the program, had two kids and a dual diagnosis—she was mentally ill and an addict as well.

"I'm a stay-at-home mother," I told her when we met. I didn't really think of myself that way, but my insurance company did.

Yvette and Julie exchanged looks. "Jesus. No wonder you're crazy."

I *was* crazy, like many mothers before me. And, like many mothers before me, I'd walked a long and winding road to proper diagnosis and treatment. Because of my illness's apparent postpartum onset, I'd been treated for it for years by my obstetrician and my internist, clinicians who never suspected any mental disorder besides major depression. (More likely, I was simply less able to cope during my postpartum period, causing the illness to reveal itself in clearer relief.) I took one SSRI after another—Zoloft, Paxil, Lexapro—in ever-increasing dosages, with effects ranging from hypomania (irritability, racing thoughts, and agitation) to no effect at all.

When I became agitated, I sought the help of my internist. The mere act of parking at the hospital filled me with rage. I picked up my ticket and drove around and around in the structure; each reserved spot or space-hogging SUV made me scream. My hands trembled on the steering wheel. Whatever this was, I wasn't sure it was postpartum depression, and I didn't think it was very well managed.

"It's like I'm angry," I told my doctor.

"Angry," he repeated. "Why would you be angry?"

I thought a minute. How could I explain? "You have small children," I said finally. "Ask your wife if she ever gets angry."

For that smart remark, I got my Lexapro increased to twenty milligrams, and I got a scrip for Klonopin.

"Are you a religious person?" he asked.

"No," I said.

"You might want to consider prayer. It might help you appreciate your life."

I fired him.

Months later, I was drunk and belligerent in the yard, swatting at anyone who tried to help me. The treatment wasn't working.

I sat in the parking lot of my son's preschool for ten minutes, deciding between my options. I could kill myself, I could run away, or I could go to the hospital. I chose the hospital. I drove myself there without asking anyone's permission; it felt like an act of defiance. Like most mothers, I had allowed myself a longing for book clubs, pedicures, and the occasional "day out." Yet it was clear that rare acts of leisure, squeezed in between working and mothering, weren't helping me function any better. When the preschool director called my cell to ask me to pick my son up—because he was scratching his eczema and had pulled off some scabs—I told her no. I was already checking in. I would be unreachable for four days. I was going to have to pass the buck to my husband. Dark tendrils of guilt bloomed in my stomach. I continually reminded myself that I was no use to my family dead.

The psychiatrist told me my medication was making me manic. That women who presented as manic (something he said was "not unusual" in his practice) usually did so a year or so after beginning treatment for "postpartum depression"—depression with a postpartum onset, anyhow—with SSRIs prescribed by a family doctor. The wonder drugs I was taking—the ones supposed to give me back my life—were making me crazier. They treated the depressive half of my illness, but the manic half ran even more rampant.

"We see this often," the doctor said.

I was Type II bipolar, he told me, and probably had been all along.

For years in my own work, I'd been trying to find the line between mental illness and wellness. I'd even written a book on the subject. Was "postpartum depression" a helpful label for describing some women's struggles adjusting to and recovering from new motherhood, or was it a falsely medicalized perspective on a problem that is at least partly political and cultural? I believe something predisposes mothers to depression, anxiety, and obsessive compulsion, whether it is our hormones, like Brooke Shields says it is, or whether it's the way motherhood impacts our earning power, our relationships, and our self-determination.

We "should" be happy and contented, but for too many mothers, political reality is bleak, perhaps more so than ever before in my post–*Roe v. Wade* lifetime. We are more often the victims of domestic violence, and even our stable nuclear families still divorce at a rate of 3.6 per 1,000. According to the 2005 census, 28.4 percent of female-headed households lived in poverty that year. Whether or not we work for pay, we are affected by a workplace culture that is hostile to family issues and refuses to restrict the mandatory workweek of its salaried employees. We have seen business interests try but fail to roll back the Family and Medical Leave Act of 1993, which guaranteed for the first time that workers can take unpaid time off, without being fired, to care for children, elders, or other family members during twelve-week crisis periods. No wonder we're depressed.

Because cultural and economic cofactors complicate mental health, I take exception, however, with the popular notion that a woman's postpartum depression is concentrated entirely within in her endocrine system and can be successfully treated by a gynecologist— a too-rosy and sexist (but persistent) ideal of recovery that rarely matches real women's experiences. A mother's mental illness—just like any other human being's—is a day-to-day struggle with a possible whole range of emotional, physical, and behavioral symptoms. To assign blame solely to our hormones smacks of the "hysteria" for which women and mothers have long been blamed. Partnered mothers without adequate support at home are statistically at greater risk for depression, as are single mothers, young mothers, and mothers of disabled or sick infants; obviously, circumstances play a role. When these mothers are told to "seek help" for their depression, they turn to the doctor they have the most access to, for political and economic reasons: their obstetrician.

We can also indict the culture of "intensive" mothering. As our public schools fail, as our most affordable foods are modified and processed, as our toys are recalled, and as our healthcare and housing costs balloon, mothers stretch themselves to nurture their children back from what feels like the brink of disaster. I once met a tearful woman who was in therapy specifically to cure her perfectionistic obsession with Dr. Sears's attachment parenting. (In keeping with her natural parenting style, he recommends essential fatty acids as well.) As I once wrote in 14-point type across a press release, Postpartum Depression Is a Feminist Issue. If we care about the mental health of women, we care about mothers.

Beyond the stigma already associated with mental illness—which is itself a political topic—mothers face a double burden. Because we inevitably involve our children in our struggles simply by being alongside them, a mother's mental illness is perceived to be harmful to her children. Certainly, some studies do indicate that children of depressed mothers may acquire language more slowly and demonstrate behavioral problems, ostensibly due to a lack of interaction. But discussions of these studies use loaded and alarmist language, rather than emphasizing that mental illness affects an entire family. In *Depression: The Innocent Victims*, author Debra Gordon establishes a dialectic of innocence and blame, attempting to "inoculate [her children] against the effects" of her depression and making apologies to them for the expense of its treatment—psychotherapy.

We would not expect a mother to inoculate her children against the effects of her cancer, or to apologize for her expensive radiation treatments. We should think of mental-health intervention as life-saving medicine for ourselves, not as bourgeois frippery we embark on simply because it's good for Junior. We need not apologize for our efforts to recover; when we struggle with the beast, we send our children messages of self-respect—that we are people, and people matter. We show them how to survive as surely as we show them how to put food in their mouths and how to drink from a cup.

So I decided to teach my five-year-old son about mental illness—an act that, to me, is profoundly political. I began in the dayroom of the adult ward at Seton Shoal Creek Hospital, where the motley broken crayons in a coffee can were. All the paper was printed or ruled, so I requested and received a short stack of printer paper from the nurses' station. I drew pictures of illness: a cartoon person sick to his stomach standing near a toilet, and a little boy with red and flaky skin. My son understands the daily routine of treatments for his eczema, which has persisted since infancy despite generous applications of every topical substance indicated for dermatitis. He understands physical suffering, the frustrating cycle of flare-ups and remission, and avoiding triggers. He understands maintenance medication and meeting with doctors.

I drew myself too, a person with an illness in her brain, and made the connection explicit. A question mark floated above my head—depressive or hypomanic, or mixed?—but I was also smiling in the pictures, because I was fighting the beast. On the last page of drawings, all the sick people in the book joined hands and stood together, fighting their beasts.

My social worker, a genial guy named Wally, hovered over me as I worked. Finally he asked if he could have a copy of my book to use with children. I told him yes, but I had to put my copyright on it first (I did), and I'd need someone to staple it for me, since I was not allowed access to sharp and pointy things.

I presented my son with the book when I came home. He read it through twice without comment (he's been reading since he was three, evincing none of the verbal delays children of depressed mothers are supposed to have) and put it aside.

"Do you understand the book?" I asked.

"Yes," he said.

At home I felt weird, floaty, having already grown unaccustomed to the house where I work, mother, and sleep. I walked from room to room just to feel the difference. I put on drawstring pants and held a real metal fork. I was terrified but determined to be strong. I would take it one step at a time, moving forward through my life with purpose and pride in my recovery. I was going to teach my son life's most important messages: self-care, persistence, and faith. I would also teach and model compassion, the first step toward a politics of radical mental health. I would teach him that inasmuch as we must protect and nurture our own selves, we must work to transform the world into a sane and compassionate place in which to struggle alongside friends. I would teach him these things not to insulate him against my failings, but to involve him in my successes.

When my son is an adult, the world will certainly need citizens with a loving awareness of mental health, for everyone's sake. I would teach him about the right to treatment, the unfairness of the stigma against mental illness, the right to live unashamed, and the need to give and receive support. I would teach him that the mentally ill are not a burden or a blight, nor holy fools, but that they are a population of everyday people who choose to medicate or not medicate, to live openly with their diagnoses or to hide them, and to greet each day with as much fighting spirit as they can muster. Each of these decisions has profound political implications on the individual and the societal level, and I hope to make my son aware of the first step: how to save a life, including his own.

My decision to live openly as a bipolar person, to reveal my diagnosis and treatment, is a political choice. I have chosen to accept the label, even though friends were already warning me about the "trendy" diagnosis of Type II bipolar while I was using the inpatient house phone to speak with them. Several women told me they'd been diagnosed as bipolar based on family history alone, when their symptoms seemed not to fit, and that they'd gone on to second opinions and effective treatment elsewhere. A school counselor who works with my husband warned of the diagnosis being applied too broadly in the middle-school population, for whom changes in mood are not necessarily pathological. Yet my skeptical friends and I do not disagree about the right of individuals to accept or reject a clinical label. Nor do we disagree that the mentally ill (for my purposes, everyone not mentally *well*) are far too often controlled like cattle, painfully isolated, or patted on the head and told to pray. We speak of them as passively *receiving* treatment provided by others, not as treating themselves with diet, exercise, cognitive-behavioral therapy, medications, or other, self-administered modalities. We are supposedly healed by doctors, not by ourselves. But mentally ill people heal themselves every day, and it is time for a politics of empowerment that begins with mothers and children—people like me, people like Yvette, Julie, Mandy, and Melissa.

When I left Seton Shoal Creek, Melissa was still there. Her new roommate was already admitted. We said tearful goodbyes and swapped clothes like girls at camp: She gave me a pair of jeans she hated because they made her butt look flat (her sister had packed them for her anyway), and I gave her a heather-gray hoodie of mine, since the air-conditioning made the ward cold. I was going home to a family, alive and well. She would not be, would never be, regardless of her own prognosis. Her situation was proof that mothers are always a breath away from tragedy; we are all susceptible at any moment to dangers so terrifying, we might break inside with one false move. There is no single answer—not in Seroquel, not in psychotherapy, not in coffee cans of broken crayons. The real answer is our strength in numbers. We are joined in our struggle like soldiers, our fight a virtuous cause. Each day we motivate ourselves into whatever action we can manage, sometimes painfully. As Ariel Gore once said, "If you wake up one dull morning and feel as if it's all you can do to get out of bed, just get out of bed."

"Write about me," Melissa said.

I told her I would.

Rebel Mom

by Tracy Thompson

NOT LONG AGO, at a feminist literary gathering in a suburb far from my home, I saw a face that looked familiar. It took me a second, and then it clicked: It was Diane, one of the social workers who had founded and led a new-moms' group that I'd been in ten years earlier. She recognized me at about the same time, and we greeted each other like old war buddies.

Was it coincidence that two women who had met in a venue devoted to motherhood met again, years later, at a gathering where the conversation kept veering off into public policy? Not really. We live in an era when motherhood seems to spawn social activism. It's certainly not the first time this has happened—the ninteenth century comes to mind—but, for whatever the reason, there seems to be a general sense these days that the rules, they are a-changin'—or that, if not, they should be. And here I am—if not exactly leading the charge, at least in there with the troops.

No one is more surprised about this than I. I grew up in a conservative state (Georgia) and in a conservative religious environment (Southern fundamentalist). My dad was a Goldwater Republican; my parents expected us to use "Ma'am" and "Sir" when addressing them. My mother kept a wooden bolo paddle next to the kitchen phone and called it "Mama's little helper"—and did not hesitate to use it on us. In high school, I was such a good little do-bee that when teachers saw me in the hall without a pass, they'd say, "Oh, Tracy, it's you," and let me go on by. I attended Emory University in Atlanta, which holds the dubious distinction of being one of the very few colleges in the country ever to host a rally in *favor* of the war in Vietnam. (It was entitled—I am not making this up—"Affirmation: Vietnam.")

Challenging the status quo, then, was not exactly encoded in my DNA. As for politics, I found it either boring or sleazy. True, I did spend the summer of 1973 glued to the Watergate hearings, but people rubberneck at traffic accidents, too, and it doesn't mean they want to *be* in one. People who were interested in politics always mystified me, even though I'd run into plenty in the years I had been a newspaper reporter.

"How can you *stand* that man?" I asked a colleague once, referring to the speaker of the Georgia House of Representatives—a sexist, racist, cornpone Buddha, in my opinion, who could be depended on to obstruct anything even faintly resembling progress.

"Oh, he's a sweetie pie," she laughed, and I shuddered; I'd rather have amputated my big toe than shake hands with that old geezer. When I went to work for *The Washington Post,* I got to town just in time to cover the indictment of D.C. Mayor Marion Barry for cocaine possession. The ensuing trial made Watergate look like a meeting of the Ladies' Christian Temperance Union. At best, I thought, politics was a necessary evil (*somebody* had to write the tax code); mostly, it was a sport for the ethically challenged.

Then I had a baby.

Becoming a mother is always a profound transformation. For those of us who came of age in the shadow of the 1960s feminist movement, I think it may be especially wrenching. For us, being female in this brave new world of possibility meant starkly differentiating ourselves from our mothers, especially in relation to those traditional wifely activities they had taken part in, such as Vacation Bible School, the PTA, women's clubs, the League of Women Voters—all of which are, of course, forms of grassroots politics. Yet the root of the word "politics" is the Greek word *polis,* or state, and becoming a mother made it clear to me that I had become a member of a boundary-free, global statehood of women united by a profound common interest: the welfare of the next generation. Watching my baby at my breast, I remember thinking that this was something women in Sri Lanka and Ireland and Bosnia and all over the world were doing *at that very moment,* and now I was a small part of that huge, intricate web; I was a mother.

The pressing need to survive that first year drove me, in the first two months of Emma's life, to seek the company of other women, and that's where I found—*thank yew, Jesus!*—that new-moms' support group. In the bland office-park conference room where we met once a week for roughly the next year, our microcommunity solved feeding problems, bore witness to one another's birth stories, compared baby poop schedules, explored marital discord—took on whatever problem presented itself that week and somehow made sense of it. For the first time, I saw the power of collective thinking: how people could sift through various points of view and get new ideas or discover common ground. At the time, of course, it never occurred to me that this was a form of civic involvement. But it opened a door in my mind.

Needless to say, becoming a mother also transformed me economically. Pre-baby, I was a productive member of society, a contributor to the economy; post-baby, I was a "dependent" on my husband. After twenty years of getting paid to run around and ask impertinent questions, the sheer physical labor of looking after an infant—never mind the emotional and intellectual challenges—seemed daunting. When I multiplied what I was doing every day by ten million (roughly speaking, the number of households in the United States with children under the age of six, according to the U.S. Census Bureau),

I realized what a truly vast amount of labor and human capital was out there—as powerful as that army of dead people in *The Lord of the Rings,* and just about as visible.

"Coming back from the dead," in fact, would be a good description of my attempts to reenter the work force after a year's maternity leave. I'd been told before I left that I might have to take a less desirable assignment on my return. When I asked about job sharing, part-time positions, and/or prorated benefits, the answers were "No, none available" and "We don't do that." In the end, I wrangled some contract work, which allowed me to work from home part-time. It seemed like a great deal. But when I divided the time I was working into the money I was now getting paid, I realized that on a per hour basis, I was making maybe 60 percent of my former salary. It *was* a great deal, just not a great deal for me.

I felt vaguely pissed off, but I wasn't sure I had a right to be. At least we had enough money so that being home with my baby was an option. Lots of moms would have been thrilled with that; millions of mothers all over the world were happy to eke out enough money to keep their kids from starving. What was I complaining about? I wasn't sure, but my inner rebel was starting to rattle the bars of her cage. In the first freelance piece I did after Emma's birth, a 1998 cover story for the *The Washington Post Magazine,* I wrote, "Motherhood these days is like zigzagging around in bumper cars. The fun-house music keeps getting louder and faster, and the moms in the bumper cars keep going in tighter little circles, and though some cars are fancier than others, we are all prisoners of the apparatus, which is a culture that treats children as sentimental objects or consumers or inconveniences—as anything but people. And I wonder: How do you stage a bumper car revolt?"

Fortunately, the computer—the Housewife's Friend—was there to help me answer that question. By the time baby number two arrived in 2001, I'd discovered a network of activist and/or literary moms, people like Judith Stadtman Tucker, Miriam Peskowitz, and Andi Buchanan. Sophie was born in January, and not long after, I saw some mention on the web of a book called *The Price of Motherhood,* by someone named Ann Crittenden. The name seemed familiar. *Oh yeah. Wasn't she a* New York Times *reporter?* (The media world, in some ways, is a small town; people keep track of each other.) I bought the book and read it on a long car trip down to Georgia to see my mom. As I read, that feeling of being vaguely pissed off kept getting more and more specific. Every page or so, I would grab my husband's arm (he was driving) to exclaim, "Oh my God! Listen to *this!*" It's a wonder my dawning political consciousness didn't kill us all.

And thus, an activist was born—or an engaged journalist, or a participating citizen; I'm honestly not sure what to call myself these days. I just know that politics is no longer an abstraction for me. I get it, finally. I understand that this fluid and often unbelievably intricate rule-making process, and the people who are elected to make it work, directly affect what I eat, what kind of car I drive, whether the son of my daughter's softball coach will live to see thirty or come home from Iraq in a box, whether we can afford to go on vacation this year or if that money will have to be budgeted for medical care. Politics is no longer a necessary evil but a subject of passionate interest. And, perhaps in part because I came late to the game, I do not feel at all vested in the way it's been played up to now. In fact, my newfound social activism seems mostly to involve questioning the status quo. There's a lot to question.

Driving to the grocery store, I catch part of a discussion on the car radio about U.S.-China trade policy, and the dearth of Food and Drug Administration inspectors for food imports; at the produce counter a few minutes later, I realize that those red grapes are from Chile. Holy cow! My food has seen more of the world than I have.

How much energy did it take to get these grapes here, and how much of a carbon footprint did that leave? Is there a place I can buy produce locally?

Or as I'm picking up a prescription for an elderly friend, I realize that her doctor has prescribed forty milligrams of a popular stomach acid–suppressant drug. A month's supply will cost $291, or $9.38 per pill. Or she could double up on the over-the-counter version, at 78 cents per pill. I ask the pharmacist: "What is the difference between two of these and one of those?" Long pause. "Different salts," she says finally. *What's going on here?*

Or I go to my daughters' school to help chaperone a fifth-grade end-of-the-year bowling party, and as the kids get herded onto the bus, I realize that the parents will all be caravanning to the bowling alley separately, many of us in gas-guzzling SUVs or minivans. "Anybody want to carpool?" I ask. Silence. Eventually, one hand goes up. *Wake up, people!* I want to say. *These dinosaur bones aren't gonna last forever!*

I am out of synch, swimming against the tide, and nowhere is this more evident than when it comes to prevailing definitions of what constitutes a "good mother."

"I'm picking Sophie up now, but Emma wants to come home later," I tell the school aftercare lady. Sophie is in kindergarten; Emma is in fifth grade. "Here's a written permission slip saying it's okay with me if she walks home."

"Oh no, I can't do that," the aftercare lady says.

"Why not?" I say. "She walked *to* school." (Our house is four-tenths of a mile from school—I've measured it.)

"Somebody might snatch her."

Statistically speaking, this is unlikely (though I can see why a casual media consumer, fed a steady diet of crime and terrorism, might see danger everywhere). What seems likelier to me, considering the corn dogs, pizza, and french fries that keep turning up on the school lunch menu, is that my daughter has inhaled too many calories today and could use the exercise. I'm in the minority here, though, which probably explains why my neighbors keep stopping to offer my daughter a ride as they chauffeur their own children to and from the school's doorstep. But it's hard to blame them for being overly cautious; some of them work such long hours, they hardly get a chance to see their kids.

"I asked them for eleven hours of time off, and she said I only had six," I overhear a woman telling her husband at my daughter's softball game. "I don't get it," she adds bitterly. "I've worked there a freaking *year*."

But here she is after a long day at work, watching her daughter play softball. She's trying, as am I, to be a "good mother," which in our middle- to upper-class, educated culture is defined largely by what sociologist Sharon Hays calls "the culture of intensive motherhood." That's the belief that a good mother makes her children the center of her world, that she is literally *there* for every possible moment of their childhoods. It's a standard I flunk, because at times I shut the door to my home office and tell my kids to leave me alone. On the other hand, there are those experts who tell me I'm spending too *much* time at home—that by "opting out" of my former salaried job (which, with commuting, would have burned up roughly twelve hours out of twenty-four), I've wrecked my financial future and set a rotten example for my daughters. No matter what I do, there's an expert telling me I'm wrong.

Agricultural policy, national defense, the healthcare system, the looming energy shortage, global warming, workplace policies that discriminate against caregivers, the media, public education, feminism, parenting and social expectations—these aren't abstractions anymore. They are issues I confront all day long. To be more precise, these are walls I keep bumping into, walls that define The Way Things Are. And I keep thinking, *Some of these walls are going to have to come down.*

And I think they will. Why? Because even though it sometimes seems like I am a one-person protest march, the truth is that I have lots of company. The proof of this is all over the Internet; it's here in the book you now hold in your hands. Motherhood got me to this place, but it's gotten a lot of other women here, too, asking the same questions I'm asking. And now that we're here, we are seeing something a lot bigger than just a few "women's issues." You start out saying, "That's not right!" to your own personal injustice, and unless you are a total narcissist, it's only a matter of time before you start recognizing that a lot of other things aren't right. In March 2007, one of my favorite people, social historian Judith Stadtman Tucker, wrote on the Mothers Movement Online:

> After a historically freakish blip of widely shared prosperity in the thirty years following World War II, America has returned to a level of income inequality not seen since the run-up to the Great Depression. . . . Not to mention that from the deadly, unjustified war in Iraq to the grim aftermath of Hurricane Katrina, it's clear the nation's leaders are not staying to the right path. In other words, conditions are ripe for a progressive social movement.

Reading those words on my computer screen in the last hour of quiet I'm going to have before the kids come blasting through the door, I find myself saying quietly, "Yeah. Yeah." And when she adds, "Trust me—we can do this," I suddenly feel a surge of energy and hope. Sisterhood is powerful, but baby, motherhood is *nuclear*.

As a Mother

by Nancy Pelosi

In the name of womanhood and humanity, I earnestly ask
That a general congress of women without limit of nationality,
May be appointed and held at someplace deemed most convenient
And the earliest period consistent with its objects,
To promote the alliance of the different nationalities,
The amicable settlement of international questions,
The great and general interests of peace.

—Julia Ward Howe, Mother's Day Proclamation, 1870

THESE WORDS ARE FROM Julia Ward Howe, who called for a day in 1870 that carried a meaning different from the cards, flowers, and chocolates we've come to associate with Mother's Day today (not that I mind the chocolates). After witnessing the devastating effects of the Civil War, Howe began what she called Mother's Day for Peace—a call to women across the globe to come together and bring an end to war.

This year, Julia Ward Howe's call is particularly relevant, not just for mothers, but for all women, all men, all daughters, and all sons. We are in the midst of a war that has taken far too many of our most precious resources—our children. It is a war the American people have lost faith in and are ready to end. It is a failed policy, and we are ready for a new direction.

There are numerous reasons to end this war—the cost of lives and limbs, the cost in dollars, the cost to our reputation in the world, the cost to our military and National Guard—but it is as a mother that I am most committed to ending this war, because war hits mothers in an especially painful and personal way. We cannot help but think of our fellow mothers as their young sons and daughters are sent off to war in Iraq, praying for their child's safety, anxiously awaiting a call, an email, a letter—anything. The relief as their children return, or the utter devastation when their children never come home. We think too of the Iraqi mothers who have lost their children, and whose children are growing up surrounded by warfare and destruction.

Women have always been the peacekeepers of our societies. When I became the first woman Speaker of the House, I was honored to assume this position and humbled by the responsibility it brought. Nothing in my life will ever compare to being a mother—not being a member of Congress; not being Speaker of the House. But I am thankful that I have the opportunity to bring my experience as a mother to this position. When I traveled to the Middle East in search of diplomacy and peace, I was there as Speaker of the House. But I was also there as a mother, carrying Julia Ward Howe's message. When I cast my vote for an end to the war in Iraq, I did so as a member of Congress. But my vote was also taken as a mother of five and grandmother of six.

We will bring an end to this war because the world is not ours alone, but our children's as well. As the adage goes, we do not inherit the earth from our ancestors; we borrow it from our children. Let us heed the call of Julia Ward Howe and make the next Mother's Day a Mother's Day for Peace, and as mothers, as daughters, and as families, bring an end to this war.

Life Under Construction

by Jennifer Margulis

"You coming to Ian's costume party?" My friend Jennifer leaned in and spoke to me conspiratorially as we gathered our books at the end of class. A skinny grad student in comparative literature, she had nicotine-stained fingers and always wore black, like all the students did.

"I don't know." Ian was boisterous and arrogant and consistently looked unkempt and unwashed, though he was smart in class—which made up for his obnoxiousness. Sometimes.

"It'll be fun. You should come."

I looked at my watch. It was three o'clock on Friday afternoon, time to bicycle back to The Shoebox, find something in my fridge to eat, and start writing a paper due Monday. But instead, a few minutes later, I found myself standing at a construction site near Emory Hospital. Dozens of men in hard hats were drilling and digging and hammering. I stopped by a temporary wire fence with a bright red sign: No Unauthorized Personnel Allowed/Hard Hats Required Beyond This Point.

"Hey," I said to a guy in a hard hat walking out.

He looked at me a little suspiciously, but not without interest. Some of his buddies joined him at the door. One punched him on the shoulder, giving him a knowing glance.

"I want to borrow a hard hat," I said, feeling my face go hot. "For a costume party. I want to go as a construction worker."

The men reappraised me. First they'd been wondering if I was coming on to them. Now they were wondering if I was gay.

"Just for the weekend." I said. "I'll give it back Monday."

"Aw, I got a tool belt you can have," another worker volunteered. "Never been used, and I don't want it back. It's too small." He patted his comfortable belly. All the other men laughed. "Give her your hard hat, Tony," someone else said.

"Give her yours," Tony shot back.

"Here." A tall African American worker stepped out from behind the others and handed me a bright yellow construction hat. "Here you are, miss," he said politely. "Bring it back on Monday and ask for Jerry."

"Thank you," I said. My face grew even hotter. The fat guy got the tool belt out of his pickup and handed it to me, still in the box. As I walked away, six pairs of eyes watched me go.

That night, before the party, I had to bore another hole in the tool belt to make it small enough to fit. I put it on over a pair of faded blue jeans, pulled my hair back into a ponytail, and wore a long-sleeved burgundy button-down shirt and the clompiest shoes I had, my hiking boots. With the construction hat on my head, I looked like a girl trying to be a boy. But the effect wasn't displeasing, I thought.

I thought I was just going to a crazy costume party, dressed as a construction worker with an empty tool belt. I didn't know I was walking across a threshold into the rest of my life.

My father taught me the word "feminist" when I was still in elementary school and said he counted himself as one. I grew up in a liberal-minded family where I was taught that abortion was little more than cutting your fingernails, "socialism" was a synonym for "enlightenment," and women could do anything they set their minds to. When my mother set her mind to leaving—choosing her prominent career as a microbiologist over her life with her family—I was ten. My two oldest brothers, twenty and eighteen, were already out of the house. My third brother, Zach, had no problem splitting his time between the city and the suburbs, but I was miserable in my mom's drafty apartment in the Back Bay, which didn't have a room for me, getting up at 5:30 AM to take the T from Boston to Newton Centre to get to school.

In high school I studied yoga and campaigned for the Democratic Party. I went to peace protests and passed out flyers showing rabbits in steel vices, their eyes forced open—animals used to test expensive makeup that I believed women shouldn't feel compelled to wear. I became a vegetarian. I joined the international Nestlé boycott, hoping someday I could visit the African villages where Nestlé shamelessly sold infant formula to women whose own nutrient-rich breast milk was better for their babies. I never shaved my legs.

Weaned on feminism, I always knew I would make my own money and have a career. I started babysitting when I was twelve and got my first job, in a bagel shop, when I was fourteen. I paid for 20 percent of my Ivy League education out of my own pocket.

I also dreamed of having children. Marriage seemed superfluous—why marry if you're just going to divorce?—but childbearing did not. Too emotionally complicated even to find a decent boyfriend, I fantasized about being a young mother and doing what my mother didn't: putting my children before myself.

Being dressed like a man at the party was strangely exhilarating. I found myself *acting* like a man: I lost my usual though often hidden shyness and worked the party like a . . . well, like a cocky construction worker. Jennifer sidled up to me, dressed like a baseball player.

"Hey, Mister," she drawled, leaning her body against mine, "how come you don't have any tool in that belt?" She giggled loudly. "I want to see your tools!"

Some smoke-filled, flirt-filled hours later I was on the dance floor, French kissing a guy wearing a black dress. He was so buff, his arms bulged over the spaghetti straps. When he told me he was a graduate student in philosophy, I had trouble believing it. How could anyone smart enough to understand Hegel and strange enough to enjoy reading Wittgenstein be so fit? At 5:00 AM, Ian ripped my birth date out of his desk calendar so the guy in the black dress—James—could write down my phone number. He called me in the morning to invite me over for buckwheat pancakes. His own recipe, made from scratch.

James says Ian's party isn't really how we met. He says at the beginning of the semester, a woman wearing a power suit, riding a mountain bike with a helmet hanging from one handlebar and a lock from the other, clipped him as he was crossing the street. The same woman ended up in his graduate seminar on narrative theory, but whenever he tried to catch her eye, she was looking somewhere else.

Two years later, we were lying in bed in The Shoebox, talking about the future. "I've got an idea," I said. "You can stay home with the children, and I'll work."

He looked surprised but curious. James's grandfather had told him he'd buy him a Porsche if he got into medical school. Most of the men in his family measure their self-worth by how much money they make. They are staunch Republicans and practicing Catholics who belong to private city clubs and talk business on the weekends. They already found it inexplicable that Jimmy Jr. was in graduate school, majoring in philosophy.

But this was my feminist solution to wanting to have children and wanting to work. I knew lots of women a little younger than my mother who had adamantly chosen to pursue their careers. Their husbands worked, too. So, in the name of feminism, they found babysitters and daycare centers to raise their children.

But I had started listening to Dr. Laura during my commute out North Buford Highway to a language center where I was teaching

English to Korean immigrants. When I first heard her on the radio I didn't change the dial, because I recognized the name: My father's third wife had once said she hated Dr. Laura. That was reason enough to listen.

And what Dr. Laura said made sense. Mothers should take care of their children. *Stop thinking about yourself and put your child first,* Dr. Laura berated when women called to complain that it was hard to balance their careers with their childcare. *Be there when your child takes his first steps, laughs his first laugh, says his first "Bah!"*

Dr. Laura spat the word "feminism" out like she was saying something dirty: mafia, placenta, nostril. But even though our religious and political affiliations didn't match, I intuitively felt that what she said was true: Children need their parents. I didn't have mine growing up—the everyday work of looking after my three older brothers and me was relegated to a series of nannies—and I was still feeling the scars. Yet I also knew I wanted to work. I was ambitious and energetic, at the top of my PhD class. A publisher had approached me about my dissertation already; the university had offered me a visiting teaching position. It felt like a political decision to have my husband stay home and look after the kids, and also like a perfect solution. Who said women couldn't have it all?

Our first daughter was born after twenty-two hours of labor on a hot evening in the middle of July in an over-air-conditioned hospital in Atlanta. As I held the smallest and funniest looking and most beautiful creature in my arms, and she made an *ut-ut-ut* noise, asking to be fed from my swollen breasts, I wasn't sure what I believed anymore about motherhood and politics and a woman's right to work. I just knew I wanted to be wherever our daughter was.

"I can't do this," I sobbed a few weeks later, trying to figure out how to put the parts of the breast pump together so that I could leave breast milk for James to feed the baby while I was at the university teaching my classes.

"I'll do it," James said, sitting beside me on the couch and picking up the unfathomable pieces. "We'll figure it out."

James has the fondest, softest memories of the time he had alone with our firstborn, sitting in the nursing chair and feeding her bottles of expressed milk, holding her to his chest as he read Baudelaire. But I remember it as a time of speeding tickets (rushing home to nurse between classes), sleeplessness, and desperation. Frantic to be with my daughter, I was angry that my "feminist" ideas and America's inability to provide a social net for mothers and newborns had driven me back to work so quickly.

So when we had our second child, it was James's turn. He got a job working for a dictionary publisher and had to leave the house before our girls were awake, sometimes returning after they were already in bed. My days were filled with the whines of two needy children: a stubborn toddler who wanted Daddy, needed a glass of milk *right now,* and refused to do anything I asked—from putting on her underwear to washing her face—and an infant who fussed *all the time.*

Every morning after James left for work, I looked around our little New England farmhouse, with its low ceilings, dust bunnies, and toys scattered everywhere, and wondered how I'd survive the day until he came home. We weren't on speaking terms with James's mother because her alcoholism had gotten out of control, and my mother acted needy and pathetic around the children, snapping at them and demanding my attention. With no family to help me, and very few friends with small children (all the academic women I knew had grown kids or were single), I was terribly lonely. I made a star chart for myself and my toddler. She would get a star if she could make it through the morning without losing her temper. I would get a star if I could make it through the morning without losing mine. Neither of us got many stars.

One dark snowy afternoon, Hesperus was whining, nothing I did could get Athena to stop her shrill crying, and I started to feel lightheaded. My heart beat so hard and so fast, I thought it would jump out of my chest. Dizzy and frantic, I started hyperventilating. I called James, who heard something so miserable in my voice that he said he'd leave work and come home right away. But the roads were icy and the commute took forty-five minutes on a good day. I thought I was having a heart attack and I panicked, calling 911. Soon, big-booted firemen were clomping through our house, their shoes tracking snow on the unfinished floors, looking for an emergency. Athena, who had just learned to pull herself to standing, bounced up and down on her legs and gave them a toothless grin. Two paramedics strapped me to a gurney to take me to the hospital. My friend Nora came over to stay with the girls, her fat-fisted baby on her hip. The first and only time I've ridden in an ambulance, I finally unclenched: There was something so peaceful about being strapped in and whisked away from my life. The incessant and depthless needs of my two small children seemed far away. Someone was finally caring for *me*.

The young resident at the hospital was arrogant and impatient. He wanted to be stitching up gunshot wounds and applying tourniquets, not dealing with a thirty-one-year-old housewife with a PhD who was having a full-blown anxiety attack but was otherwise in perfect health.

James felt desperate, too. He spent all day wishing he could be with his family, worried that he was missing something he would never be able to recapture, wondering why he was working with words all day instead of taking care of his girls.

One night after they were finally asleep, and before the inevitable pitter-patter of feet that would signal a bedtime visit from Hesperus, we talked it over. James's working full-time and my staying home wasn't working. My working full-time and James's staying home hadn't worked, either. We both wanted to be with our children. And we both wanted to work (something I was only able to admit once I tried being a full-time mom). But neither of us wanted to do one or the other exclusively.

So many of our friends either work or stay home full-time and seem happy with their choices. I know that everyone is different, and that women and men have different degrees of attachment to their children, depending on the child, their life circumstances, genetics, up-bringing, and lots of other factors that are hard to name or measure. But I wonder if women in America are really better off than 1950s *Leave It to Beaver* housewives were. Instead of having to excel at vacuuming and lunch making, we have to excel in the workforce *and* at home. Without a social structure in America that allows women and men to take paid maternity or paternity leave for the first few years of their child's life, they must either leave their family to return to work when the baby is a few months old, or experience the isolation and depression that sometimes come with staying home full-time in an individualistic society where family no longer participates and the spouse is away for most of the day. Financial pressure often drives us to make decisions that are best for our family's bank account but not for our mental health.

James quit his job, and we started a writing and editing business. Our office was the walk-through room with no closet be-tween our bedroom and the girls' room, and we did grant writing, translations, editing, and ghost writing from our shared desktop computer. At first, we made so little money that we applied for food stamps and heating assistance, but slowly our business began to take off. I got a book contract, and we both started getting magazine article assignments that would actually pay the bills. Maybe it wasn't a coincidence that Hesperus turned from a difficult toddler into a charming little girl and Athena outgrew her fussiness at the same time that my husband and I carved out a way to be home with them. By then, another baby was on the way.

"Is Jerry here?" I asked a construction worker a bit nervously that Monday after Ian's party.

"Now, what would a nice little lady like you want with Jerry?" the worker teased, then turned to holler: "Jerry! Someone's got something for ya!"

Jerry appeared at the gate. "Thanks for the hat." I handed it up to him.

"How was the party?" he asked.

I could feel myself blushing. "Good. It was . . . interesting."

"The hat do the trick?"

"I think so."

Of Volcanoes and Ruins and Gardens

by Violeta Garcia-Mendoza

I KNOW IT'S A PRIVILEGE: this ballot, the fact that the American government deems me person enough to be counted. I am Hispanic, a woman, and one not even fully of this country, born abroad as I was. I can never be president. Still, I can determine who will be.

Maybe it's fair, then, that the American government has a say in when and how I fulfill something vitally important to me: becoming a mother. When my husband and I decide to make our family through adoption and to seek a child from Guatemala—a country whose language and culture best match the Spanish/American blend of our marriage and everyday life—we must follow the chutes and ladders of bureaucracy. We must outline our histories and our intentions on reams of paperwork for a progression of government workers to approve or deny. A yes or a no, my motherhood caught up in a vote of sorts.

I come of voting age in one of American history's most politically divided times, just after the new millennium and the contested 2000 election. Soon after, planes irrevocably alter the skyline. The president draws a line in the sand, demarking on national television who is with us and who is against us. Armies march across borderlines, invade cities where I've never been. Across the country, debates break out over party lines. Strangers across the world lay more bodies to rest in the mournful grids of their cemeteries.

I feel overwhelmed by the political scene. I picture men in suits shouting. My mind paints the sphere of politics as a virile, dark-paneled office, with too many picture frames and trophy heads hanging on the walls. It's a place I'm sure I don't belong, circuitous and soft as I am.

A few years later, my husband and I are waiting for the sky to open, waiting for the seasonal rains to pour into the lap of these mountains, here in Guatemala City. This afternoon, the water will run brown through the faucets. The roar of thunder in the distance will serve as background music to the cries and coos of the new daughter we will meet for the first time.

What has brought us here is the same thing that brings many Americans to this country—parenthood. Or, in more concrete terms, adoptive parenthood: an incompliant body, a ream of paperwork, a handful of photographs, hope.

On our first drive through the city, the weapons I see everywhere remind me of what could go wrong. Men wear guns slung across their bodies as casually as if they were backpacks. I watch them standing against buildings, riding in the back of a truck beside our car. They walk so confidently in spite of the burden that I wonder if, when they undress, they stumble to their beds without that weight. Watching them, it occurs to me that not only do I not know how to shoot a gun, I don't know what to do if a gun goes off. It has not been a danger anyone's ever warned me against.

What could go wrong here is the same as what could go wrong at home: natural disaster, war, illness, loss. But in Guatemala, shoring up against it operates at a different pitch. Families do more than just collect canned goods and flashlight batteries, Purel and condolence cards. Here, the sidewalks are cracked in a visible history of earthquakes. Here, our friend points out where Hurricane Stan caused hills and crops and homes to give way in a landslide. Almost everyone we meet can tell us of someone they loved who was murdered, who was made to disappear, or who fell ill, never to recover. Of people who needn't have died. On this weekday afternoon, we drive past dozens of older women filing slowly into churches.

In Guatemala, as at home, I take in the drama of other people's stories. I am naturally shy, a woman, a writer. People expect me to listen and watch, and I do. I am comfortable pressing my ear to the ground. I think of anthropology, that art of chronicling societies as an embedded observer, and on this trip, I tell myself that's what I'm doing. I file the story of a murdered son beside the story of a drowned son. Genocide beside racism. Famine beside hunger. I bear witness to the stories. I remember them.

But I fear I will not remember them urgently enough. Not as if they were my own. I fear that after this trip, my husband and I will disembark onto American soil with a hundred other people who've just seen what we've seen. I fear we will join the stream toward the Metro, the food court, the short-term garage, already forgetting.

Fear begins to gnaw at me that witnessing isn't enough. That I can't save the world with something as passive as remembering, as simple as storytelling.

A few months later, friends who've just returned from a trip to Guatemala—to visit the child they'll be adopting, just like us—call to tell us about their trip. There was new construction at the airport, their hotel's breakfasts were delicious, they had a hard time fitting the painting they bought of the Antiguan Arch on the plane home. And then my friend hesitates and says, "There was something else, too. The hotel shuttle wasn't outside the airport this time. Someone had to call it for us, and we had to wait." She pauses.

I know what she's going to say.

"There were so many children there, begging. I didn't know what to do. The airport employees told us not to give them anything, but . . . I couldn't *not* do it, with what we were there for."

When it's time for us to return to Guatemala to bring our daughter home, my concern is, first and foremost, to have everything go smoothly. Instead of staying with friends, I book the Real InterContinental, which puts us closer to the airport and to the embassy. Last time, our friend picked us up and whisked us away immediately, but this time we will be waiting for the hotel shuttle. As we join the muggy crowd of people in the airport corridors, a shapeless anxiety forms in the pit of my stomach. I dread what's coming before seeing it with my own eyes.

I don't expect the street children to whisper. I don't expect them to approach us like they do, bumping against each other somnolently, like fish. Opening and closing their hands instead of their mouths. Some of them hold hands with a smaller sibling, tethering themselves together to make sure they don't get separated in the crowd. They try out a handful of English words on us—"hello," "please"—before they learn I speak Spanish. Then they ask for money for milk, for medicine. Their skin is dull, inflamed in places, their lips chapped, hair tangled and matted; their feet are bare. They don't swarm but quietly press against us with their soft *por favores* and *gracias*.

My husband and I place American dollars in their palms, meeting their eyes and nodding as respectfully as possible. An airport attendant walks toward us, shouts and kicks one of the kids. He tells us to stop giving them money. When he's walked away, we resume our handouts.

Our singles run out before the shuttle comes, and I try to explain to the children that we have nothing left. They are incredulous; something sparks and hardens in their eyes. The attendant returns to shoo them away. I watch the children dart across the slick streets, where traffic rushes toward them in both directions. There are no mothers to hold their hands, to keep them from the sharp edge of danger.

I almost step off the curb after them. Mothers turn toward a newborn's cry anywhere, instinctively, whether or not it is their own baby crying, and I'm only *almost* like them.

Adopting internationally is more political than I bargained for. Throughout our process, sensationalist stories break: news of corrupt adoption practices, of stolen children. World groups speak out against governments that allow children to be adopted outside of their birth culture. Some Americans decry international adoption as bringing more "foreigners" into the country. I view this lust for scandal and this clubhouse mentality with dismay and outrage, from the fringe of American identity. Having lived inside and outside of this country, I know the price and promise of this place.

It surprises me what gets left behind. There's little discussion of the social policies in Guatemala that lead many Guatemalan women to relinquish a child. Of Guatemalan women, particularly Mayan women, with little opportunity for education or fair employment under the current system, with no reproductive choices available to them. Of babies placed under the wheels of buses when women are denied the option to relinquish a child for adoption. Of nights when government-trained men march street children to the jungle and make them disappear. It's a privilege to be unaware of the dramatic circumstances that cause a need for intercountry adoption, or other types of immigration; it's a crime to not be willing to even imagine them.

The choice to adopt our daughter is so much bigger, more complex, than I anticipated. It involves politics—questions of who may mother, under what circumstances, and where—voiced in both countries, but no good answers. First families, foster families, adoptive families are excluded from the formal debate; instead, discussion ebbs and flows between so many men removed from the mess of women's bodies, of poverty, of love. The men who decide the fate of intercountry adoptions don't have their backs up against the wall; nor are they leaping in faith. Politics do not do this the justice they must.

I need to make the journey to motherhood manageable again, in the face of the press and the tangle of international relations between the United States and Guatemala. I don't know how to battle. I want to make a little altar to Guatemala—a place to sit and think about this staggering place of volcanoes and ruins and gardens. A place to pray for our daughter, for her first family, for her foster family, for the friends we've made. Instead, I decide on a portable altar, a shard of jade my husband brought me from his day trip to Antigua Guatemala. A prayer stone, its touch grounds me. I close my fingertips around it, listen. I speak what I know, make the difference I can make.

The American embassy in Guatemala City looks a lot like our local Department of Motor Vehicles: steps, turnstiles, long lines. The dry smell of paperwork. In this bureaucratic palace, the American government will issue our daughter her citizenship status so she can emigrate home with us.

Most of the waiting room is taken up by others like us: American families with Guatemalan-born children in tow. Men and women wait to sign the final paperwork offering America to their child as a promise; but also, in this place, promise to honor, not forget, the soul-shaping influences of the Guatemalan landscape—geographic, cultural, social, and otherwise—that have converged tragically, and joyfully, in this moment. We smile across the room at a couple who later tell us they're from Kentucky. They tell us they got on a plane for the first time in their lives to bring home their dimpled son. We exchange small talk with others: a thirtysomething single mom, a military family, a radiant woman with a chronic medical condition, a young couple who plan to adopt before trying to get pregnant, an older couple with grandchildren slightly older than their new daughter.

This is a private moment for all of us, not a demonstration for or against anything. But it could be; all of us in the same moment, we are also committing, together, the same political act: loving outside the borders.

My husband holds our daughter in his lap on the first leg of the plane ride home. She's quiet but awake. We tip bottles of formula to her mouth and talk to her and show her a small purple dinosaur and a bunny with a rattle in it. On the second leg, she's on my lap, and she sleeps. In the darkness of the cabin, lightning flashes far below us like the glow of upside-down stars. I kiss our sleeping daughter. Her dark, wispy hair against my lips smells of pureed leeks and baby shampoo, and it startles me, how I can now take part in this intimate gesture.

It takes months for this intimacy to be consistently reciprocal. Slowly, I notice how Maya begins to take my hands in hers when she settles into bed between us after a teething nightmare. She nestles into the dip of my underarm and places my hands across her tummy. During the day, she runs up to me to let me receive her sloppy open-mouthed kiss. She offers me a drink from her sippy cup and gives a belly laugh when I take it. She takes her fingertips to my eyelashes, as assuredly as if they belonged to her. She sneezes into my hand.

It's the opposite of pregnancy, maybe. If I had given birth to her, her birth would have begun a slow process of releasing her into the world; having adopted her, we've begun the process of letting each other in, of allowing ourselves to become inextricably linked. We were born six thousand miles apart and share not a single genetic secret; we share only circumstance, a chain of moments. It is enough. I'm in awe of the way the perceived boundary lines between us fall away. The space that carries my love for her is so vast, it feels like a cove carved out in me; so big, it's startling what else it lets me carry.

Motherhood bears gifts: patience, the necessity of being present, the sharpest sense of compassion. Adoptive motherhood bears the secret that the lines we erect to partition ourselves off from others, to protect ourselves against the heaviness of the human experience, are arbitrary. I believe in these things.

The first year of motherhood is enough to startle me to action. Suddenly, I no longer feel paralysis, or inadequacy in my political roles as mother, as woman, as person. With an expanded worldview, I no longer feel unworthy of raising my voice on behalf of the people I love—everywhere. Political action and thought become certain consequences of the maternal. The system in which these are housed is beside the point. I become an activist, an advocate—a more realized voter and mother.

And a fearless storyteller. I am altered by the gravity of what I have borne witness to through my experiences with Guatemala, that land of volcanoes and ruins and gardens. I return to these stories as if they were intimate and urgent, wise and heavy as a prayer stone in my pocket. As if they were my own.

Mothers Against Faith

by Marion Winik

Many people think it's grace to be able to believe in God. To be faithless is to be spiritually impoverished, with only logic's cold sun for warmth and science's heedless molecules for company. But while I'm all for logic and science, my atheism is less an intellectual attitude than a spiritual intuition, born in my heart as much as my head, something I feel as much as conclude.

In fact, until recently, I wouldn't have described myself as an atheist, because it sounds more certain than I am. Though no argument for the existence of a deity has persuaded me so far, all I know for sure is that I don't know; the word "agnostic" seemed to reflect that perfectly. But my drift toward a more definite position picked up momentum on September 11, 2001, when the violence of believers jumped its historical and geographic confines and came to live in my neighborhood, came to do mayhem in the city of my birth. Out of my tears and shock that day came a clearer sense of how faith gives permission for people to do horrible things to other people.

Part of it can be blamed on specific religious tenets about life after death, the notion that people who act in service of their God will be rewarded in the great beyond. Part of it is more general symbolic thinking, the substitution of the conceptual for the real. It was said over and over that the World Trade Center and the Pentagon were symbols of U.S. policy. To me, they were buildings full of people. Which were destroyed, while the policies lived on unscathed.

In the wake of this event, I fantasized about organizing some new political action groups. I wanted to found Mothers Against

Symbolism, Mothers Against Religion and Ideology, Mothers Against the Afterlife. And finally, after our country chose its course of response, Mothers Against Indiscriminate Revenge. Why mothers? I guess for the same reason mothers are against drunk driving—because that could be my kid out there. It could be your kid. It's somebody's kid, that's for sure, and a random death is not good enough for anybody's child. When you spend so much time taking care of people, it's hard to see them senselessly wiped out, just because they were in the wrong car, the wrong building, standing at the wrong bus stop in the wrong city.

Even as the attacks clarified my differences from those who live by theology, they also helped bring into focus what is most sacred to me. Which is simply human life. To me, it's like this. If your political ideology or religious belief is telling you to go kill people, there's something wrong.

Of course, there are many right things about any given religion, and if living in a Christian country actually meant that we do unto others as we would have them do unto us, that we turn the other cheek, that we don't throw the first stone, I would make my peace with it. But though there are Christians whose lives embody these beliefs, and I even know a few of them, on the whole, this doesn't seem to be the gist of our national religion. In fact, the argument made to the Supreme Court in 2004, that the phrase "under God" in the Pledge of Allegiance is divisive, reflects what I see as a larger truth about God. The notion of God has been splitting people into fierce factions for a long time, and the ripple effect of their competing beliefs seems not just anti-sacred but unbelievably dangerous.

I'm not just talking about Islam; I'm talking about all religions. Even the box office figures of *The Passion of the Christ* made me nervous. If we leave now, I half joked to my Jewish friends last year, we'll be like the Goldsteins who got out of Germany in '29. And, of course, I have my problems with Israel, too.

Actually, it's not only that I don't believe in God. It's that I'm against him.

Since I was not struck dead after typing that last sentence, I'll go on.

As for the cold sun and the heedless molecules, I'd like to put in a word for the spiritual side of atheism. I still have all the emotional experiences that lead people to faith: I feel small; I have questions; I am grateful; I need strength. And I constantly see things that hint at the presence of secrets I do not know. The ones that bewitch me the most are not the inexplicable nightmares, but the tiny benisons. The appearance of butterflies, the taste of peaches, the possibility of simultaneous orgasm. The love between people and animals, the generosity of strangers, the million acts of kindness and friendship that have no component of self-interest—life's moments of undue sweetness do make it seem as if something out there takes a fond interest in us, not just as a species but as individuals. Though other times that something seems just as intent on our cruel destruction.

No matter how they enchant me, these phenomena don't lead me to faith. I experience something quite a bit less definite, a lighter-than-air sensation that flutters and hovers in my breast like the hummingbirds around the bottle of ruby-red sugar water my husband puts in the back yard.

Faith moves mountains, they say. That may well be true. It certainly knocks over buildings. Wonder, I think, might be a gentler way to live.

Well-Behaved Women

by Jennifer Niesslein and Stephanie Wilkinson

You see these bumper stickers. Honk If You're Horny. Visualize World Peace. Well-Behaved Women Rarely Make History. You don't honk; your horniness is a private matter. You don't think it's wise to visualize anything when you're behind the wheel. You purse your lips a little at the last bumper sticker, presumably slapped there by the rebel in the SUV, the one who is destined for History. It grates a little, if you're like us.

We're well-behaved women, for the most part. We came to the magazine we founded, *Brain, Child,* as interested readers. We came as editors and business owners. Foremost, we came as literary types, more interested in the good story than the political point.

We were very serious. "Motherhood," we declared in our mission statement, "is worthy of literature." Worthy of *literature.* We didn't want to be political. Or, if we did, we wanted to be political in that personal-is-political kind of way.

We wouldn't be dissuaded. We went out to lunch with a contact in publishing. We sat at the table and picked at our crab cakes, our salads, our crème brûlée. Our babies kicked their legs in their bucket seats next to the booth. "I'd hate to see you lose the money," the professional warned us. "I mean, this is something that would appeal to the two of you, but is there a market for it?"

Later, at a party, we met a guy with a kid our kids' ages. "So you have a magazine about being a mother?" he asked. "So you, like, read little poems that mothers write about their kids or whatever and publish them?"

Sometimes being a well-behaved woman is trying.

This is what we actually do: We publish a magazine that is composed largely of personal essays by mothers. We run pieces on the maddening process of potty training, on what happens when a mother's drinking buddy joins AA, on weaning a toddler, on swearing off swearing, on finding happiness after divorce, even when that happiness is painful for your kids, on losing faith, on being a deaf mother, on life after the death of one's child.

We also run news, in-depth reported pieces, and book reviews. This is where it gets tricky. Because if you follow mothers' issues for more than, oh, a month, you find that there's only so far you can report or edit the news without it affecting your own life.

One of us, after researching the link between autism and vaccines for a story, decided to space out her son's vaccines so he didn't get the full-on cocktail. Did you know that if you do that, you'll get a registered letter from your kid's school requiring you to sign an acknowledgment that, in case of a measles outbreak, they can expel your child?

One of us, after working on a feature about the history of artificial hormones, decided to pitch the birth control pills she'd faithfully been popping for years. (Later—years later, after her long and tiresome run of condom use—we ran a feature on the dearth of birth control marketed to mothers.)

After running a piece on premature puberty, both of us switched our children to organic milk from cows that weren't pumped with hormones. We make a living reading essays written by other mothers, after all, and neither one of us was especially keen on breaking into the world of training bras, deodorant, and hormone-fueled diatribes against our parenting skills any earlier than we had to.

Clearly, we were changing lives. Our own, anyway.

As a wise man once said, "Money—it's a drag." You don't go into journalism for the money, and if you start up an independent magazine, you are obviously a) bored and independently wealthy, or b) committed to your ideals. We were neither bored nor rich.

Brain, Child grew until the ratio of blood relatives to regular subscribers in the database was close to nil. The official office moved out of Stephanie's basement into a real place where we paid rent. Around this time—let's say 2003—other women writers and editors were also finding themselves in the "b" category, as in Be Aware of Mothers' Lives, or at least Be Aware That We Will Kick Your Ass If You Condescend to Us Again. Some were looking, in a very overt way, to overthrow the patriarchy; other just wanted to rid the world of mom jeans.

As for us? We were figuring out what kind of role to take in this brave new world where mothers were suddenly speaking out on matters like expanding the Family and Medical Leave Act, welfare reform, and other political issues. *Brain, Child* definitely covered these things, but would we take a stance?

"We're *literary*," one of us said, clinging to the mission statement as if it were the official security blanket of English majors.

"But we hope to make a difference," said the other, the one with Puritan do-gooder blood in her veins.

Every once in a while, the phone would ring with a potential subscriber asking the Formula Question. "I'm considering subscribing to your magazine," the caller would say. "But I wanted to be sure that you don't run ads by formula companies."

As a matter of fact, we haven't. But we wouldn't turn one down based on ideology, either. Between the two of us, we have five years of breastfeeding under our brassieres; at the same time, we believe our readers can make decisions for themselves and know the contexts of their own lives better than we do—or anyone else does. We would explain this to the caller—yes, we cover political issues; no, the magazine itself isn't tied to one political philosophy. Sometimes the call would end with a collection of a credit card number, some-times not.

We got it from the editorial end, too. We learned to be wary of cover letters that began, "I'd like to write a feature that advocates for [fill in the political hot topic here]." No matter how fabulous the writing, we knew it would end in heartbreak all around if we assigned a reported piece to a writer who also wanted to be an advocate. There would be pleas (from us) to get some quotes from the other side of the issue. There would be the barely bit-back anger (the writer's), suggesting that we didn't understand the *importance* of the political hot topic. There would likely be a parting of ways and grumbling and talk of one's blood pressure. We wanted to avoid this scenario.

This reluctance to embrace causes—even ones you personally believe in—has the potential to get you a reputation as, say, a cold fish. If we had a nickel for every time someone said to us, "I'd love to see *Brain, Child* become more overtly political," then we'd be able to take ourselves out to a very nice dinner indeed.

But there is a line for well-behaved women, particularly ones who consider themselves, first and foremost, journalists: It's the line between pushing for a particular point of view and providing the forum to bring issues to the table that, really, aren't invited to the mainstream tables. It comes down to this: We want our own freedom of the press—a political issue if there ever was one, by the way. We want the freedom to run pieces that are political, apolitical, neutral, or even counter to the conventional wisdom of the emerging moth-ers' movement. In a weird way, knowing our place has been, for us, a triumph.

As we write this, the current issue of *Brain, Child* includes a feature on antidrug messages for the K–6 crowd, an essay about caregiving for children and elders, an essay about a weird man and his snake at the park, a piece on an abortion clinic that offers prayers after pregnancy terminations, an essay about one woman's struggle to raise a successful black son. In other words, your basic hodgepodge of apolitical, political, and that gray area of However You Want to Take It, Ladies.

When you get down to it, some would argue, every time a mother's voice is heard—*this is what* my *life is like, this is what* I *struggle with,* this *is what makes life worth living*—it is a political statement, because we've been invisible, dismissed, for so long. The two of us believe that—and have to believe it, really—to a certain degree. But we also recognize that what we do is limited. We provide a stage and hope that players—ones who can take it to the next level, the lobbyists and activists and policymakers and voters—will jump on it.

Months ago, *The New York Times* ran a piece on the mothers' movement. The big color photo accompanying it featured Kiki Peppard, the Pennsylvania activist who has worked for years to get a maternal employment discrimination law passed in the state. Peppard was holding a magazine in her hands. It was at an angle. We're sure that most *New York Times* readers couldn't tell what magazine it was, but we knew—it was *Brain, Child*.

We can recognize a metaphor when we see one. Well-behaved women might not make history. But we're hoping with all our journalistic hearts that we can make a difference.

The Secret Lives of Babysitters

by Sarah Werthan Buttenwieser

IN PROGRESSIVE WESTERN MASSACHUSETTS, having a strong commitment to politics is commonplace. Countless large-scale resistance
movements began here: against nuclear arms, the Cold War, apart-
heid. The annual Gay Pride March, which our family always attends,
is a civic event that compares to other towns' Fourth of July parades,
drawing thousands. Graffiti has been emblazoned across the majority
of stop signs, turning them into STOP BUSH signs. From this bluer-
than-blue corner of Kerry's home state, my husband's and my kids—
the eight- and five-year-old, at least—are already politically involved.

When Florida's bogus election-count story broke several years
ago, my eldest son, Ezekiel, was in preschool. Months later, Ezekiel
piped up from the back seat of the car, "They should count those
votes," his high-pitched voice emphatic. He'd heard all about the va-
garies of vote counting during dinner conversations. "I mean, if they
count the votes and George W. Bush has won, well, then *all right,*
he should be president. But if he did not *actually* win, then Al Gore
should get to be president."

Just before the 2004 election, I bought back from five-year-old
Lucien, our middle son, his unwanted Halloween candy, giving him
money to donate to a good cause (something we do each Halloween).
He and I delivered the proceeds to the local Kerry for President office.
The following January, Lucien, having learned about the Civil Rights
movement in kindergarten, quizzed every person who came through
the door: "Did you know that white people hit black people just for
being black? And spat on them? Can you *believe* that?"

Not surprisingly, given where we live and who we are, our babysitters are more likely to be Green Party backers than mainstream Democrats. A creative, quirky group, they've arrived with magenta hair, pierced eyebrows, and tattooed ankles, and from our household, they have ventured forth to paint in drafty studios, attend yoga retreats, DJ at local bars, return to college, and teach English in South Korea. With our kids, they raise topics as diverse as karma and nonviolent resistance, Buddhist meditation, tarot, Italian cooking, knitting, reincarnation, and ecology. We've admired their art and have given money to their causes, such as prisoners' rights and the local gay youth center. Recently, we even helped Lauren come out to us when she was too shy to do so herself.

Jill, another babysitter, went to the university and had blond hair (perhaps with a little bottled assistance), wore jeans and sweatshirts, spoke often of her tall boyfriend and his slovenly roommates, and liked studying. If anything, by our standards, she seemed very *normal.* So imagine my surprise when one day my husband, Hosie, called out from the bedroom, where he was reading to the baby, "Guess what?"

I was just coming through the door with a load of laundry in my arms. Before I could respond, he announced, "Jill's vice president of the Young Republicans club."

"That's . . . fine," I replied hastily, scrambling to cover my shock. Before I had even uttered a word, my body had stiffened like a cat's. My eight-year-old, Ezekiel, picked up on that immediately and began looking wild-eyed and frantic. I'm not sure he believed we hated Republicans—exactly. Then again, he might not have been too sure about that.

He pulled on my arm and launched right in: "I want to know what makes someone want to be a Democrat or a Republican." He was earnest and emphatic, his voice bordering by then on shrill.

"I want to know, from *both* points of view." To my kids, Jill was Jill: happy to play games and share her lap. He concluded with a lower, stronger voice, "I want to understand each side."

"That's a great idea," I replied, thinking that he deserved my wholehearted reassurance and simultaneously wondering how in the heck we'd wound up with a Republican babysitter with Young Republican credentials. In truth, we'd found her through our first-ever ad in the paper—all the other sitters had arrived word-of-mouth—so Jill arrived without one thing we were used to in a sitter, which was her inclusion, even tangentially, in our social sphere; she wasn't Jennie's girlfriend's sister, like Emma; or the renter of Paula and Deb's house, like Senta; or the student teacher who did lunch duty at the kids' school, like Katherine.

Simply finding a Republican babysitter in this town is a rare feat. At the University of Massachusetts, where Jill majored in sociology, there are twenty-five thousand students. Over 800 belong to the Radical Student Union, compared with only 160 Young Republicans.

Meanwhile, Hosie—oblivious to Ezekiel's distress—teased Jill about his intention to sway her vote. "You know," he promised/threatened, "we'll get you voting Democrat."

I tried to sound convincing when I chimed in, "Or not."

As I lay awake that night, I wondered: What did it mean to be a Young Republican, anyway? Did Jill back the war in Iraq? Oppress gay people? Oppose abortion rights? Support tax cuts for the wealthy? Back the NRA? Was it detrimental to have someone whose beliefs were, in so many ways, antithetical to ours watching our kids—or was this diversity in action? The question I really had to answer was whether I believed that our job as parents was to expose the kids to all points of view—or whether I thought we were ultimately responsible for imparting to our kids a worldview that reflected the benefit of our judgment and perspective.

Up until that point, I'd never considered censoring anyone from sharing his or her beliefs with my kids. The truth was that some of our babysitters had dug into issues we might have been happier to leave alone, including a large dose of reincarnation, God from a conservative Jewish perspective, and the merits of tattoos. Similar questions had come up when our kids were exposed to how some of their friends' households operated: television (our kids didn't watch), Power Rangers (we didn't have any), weaponry (we didn't have that, either), certain forms of brightly colored and highly artificial food and drink (the brightest we ever had was cheddar Goldfish crackers). I really didn't want to censor anyone now, and I didn't want to raise my kids in a bubble. Yet as I lay there, I did ponder wording future ads differently: *Republicans need not apply.*

I decided not to worry about Jill's political leanings. It being a presidential election year, talk turned to politics and the campaign trail on a fairly regular basis. There was some good-natured ribbing between us and Jill, to smooth the glaring divide between party affiliations, but politics wasn't at our collective center stage. Mostly, she played with the kids, and in turn they enjoyed her a great deal.

Then one morning, per usual, I was racing around, making kids' lunches for school. Jill was hanging with the kids at the kitchen counter, she and the two of them eating English muffins. The little guy was in his booster seat, with some peas and Cheerios strewn in front of him. Lucien began, "Jill, I have a question for you." The gleam in my five-year-old son's eye appeared slightly mischievous. He had before him half the English muffin and a few slices of pear. "Name one good thing George W. Bush has ever done."

There was a beat—just one beat—of silence. *Oh brother* (or one of its less polite counterpart phrases), I thought to myself. *Here we go.*

"He signed the ban on partial-birth abortions," she flung back at him.

I was so stunned, I nearly dropped my peanut butter–coated knife. Maybe politics is fair game, but the abortion issue—something so confusing to explain to very young children—was still off-limits for my kids. I hadn't begun to figure out how to talk about abortion with them yet.

"Jill, can you grab me a couple of plastic bags?" I pointed to a drawer, hoping to divert attentions to school preparations. *Her back was against the wall,* I reasoned. *Who expects a kindergarten student to pose a question like that at seven in the morning?* "We forgot to give you some water, Lucien. Jill, could you get him some water?" I found myself speaking loudly and deliberately, as if without direct words, but with the way I used other words, I could steer Jill onto safer ground.

I couldn't look Jill in the eyes. I felt as if she'd slapped me in my face. But I also knew that she hadn't tried intentionally to do so. She'd responded inappropriately (in my view) to a leading question. We'd all kind of joked about our political differences up until then, as a way of living with them. Sometimes the kids teased our other babysitter, Aaron, a vegan, when they were eating cheese, and the ribbing with Jill wasn't—at least for them—dissimilar. Whatever I said to Jill that day on the subject of abortion would sound like I was trying to change her opinion, so I kept my mouth shut. But I went over the possibilities of what I might say again and again: *every woman's right, equality, think about a woman's health or something like rape or incest, you can never put yourself in another person's shoes,* blah blah blah. Meanwhile, I told myself that the subject of abortion would not come up again in front of the kids, because I just wouldn't let it.

Still, I spent much of the day blathering to friends about what had happened and how offended I was. (Good friends, they were incensed too.) Could such an inappropriate outburst constitute grounds to fire her? By then, we'd been through irresponsible moments with plenty of babysitters—not showing up when scheduled, underdressing a kid when it was cold out, offering dessert first—and we'd weathered many of their troubles: from major depression to a failed babysitter/babysitter romance that began (and ended) in our house. We'd worked out ways to use those hard experiences as opportunities for growth—babysitters' and ours—and we'd never fired anyone for a single lapse.

Besides, politics aside, the day-to-day with Jill was easy. She arrived not on time but *early*. Neither mean-spirited when the kids ceased to cooperate nor freaked out by our middle son's preference to shed his clothing on a regular basis, she took our vegetarianism and television-free household in stride. She even adopted some of our healthy foods into her diet, stunning her roommate by stopping at Whole Foods for cereal and other items. I decided to let the partial-birth abortion comment go and move forth, prepared to censor her if necessary. From that point on, I also tried harder to steer the conversation—including the kids' questions—away from politics. While Jill and Hosie still traded a few teasing barbs on occasion, for the most part, the less political, less heated approach to babysitter/children/parent harmony across the blue/red divide worked just fine. After all, save for these disagreements about certain issues—critical as they are to me—I liked Jill, and I did trust her with my kids.

Months later, when we were cleaning up the kitchen together and the kids were playing outside, Jill asked me for some help in finding a holistic doctor. She was very upset, having just received an abnormal Pap smear. Given her family's history of infertility, she certainly had little reason to fear—in theory, at least—an unplanned pregnancy. Just the opposite, her fear was infertility, and the abnormal Pap could be a signal she, too, would be afflicted. But during the two years I'd spent as an abortion counselor, I'd watched Catholics, anti-choice activists, teenagers, college students, married mothers, and single forty-year-olds all making decisions they had never before envisioned for themselves, in both directions (more often abortion, but certainly sometimes baby). At twenty, Jill did not yet know what situations she or her friends might find themselves in. Although Catholic and conservative in some ways, she was, it turned out, also for gay rights, and she did spend the night at her boyfriend's apartment frequently, and there was no talk—as far as I knew, and Jill talked a lot, so I think I would have known—of a sparkly ring going around her finger.

Jill initiated our conversation because she trusted me. She adored my kids, and she admired my parenting of them. So, while I tried to portray my own feminist epiphany as personal, rather than political, I did describe having an abortion during my senior year in high school. I said that not until that moment had I realized how much I wanted college, career, falling in love, getting married, *and* having children. I said that, like her, I'd been a big-time babysitter, not only through high school and college but also after college, when I continued to care for friends' kids. Of my own children, I said how grateful I felt to have these children she knew and loved when I was ready to raise them with my chosen partner. To her credit, she listened with respect.

Jill babysat through the winter and spring without further political incident. The summer before the 2004 election, she announced that if John Kerry were to choose John Edwards ("He's so *cute*") as his running mate, she might be swayed. And thus our lone Republican took her place alongside the artists and vegetarians and environmentalists, perhaps our quirkiest babysitter yet.

Okay, so she didn't actually vote for Edwards and Kerry.

Thankfully, Jill wasn't slated to work that Wednesday after the election, when our entire town took on the ghostly pall of mourners, and moving to Canada was the hot topic at the kids' school and in the cafés.

The strange thing was, Jill never showed up again. I called her, I emailed her: no response. Did she just feel guilty for Bush's having won? This is really the only explanation I can come up with, to this day. It surprised me to realize that she'd likely wrestled with our differences as well, something I hadn't considered before she disappeared without explanation or proper goodbye. The kids were confused by her sudden absence and a little upset for a couple of weeks, but they rolled with a change in babysitters, as they tend to do. And I found myself feeling a little peeved, a little guilty, a little relieved.

What was odder was this: Months later, Jill used me as a reference for a job. What's more, while explaining that she'd bailed on us in an abrupt fashion, I still gave a positive recommendation.

My Bus

by Karen Maezen Miller

I ALWAYS KNEW where it would lead.

As we cruised down the street on the morning commute to nursery school, my two-year-old would pipe up from the back seat whenever the yellow bus rumbled into view.

"My bus, my bus!"

"That's right," I would carefully rejoin, "A *bus,*" affirming the noun, but not yet the pronoun, not the possession, not the slightest quiver of possibility that the public school just down the street would one day be hers. Years before the question of schools could reasonably be raised, I already felt the fluttering clutch of resistance to her baby-talk claim.

Which school for my daughter? I waffled. *Haven't a clue,* I'd think. *Never given it a thought,* I'd shrug, although I'd given plenty of thought to how brilliant her future would be. How bountiful her birthright. How predestined her success. Although my husband and I were public-school progeny, those were different times in different places with different kinds of parents, we thought. Our parents had neither the privilege nor the need for a choice.

Our school district was as underfunded as any, and especially ill-favored by those with a chance of escaping it. Decades earlier, forced busing had decimated enrollments. As incomes and property values rose, the middle class that had once populated neighborhood schools was nowhere to be found. Sixty-three private schools educated more than one-third of all children in the district. Competition for admission was severe; tuitions were stratospheric. But for parents like us, parents who could pinch and scrimp their way to having a choice, there seemed to be no other choice.

This was the state of education in our country. This was the state of our country, in which the newly elite lived in fear of being left behind with the mass of others we had falsely promised to never leave behind. This was the road the yellow bus traveled twice a day: hauling mostly Hispanic kids to and from the apartment buildings that rimmed the industrial fringe of our suburb; collecting them on the littered streets at frosty dawns and delivering them to our quaint hometown school in our million-dollar neighborhood, made empty by a herd of us heading the other way.

I was not, I thought, unduly anxious about my daughter's prospects. I was not among those employing literacy tutors for my three-year-old. I did not use an Excel spreadsheet to track the application process to private kindergartens. I did not angle playdates with the grandchildren of private-school directors. I did not donate a wad of money to the schools at the top of my wish list. I did not even make a list. I simply believed that one day, when the luminous sheen of my daughter's wonderfulness was made known, something fantastic would happen.

"Who's John Kerry?" she asked one day, seemingly out of the blue. It was not out of the blue, but rather right out of the red, white, and blue bumper sticker on the SUV in the preschool parking lot. She pointed to it and revealed that, while I wasn't looking, she had begun to read. It seemed early, the reading, and early too, the electioneering, although I happily took both signs as foretelling a fabulous outcome.

I had been crushed by the presidential election of 2000. Heartbroken, enraged, and then quietly, insistently, optimistic again. Four years was unimaginable, but four more was entirely impossible. Not with truth on our side. Not with smart money. Not with the

Internet. And so I found myself doing what I'd never done before, not in my more than twenty years of informed, and sometimes impassioned, voting. I took the phone calls. I made the phone calls. I sent tens of dollars. I sent hundreds of dollars. I walked the precinct. I wore the button. I slapped on the bumper sticker, then saw the stickers everywhere, and not just in the parking lot of our high-priced, progressive preschool. Democratic values were alive and never wealthier, it seemed. The republic would be saved.

We took our daughter to the polls on election day of 2004. And what seemed to matter most going in—truthfulness, courage, effort, and ideals—mattered nothing in the end. One measly vote in one dinky town in one irrelevant state didn't count for much. The republic was not only broken, it was no longer ours to fix.

"Have we *ever* voted for someone who won?" My daughter's response reflected her brief life history of losing, zero for two, in presidential contests, but the dejection was universal. We had come to the irretrievable end of hope. And the loss, we realized, was truly hers.

My daughter turned five. She sparkled and charmed. She beamed wonderfulness.

It was time for her to take her rightful place on the cusp of her illustrious career.

We applied to the top-ranked private school in the city. They did not take us aside and tell us that her DNA qualified her for automatic acceptance. We applied as one of four hundred hopefuls paying a $250 fee for a shot at five openings. They did not whisk us to the VIP entrance. We stood, anchored by the weight of our foolish faith, clutching cups of bad coffee, with a hundred other no-chance parents one Saturday morning while our well-dressed children were taken away en masse for their "evaluations." They did not immediately dismiss the others in favor of a clear and unanimous winner. We watched, stunned and deeply ashamed, as our baby girl bolted from the interview room in hysterics, hollering, "Never bring me here again!"

They did not call us back.

While our first choice had failed us, we were still shopping our options.

It is understandable that in our colossal engine of American enterprise, every aspect of life has been reduced to a sales transaction. Everything is a product, every product is a brand, and every brand is a shiny bauble of marketing assembled by campaigners more clever than we.

So it was uncomfortably obvious to us, while my husband and I toured the second tier of private schools, that we were the *customers*, and we were there to be *sold* something. We were being sold an educational philosophy. We were being sold a community. We were being sold social values. We were being sold security. We were being sold success. We were being sold a different kind of world, fabricated out of kids who looked alike and parents who thought alike. We were being sold on the most ambitious and fearful part of ourselves. It seemed phony and even un-American.

Of course, it wasn't un-American in the least. It was the dark and corruptible soul of America. We whispered to each other as we paraded the pristine hallways, "Where are the schools like the ones we went to?" We might as well have been asking, "Where is the country like the one we grew up in?"

In our newly cynical view, all the assurances of product excellence and consumer protection seemed disingenuous when applied to education. We were aimless and unconvinced as the decision deadline approached.

Then our daughter took the wheel.

After three years of schlepping sixteen miles round-trip to a fancy preschool, pushing on even farther to the rarely accomplished

playdate, and routinely crossing multiple city limits to attend a birthday party, my daughter staged a mini-revolt. "Where are my *friends?*"
she wailed on one particularly woeful weekend, stuck in the wonkish
company of dear old Mom and Dad. Looking up, we saw her point.
We had gone hunting for her brilliant future, and we'd overlooked
her front yard. We'd been chasing her birthright and had ignored her
birthplace. *This* was where she lived. This was her world. This was
where she wanted to belong. Where *were* her friends? We scheduled
a visit to the public school down the block.

There, in the porticoed walls of an eighty-year-old building, on
a rolling lawn under leafy grandfather trees, amok with hundreds
of ordinary urchins, awash with the inimitable aromas of dirt, dis-
infectant, and cafeteria lunch was the school like the schools we remembered. The hallways were a little scruffy. The classrooms were
bustling. The teachers were educators. The parents were participants.
The kids were just neighborhood kids. The money was scarce, but the
opportunity was wide open and free.

We were reminded, once again, that this was the best our country could offer. It was the best our country had ever offered. And we
had turned out okay.

The night my husband and I made our choice, it wasn't even a choice.
We looked at the letters from the fine private schools inviting our
daughter inside. We knew their curriculum was excellent, but it no
longer seemed good enough. We knew what they offered was valuable,
but it no longer seemed worth it. Still smarting from our disillusionment with our own government, we resolved to live, really live, the
values that were no longer so self-evident. We would save our money
and invest our daughter in democracy. The bus, after all, was hers.

We would need to be attentive and involved, but we would be
doing that no matter where she went to school. We would need to

enrich her education with extras, but this way, we still had enough in every paycheck to afford them. We would need to trust people of all stripes and believe in the ability of each person to reach the stars.

We would need to be brave, but we could: We were born in the home of the brave.

On the first day of kindergarten, my daughter's teacher stood before an array of beautiful faces. She spoke loudly to reach the pack of teary parents spectating at the back of the room.

"Our job is to create citizens," she declared, and turned to face the flag.

That morning, I placed my hand over my heart and spoke the old pledge with newfound allegiance. The school for citizens had created one more.

On Receiving Notice of
My Stepdaughter's Pregnancy

by Mary Akers

I WANT YOU TO HEAR the voice of an angry stepmother as you read this, so go ahead and settle into it. You know the voice I mean: that extra-tall mocha raspberry voice, with the hint of an edge, the little bit of burn from sitting too long in the pot, from forgetting to remove the dripping dregs.

You remember your stepmother. The woman who first met you when you were thirteen, when you were already mostly formed but still impressionable. The woman who is twelve years younger than your mother, who you thought was so cool, who highlighted your hair in a classy way (when Dad was afraid you might look cheap), who talked to you about boys and choices and gave you the book *Our Bodies, Ourselves* even as you marched in antiabortion parades sponsored by your mother's nameless church, the church you swore was a cult.

The woman who saw what no one else in your life would see: that the cuts on your arm were too symmetrical, too measured, too *clean* to be the cat scratches you claimed they were. The woman who talked to you for hours, crying, "You're my girl, sweetie. I can't let *anyone* hurt you. Not even you."

The woman who urged your father to get you into therapy, who talked you through two pregnancy scares, who spent long nights worrying, struggling to understand, trying to interpret for your father just exactly what you meant when you said the things you said. The woman who sat by helplessly and watched from the corner of her eye as you chewed your fingertips ragged in the National Cathedral during Easter services; picking bits of your own flesh away, devouring them like a ravenous bird. The woman who introduced you to tofu and salads, offered to exercise with you, then watched as you chose, instead, to overeat with an obsessive, focused joy, filling your skin to its bulging capacity and beyond.

And I am still your stepmother: that woman who loves you and cares what becomes of you. But I am angry now. Angry at the hours pulled from my own life—and my other children's lives—trying to help you in yours. Angry when I finally understand that you have been wedded to your suffering for years, so enamored of the attention that you have chosen to make your whole life a buffet of pain. "Long-suffering," as your mother's no-name church might say. As if it were a virtue.

That very same church where you have found such welcoming arms now that you are pregnant. That church where so many other young women are having babies—while still babies themselves, without benefit of husbands or education or money—and everyone is sympathetic, encouraging, reassuring them that they are doing the right thing. Your mother's very words to us: "She's doing the right thing."

To which I want to reply, "For whom?"

When you learned about the possibility of *this* pregnancy, you did not call me, crying, to talk for hours. This time you decided that the greater attention was to be gained in carrying the child to term, having the baby with this man you've known for approximately as long as you've been pregnant. This man who left high school to sweep and empty trash in a fast food restaurant. This man who has encouraged you to stay single, so that you can have the baby on the government's dime.

And when you *did* finally tell me your news, it was an afterthought, at twenty weeks—after you had told your mother, your church, your work, your landlord, your teachers—and (coincidentally) the time just beyond which the only choice to be made was *where to deliver.*

I want to talk with you about the politics of your decision, about owning your own body, and about the dangers of a government that would tell women what we can and cannot choose, would mandate that the slip of one passionate moment commutes every other desire. But I understand I cannot reach you now; your mind is made up, your body has decided. My words would be taken as a polemical rant, as the one small dissenting voice in a tide of fervency telling you what you want to hear: that your decision is *right,* is morally superior, is godly. To swim against that tide would be to risk what remains of our tenuous relationship.

But I wonder: Will that tide still lift you up when you are a struggling single mother? When your baby is sick in the middle of the night? When colic and loneliness and tears threaten to sweep you away? Imagining the difficult years ahead of you makes me sad—the struggle, the heartbreak, the suffering. Except now I understand that it is the suffering you need, that you crave. It is your updated version of cutting. Cutting, without the knife.

Together, we, your family, will feel the ripples of this for years. You've brought this on us all. And the baby. Let's not forget the baby. What choice does she have, being born into poverty, of an immature, uneducated, unmarried, suffering mother?

Suffering. You tell me your feet hurt from the long days of standing behind the register at work. You are tired. You feel nauseous. Your ankles swell. And instead of being sympathetic, anger rises into my temples. You tell me, in the food court of the mall, that yes, things are difficult now, at twenty weeks, but that it will get better when the baby comes.

And I want to stand on the table and shout. "No, it won't! It won't be better. It will be worse. *Now* is the easy part. From here on out, you will never be just yourself again. You will be a mother with her baby. You will be tired from lack of sleep. You will have even less money when you are buying diapers and medicine and childcare. *Now* is nothing. *Now* is easy."

Instead of yelling, I say it gently.

And you flush and say, "Whenever I talk to my mom about the baby, she's excited, she's happy for me. Whenever I tell you and Dad things, I feel like you are mad, like you think it's bad. Why can't you be happy for me?"

Just so I'm clear: Which aspect of this would you like me to celebrate? The decision to have a baby at eighteen? The decision to have a baby without a husband? The decision to drop out of college to become a mother? The decision to bring another small, innocent being into your circle of suffering? The decision to go on welfare? Please, I would just like to be clear about which one of these things I am meant to rejoice in.

Yes, I am angry. Teeth-on-fire angry. Angry for the years of emotional blackmail, angry at your mother, who calls this baby *God's will*, angry at the baby's father for being stupid, at the Chicken Church that preached abstinence ad nauseam, then held up other young mothers as heroines, as martyrs.

But especially angry at your mother—you remember her. The mother who locked you in your room, nailed your window closed when you snuck out to be with your boyfriend du jour, but who wouldn't give you birth control, because premarital sex is a sin. That warden mother you swore you hated, who, when you tried to speak openly with her about sex, threw her palms heavenward and implored, "Jesus, cut these lies in two!" And we rolled our eyes and agreed she was nuts. The mother you now visit often and breakfast with and watch movies with and talk to about the beautiful perfect little baby girl in your belly, the baby that will transform all of your lives into goodness and light the moment she is born. The little princess who will love only you and worship you forever. The tiny doll you can dress up and carry around, that will never cry or make a mess or break your heart.

And I am angry at my shallow, shallow self. I hate that I am embarrassed to tell people the path you have chosen, that I feel the need to explain, as if there were an explanation. That to others, I say your mother is to blame as if I were not a mother myself, damaging my own children in their very own unseen ways every day. If I were a good person, I would not be jealous that you love your mother again. You need her. I should be grateful for her input and support. But I am angry.

Perhaps she is right. Perhaps it *is* God's will that you are pregnant, and I should pray for serenity. But not today. I cannot let go of this anger, because it is a shield that keeps me from seeing how *I* have failed you. In five years of trying, I never managed to help you through the thickness of your own private despair. I never managed to convince you that you were worthwhile and worthy. I never managed to make you want more from life. I never managed to protect you from yourself.

All I am left with is this pathetic, fragile hope that maybe you are happy, that maybe this, *this,* will finally make you happy.

I keep trying to believe it.

Instead, I circle back to helpless rage: You are eighteen and I have to let you go, let you be who you will be, even if that means an unwed mother, college dropout, working at McDonald's in a dead-end town.

I have to decide if I will love that person as much as I loved the suffering girl. Except there is no choosing, love being what it is.

Take your journey, dear stepdaughter. I have not saved you from yourself, but at least I have loved you. Know that I have loved you.

Shown the Ropes

J. Anderson Coats

IT'S GRADUATION DAY at Bryn Mawr College. Girls in black robes fidget in a long, meandering line that snakes around the statuesque Gothic structures in which they studied only days before. Many students cradle bouquets of flowers from boyfriends or proud parents, and some hold small gifts wrapped in shimmery paper with trailing ribbons.

I'm in line among the graduates, but I'm not holding flowers or a present. I'm holding a coloring book, a rock with a purple stripe, a half-eaten package of peanut butter crackers, and a stuffed cat that's missing one eye. My three-year-old son is climbing up my leg, trying to reach the red tassel dangling at my ear.

I'm twenty-two years old, and in half an hour I'll graduate magna cum laude with departmental honors.

Even now I stand out, but I'm used to that. I'm used to smudgy chocolate thumbprints on my copy of Froissart, and Richard Scarry paperbacks mixed up with Cicero and R. R. Davies. I'm used to making hay in the shadow of the debt I owe to progress. Fifty years ago, when married pregnant women were excluded from campuses with much less pedigree than this one, a girl like me with a wide-eyed toddler would have met the smooth oak of the admissions office door.

Shadows and all, I am here because I *belong*.

I was a high school hotshot, trained up as a fish of many colors in a nondescript pond. My GPA was through the roof, and my constellation of achievements glowed on applications. I was the one coming

94

back with a PhD and a Pulitzer, not necessarily in that order. No one looked at me too closely, though. No one could see despair already coating what lay ahead with a faint silt of *don't give a damn*. I wasn't six months in the Real World before despair caught up with me and I went down.

Barely out of high school, I met a man in January and married him that November; our son was born the following March. Before the baby was a year old, we were three thousand miles from home, scraping together something of a life in a jumble of interstates and strip malls.

I cried away long afternoons in slants of powdery sunlight while the baby slept and my husband tiptoed through his workdays, stiff in an unfamiliar husk of oxfords and wingtips. I trudged the apartment's fifteen bland carpeted feet from glass slider to bedroom wall, the baby snuffling into my shoulder and winding tiny damp hands through my hair.

Down I went, down and down, far away from anyone who might notice.

I have no memory of those years. It hurts to write—it hurts to think—that a modest collection of static photographs must stand in for lustrous memories of first steps and splashy sink-baths. That all I have left of his earliest years is limited by what I managed, for form's sake, to absently freeze on film.

I could look up through the delirium of *Sesame Street* and squeaky books and see myself as I once was, the clever, bookish girl who made rag quilts and read Chaucer for fun. This was not how it was supposed to be. I was supposed to spend hours researching delightful obscurities in dusty libraries while my baby amused himself with recycled butter tubs.

Instead, I could barely leave the house. I could barely get up in the morning. I could barely think.

I'd given myself up as permanent baby furniture and washrag and busybox when my acceptance from Bryn Mawr arrived in an embossed ivory envelope.

Looking back, I always picture my entrance into college as a rope dangled about five feet above my head, a single knot tied at the bottom and greased with a thousand kinds of *can't*.

"Grab on and climb up," said a disembodied voice from the clouds on high, where the rope disappeared. "We'll see you if you get to the top."

I would get only one try, and if I fell, I would land where I started, down with the mushy saltines and discarded sticker charts in a dismal suburban zoo exhibit. I would never get this chance again. I swung my baby onto my back and jumped. I caught that rope and held on tight.

Everything about Bryn Mawr was right: the Gothic architecture and the endless rows of books, the brisk and businesslike atmosphere. Wool and leather, old paper, stone and climbing ivy. It was like coming home.

My colleagues were poised, sharp, and intense. They'd prepared themselves to be here their whole lives. They had manicures, digital assistants, and monogrammed luggage. They'd been taking Latin since first grade.

I didn't want to fit in, to wear ballet flats and call professors by their first names without a hint of discomfort. I wanted to *belong* beneath roundel windows in glossy-paneled classrooms. But I stood apart from day one, separated from the world I climbed toward by commuting more than four hours across two states.

I came among them hungry, restless. This was not my birthright. This was more than books and tests, the Dean's List, a degree inscribed on honest-to-God parchment. This was reconstruction, building myself again out of the rubble of hotshot relics and the mental erosion of a thousand powdery afternoons.

My kid, however, was not content to cling to my neck and quietly contribute to my rebirth as a thinking, sovereign citizen. He performed every act of malfeasance in a toddler's considerable arsenal to distract me from the furious paper writing and underlining that stood in for self-determination.

"You not read dat!" He pulled Foucault from my hand and heaved it behind the sofa like a soiled diaper.

"Play Tubbies now!" he whined, threatening a stack of library books with a pink highlighter while I patched together a response to a reading finished the previous midnight.

He clung to my leg and screamed Jack the Ripper when I brought him to daycare, a cheerful home filled with toys and playmates and an amiable basset hound with a fondness for cookies.

His angry screams carried across the daycare's lawn and earwormed into my head among the statistical analyses and colonial discourses. I'd sit in the driveway, crying hard enough to hurt. I'd drive to school four hours across two states, white-knuckled and wishing like hell that he could know somehow that Bryn Mawr was as much for him as it was for me, that Mama numb and bereft of herself was not the mama he wanted or deserved.

I went to class, kept my head down, and went up the rope hand over hand. I conjugated, analyzed, challenged, debated, deconstructed, and conjectured. I told no one about my son, not colleagues nor professors. Inevitably it would change how they treated me, how they conceived of me as a student and as a human being. And I wanted none of it, no sympathy, no pats on the head, no special treatment. I would fly or fall, and whatever became of me would be my own.

I managed to lay low during the autumn semester, but in spring I had to turn in a paper on a day when I had no class and my husband was at work. Which meant I had no daycare. There was no way around it—I had to go in to school. And I had to bring the kid with me.

It was all over. Everyone would know. They'd take one look at the volatile toddler attached to my hip, and all at once I'd be a different person. The careful facade I'd spent precious hours bricking into place, the effortless arguments and sleek papers, would crumble in a single juice-sticky blow.

Not if I could help it.

I spent the whole drive planning. It would be quick and precise, a commando raid worthy of Sun Tzu. Race in. Slide the paper under the professor's door. Duck out. Invisible. No one would know.

The kid was surprisingly eager to see Mama's school, a place he understood only in relation to its removing me from his world. He stopped to introduce his blanket and toy cat to the planters and brickwork. Some girls turned to look at us, but most breezed past like a toddler was part of the scenery.

I began to relax.

We hurried into the history building and crept down the long windowed hallway, the kid stopping to peer out each window and tell me about the cloister outside. The hall was quiet, a long paneled expanse of doors covered with flyers for summers abroad and enrichment programs in far-off and unreachable places.

I slipped the paper under the professor's door and turned to go.

Around the corner came one of my colleagues, a whip-smart New Englander who kept me honest in Chaucerian Texts.

Oh, bloody hell.

She waved cheerfully, then her eyes flicked down to my kid, tormenting the flyers on the professor's bulletin board. When she knelt to slide her paper under the door, my kid chirped, "Hi!"

I was sunk now, so I greeted her and we chatted about the mid-term and "The Miller's Tale" while my kid stomped to hear his steps echo and swung his toy cat by the tail.

"And who is this?" she asked, not unkindly, tilting a thumb at the errant and moderately destructive toddler at my knee.

"This?"

It would be easy to lie. It would be easy to say he was my nephew or my little brother or some kid I was babysitting. But I looked down at the little baby curls on his neck and his shy dimples, and I pulled him close.

"This is my son."

"Wow," she replied, and a look of mild awe crossed her face as she hitched up her backpack. "See you Tuesday!"

And I watched her disappear down the dusty corridor, her ponytail swinging and her pack slung over her shoulder, no herding, no negotiating, no pulling anyone by the hand. I knew then that I never *would* fit in among these effortless girls with their uncluttered days and late giggly nights, the broad sweeps of time devoted to summers in Paris or Wall Street internships, their patient air of unquestioned success.

But I looked down at the corner of my paper protruding from beneath the professor's varnished door and my son's grubby sneakers raising ancient dust, and I knew too that I did in fact belong here, twined around the ivy with brickwork in my soul. I belonged here for the simple reason that I could make the climb, grease or not.

That I did so with a toddler on my back made me a pioneer, much like last century's girls who wanted more than just to marry, who peered out of black-and-white worlds framed on the history department walls as they stood in familiar robes, lined up around familiar Gothic buildings.

People could know, and it wouldn't matter.

The climb was easier once I stopped worrying how I looked making it.

It's graduation day at Bryn Mawr College. Today I'm at the top. My hands are cut up from the climb. The kid on my back got ten times as heavy and took way fewer naps. I wrote my senior research thesis while taking two writing-intensive history classes, toilet training the kid, and buying my first house.

But up I went, because I knew exactly how far down I could go.

I don't leave here with a Fortune 500 gig or a slot at Harvard Law. I don't leave with a dormful of friends or a shoebox of photographs from May Day.

I leave whole.

I leave enmeshed in a prestigious, uncompromising community that rolled the dice on an underage autodidact with more secrets than pedigree, a community I'm proud to claim as my own because it offered the rope without condition, without favor, without slack. A community that gave me the chance to fly and let it be my own.

Tomorrow will be another climb, and I'll have to shoulder my way into grad school or a nine-to-five. I'll have to want it twice as bad and work twice as hard.

But this too is what I leave with: an overarching sense of the possible.

Today I'm at the top, and the view from the clouds is something else.

In Albania

by Mona Gable

HIS EYES TOLD ME EVERYTHING. Pale green and luminous like colored glass, they were wet with tears. "I missed you, Mommy, so much," he said, gazing up at me. He was clutching a bouquet of carnations and daisies and a Mylar balloon with the words "Greatest Mom in the World." He'd worn his best shirt, a blue cloth oxford, and run gel through his sandy hair. I had on rumpled khakis and a T-shirt I'd been wearing for the past twenty hours. All around us, people in the terminal at Los Angeles International Airport were smiling at us, as if to say, *How sweet, the little boy reunited with his mother.* I had my nine-year-old son back, but it was hard for me to rejoice. I had just returned from a country where thousands of mothers would never see their sons again.

It was June 1999, and for the last ten days, I'd been in Albania as a journalist, following a team of UCLA doctors and nurses on a relief mission. Since early spring, 800,000 ethnic Albanians had been driven from Kosovo in a campaign by Slobodan Milosevic, then president of Yugoslavia, to rid the province of its Albanian majority. Over a decade-long series of wars in the Balkans, the Serb dictator had left more than 225,000 people dead and had almost single-handedly scattered millions of refugees. Two months before we arrived in Albania, NATO had launched air strikes against Yugoslavia in an effort to force Serbia to withdraw. But Milosevic had not relented.

Most of Kosovo's ethnic Albanians had fled over the rugged mountains into the neighboring countries of Macedonia and Albania. Of those refugees, thousands were doctors and nurses who'd been stripped of their medical licenses and jobs during a Serbian crackdown in the late 1980s. Some had found work in Albania with International Medical Corps, or IMC, a Los Angeles–based relief agency providing medical care in the region. While I was there, the Americans were paired with the Kosovars and with some local Albanian doctors in medical teams. Every morning, we'd set out in Toyota Land Cruisers from Albania's capital of Tirana and head for the refugee camps, returning just before dusk.

Albania was not my first time in a war zone. I had covered the conflict in Nicaragua in the early 1980s, had seen bombings and met *campesinos* who'd had their crops burned, had spoken with Sandinistas who'd been tortured by the National Guard. As a journalist, I thought I had become somewhat immune to such violence, but I failed to take into account certain things. When I went to Albania in May 1999, I was no longer single and in my late twenties. I was no longer unattached and rootless, with no one depending on me. I was the mother of two young children.

The lens of motherhood would filter everything I was to witness, from the gypsy children who pursued us in the filthy streets of Tirana, begging for *leks,* to the two-year-old boy at a camp in a grim former veterinary clinic in the northwestern corner of the country. Dressed in a pair of overalls with hearts and bunnies embroidered on them, he sat in the lap of his grandfather: an elderly man in a conical Muslim cap with the thick gray mustache common to many ethnic Albanian men. The boy had a ragged cough, and as one of the Albanian doctors listened to the boy's lungs, the grandfather tenderly stroked the child's head, tears in his eyes. The grandfather was the boy's only relative in the camp. His mother was missing, maybe dead. No one seemed to know.

My job as a reporter was to take down such stories, to be detached. But that morning, as the boy and the grandfather waited for the doctor, I had to look away.

In camp after camp, the stories ethnic Albanians told me were chillingly the same. Serbian paramilitary bursting in the door and demanding money, giving the terrified inhabitants only minutes to get out. Boys and men being dragged off to God knows where while their mothers and sisters and wives begged for their lives. Families fleeing when their villages were shelled by Serbian military and escaping to another village, only to be burned out there. Middle-aged women whose eyes were dead because their teenage sons had been shot.

I'd read the newspaper accounts, of course, had followed the reports of ethnic cleansing on the evening news. But hearing the stories up close turned my stomach. "I growed the boy and they killed him," one grieving mother said through my Kosovar translator.

We were sitting in the shade of a scrub pine at a shelter for four hundred refugees, about an hour's drive west of Tirana. The sun was fierce and cows grazed in a verdant field nearby. NATO troops were now in force in Albania, and as we were talking, two American-made Hueys rumbled overhead, causing the children near us to startle and reflexively look up to the sky. A sign, I later realized, of war trauma. A thin old man in a beret hobbled by on crutches, his foot bandaged: evidence of a grenade attack that had also killed his daughter and son.

One mother told me that she—like dozens of the ethnic Albanian refugees I met—had a son in the Kosovo Liberation Army, or KLA, the rebel group fighting for Kosovo's independence. She had no idea if he was alive, and she was taking Valium for depression, a common opiate in the camps, since antidepressants weren't available. As we talked, dozens of women crowded around, occasionally interrupting to help my Albanian translator. They wanted me to understand exactly what had happened.

Yet while I listened to their stories, I thought: *How could I?*

The contrast between my own life as a mother, fraught mostly with worries over school and bedtime and meals, and theirs was simply staggering. I had never been forced to flee my home, had never lost a child to disease, had never lost a child to war.

The leader of this camp was a thirty-nine-year-old elementary school teacher from Pristina, Kosovo's urbane capital. Slender and articulate, he could have been someone I knew when I was a teacher fresh out of graduate school at Berkeley. His voice was level as he told me how he and his wife, four children, four brothers, and several relatives fled after fifteen Serbs in black masks appeared one night at their front door. By the time they escaped, every house on their block was in flames. "It all happened so fast," he said, looking away. They were blessed. They'd had a car and were able to drive all the way to the camp here in Maminas, outside of Tirana, without incident. That is to say, without being robbed or taken away and shot.

It was eerie to walk into a camp of, say, a thousand and see so few men. In April 1999, the month before I arrived, a delegation from the Commission for Refugee Women and Children had reported that 70 percent of the refugees in one camp were children under the age of fifteen. The report said that "most of the refugees had arrived with only the clothes on their backs, and at risk for infectious disease and severe diarrhea."

The babies especially got to me. Perhaps because their illnesses—blistering skin rashes, ragged coughs, eye infections—were both so commonplace and so clearly preventable. Perhaps because I remembered so vividly my own children at that age and the countless visits to the pediatrician, and the shots the nurses gave them, and how I dreaded seeing their tiny bodies afflicted with pain.

Albania was hardly equipped for such a monumental humanitarian crisis. The level of medical care, one prominent Albanian ophthalmologist told me, was fifty to one hundred years behind that of Western nations. The country was still struggling to emerge from the chaos wrought by Enver Hoxha, the Stalinist dictator who ruled Albania from 1945 until his death in 1985. Under Hoxha, Albania had been closed to the world, sealed off, its citizens banned from travel. There was not even a railroad connecting the country to the outside. Fearful of a nuclear attack by the West, Hoxha had forced Albanians to build thousands of steel-reinforced concrete bunkers in lieu of badly needed housing. The attack had never come and the dictator was long gone, but the bizarre concrete domes remained, littering Albania's steep mountainsides and lush plains.

When communism collapsed in 1991, the country descended further into economic ruin. In an explosion of violence, mobs destroyed shops, factories, libraries, government buildings—any concrete reminder of Hoxha's repressive reign. Tirana University, the center of the country's academic life, was forced to close for a year. Since then, little of the damage had been repaired. For the first few days I was in Tirana, I could not figure out why the city felt so strange. Every afternoon, after we'd return from the camps, I'd leave the hotel and go for a walk in the dusty unpaved streets. I eventually recognized what so unnerved me: Tirana had been utterly stripped of culture. As far as I could tell, there was not a single museum or theater or movie house or cultural institution. We could pay a few *leks* to climb to the top of Tirana's grand mosque, but Tirana's Opera House, a once grand marble building of Italianate design, was boarded up, its walls scarred by graffiti.

The camps reflected Albania's staggering poverty. Thousands of the refugees were living in "community centers," decaying concrete buildings that had once been factories or schools. If the refugees were lucky, the center had more than three bathrooms for 150 people. If they were lucky, the plaster on the walls wasn't crumbling and there was more than a single lightbulb in the long hallway. If they were lucky, there was a room that served as a working kitchen of sorts: a pair of burners set on a table.

One morning we were in Shkoder, a town of concrete housing slabs and rusting verandas near the Montenegrin border, where an abandoned factory housed seven hundred refugees. Crammed into one of the dank, windowless concrete rooms were twenty members of a family, including an old woman lying on a cot. She could not get up because of a fractured hip, and because the medical team had no surgeon, there was nothing they could do for her. Amid the tangle of metal beds and bags of clothes and the knot of doctors and refugees was a beautiful, hand-painted wooden cradle on the floor, covered by a white cloth. I had not noticed the cradle, but then a woman lifted up the cloth and we all gasped. Nestled inside was a two-week-old girl. She'd been born on the road to Albania, near the border crossing in Kukes. Her name was Liberty.

During such moments, I tried hard not to think of my daughter and son back home, of my daughter sitting on the floor, playing with Lego sets, and my son at the table, shuffling Pokémon cards. Yet I would find myself ambushed without warning. One afternoon, passing through another small town on the plains, we stopped to have lunch. I was walking along a crowded sidewalk with one of the UCLA nurses when I stopped suddenly and cried out.

"What's wrong?" she asked.

"I just saw a boy who looks exactly like my son."

Another day I might see a girl in the camps who reminded me of my seven-year-old daughter. The girl did not even need to look like her; she only had to be wearing a pink T-shirt or her hair in a ponytail or to smile a certain way for me to be struck dumb.

Many of the young Kosovar women in the camps reminded me of my nieces, they were so poised, so full of life. One, a slender girl of twenty-two with long brown hair and jeans, took my hand and guided me to her room, a hovel in an abandoned factory she shared with her mother and six sisters and several relatives. Even so, the place was immaculate, their belongings neatly organized in plastic bags hung on the wall. After settling me in a chair, she made me Turkish coffee and then served it in demitasse cups. She did not speak English and I did not speak Albanian, but as we sat there sipping the strong black coffee and holding hands, it seemed to me that we were friends.

On the morning before we flew out of Tirana, the medical teams gathered on the roof of the IMC building to say goodbye. We were exchanging addresses when Vjollca, a Kosovar nurse I had grown close to, reached into the pocket of her jeans and handed me something. It was a silver hair clip with the words "I Love You" on it. "You must come visit me in Kosovo," she said, smiling through her tears. I hugged her, promised her that I would.

I have thought of Vjollca often since that spring of 1999, have thought of my promise to her that morning on the rooftop in Tirana. I feel a connection to that troubled part of the world, a connection I never would have imagined. When the war in Kosovo ended not a month after I left, and Kosovo became a U.N. protectorate, I wondered if she and the other ethnic Albanians I knew were on their way home. I also found myself thinking of the thousands of children I had seen in the camps: in particular, one blond eight-year-old girl whose aunt had neatly brushed her hair and fastened it with clips. She had a fever of 103 and, like so many children in the camps who had endured the two-week walk into Albania over the mountains, had a bad case of tonsillitis. Perhaps because I live in Los Angeles, have spent a good portion of my life at some beach or another along the Pacific, I also distinctly remember this: She was wearing a blue T-shirt with the word "surf" on it.

In Albania and long after I had returned to Los Angeles, I also often thought of notions of home. As I write, I am sitting in my office, a drafty room off our garage. There's a shabby old sofa, photographs of news stories, children's drawings and wedding pictures, a poster of a swimmer in a pool from the 1984 Summer Olympics. An etching of the spiral staircase in the Trinity Library I bought when I was in Dublin one fall. Books spill from shelves everywhere. The hair clip from Vjollca is here, too, somewhere near a stack of folders on my desk. None of this stuff means much to anyone else; it means the world to me.

Through a small window above my desk I can see my house: a 1926 Craftsman bungalow painted in shades of rust and green. We moved here when my daughter was six months old, my son a toddler. I have lived in this house for more than twelve years now, lived in it through the 1994 Northridge earthquake and fires that burned hundreds of acres in the nearby San Gabriel foothills, through rainstorms that flooded the basement. I feel almost an irrational attachment to my house. It would take an act of God for me to move out.

This is what I say. But it's easy to say such things in the abstract. If the enemy were to come in the night with guns, I now know that seeing my home go up in flames is not the worst fate imaginable. The worst fate imaginable would be seeing my son taken away or shot in front of me. This is what the mothers of Kosovo taught me. It is a lesson I will not soon forget.

All they wanted was for their children to be safe. All they wanted, the refugees told me over and over, was to go home.

TEACH

So when the great word "Mother!" rang once more,
I saw at last its meaning and its place;
Not the blind passion of the brooding past,
But Mother—the World's Mother—come at last,
To love as she had never loved before—
To feed and guard and teach the human race.

—*Charlotte Perkins Gilman*

Twists in the Plot

by Jennifer Brisendine

THERE'S A LITTLE WAR silently spiraling in Room 112. Arms folded, I stand in wide-heeled shoes that boost my petite frame a good two inches. When you teach high school students who sometimes tower a foot above you and outweigh you by a hundred pounds, every inch helps.

My fifteen students in fourth-block Junior English do not sense my growing rage . . . or if they do, they demonstrate no reaction. I suspect they would be surprised or perplexed to know that I'm fuming. *But we're in our seats,* they would say. *We're not talking. We finished the* Gatsby *test and we're being good.*

But you are not reading, I would rant back at them. *You are not reading the assigned story.*

This is close to completely true. One student, Girl Who Should Have Taken Honors, is dutifully reading James Thurber's "The Catbird Seat" and answering accompanying study guide questions. Another student, Prefers Adidas Apparel, is flipping fitfully through the pages. Others are staring ahead, watching the windows, glancing at the clock. I'd bet money that Suspected Text Messager has been peeking at a phone hidden in his jeans pocket. Every time I begin to walk toward him, he removes his hand from the pocket and makes a face at the words in front of them, as if they are written in Portuguese. Around the room, there is doodling, daydreaming, dazing, and even drooling. Can't Stay Awake has drifted off again. They are not reading.

When the bell rings, they leave, unconcerned about the test they have taken and the story that went mostly unread.

"See ya, Miss B," Good-Natured but Failing says. "Have a nice weekend."

I seethe, wanting to scream. I don't answer.

Throughout four years of college and ten-plus years of public school teaching, one bit of advice has been overwhelmingly popular among professors, veteran teachers, administrators, and retirees: Choose your battles. I look around the empty room.

I choose this one.

If my teaching career were mapped out on a Plot Triangle Diagram, here's how it would go:

Exposition (introductory information): I want to teach. I love literature and writing. I get a teaching degree. I pass the tests, get a license, and find a job.

Inciting Incident (early conflict that promotes interest): I begin teaching and immediately wonder what the hell I was thinking. The workload is insane, the students unmotivated. I inspire a love of life-long learning in no one. But I dig in. I try harder. I embark on a ten-year quest to find the perfect balance of discipline, instruction, enthusiasm, humor, and wisdom.

Rising Action: I leave a large county system in Virginia for a small Pennsylvania district, eventually settling in to teach at the high school from which I graduated. I dig in harder; I will stay. I will teach my heart out.

Discoveries: I discover that a single student can turn an otherwise decent group of kids into an off-task, disrespectful zoo. I discover that every few years, a teacher is blessed with a perfect class: optimistic, eager, willing.

Plot Twists: Among many, these are the two biggest and most complex:

In 2001, the current version of the Elementary and Secondary Education Act, the law known as No Child Left Behind, was passed.

In 2004, I had a baby boy.

Because of the effect the second event had on me, it was a few years before I understood the full impact of the first. Among other things, No Child Left Behind called for an increase in the use of standardized testing to determine yearly progress. Following a heady year of pregnancy and maternity leave, I returned to my teaching position in a half-time capacity, unaware that while I'd been far away, enjoying my baby—learning to nurse, changing diapers, and reading picture books—the rules of the game had changed.

"Because there seemed to be some . . . *hesitation* with the reading of the short story last class, we're going to try again." I count off pages and hand piles to front-row students.

Huffs and puffs, groaning and slouching. A few brazen comments—"Stupid story." "I didn't get any of it." "If we don't read it out loud I'm gonna fall asleep."—which I ignore. On the overhead projector, a prepared transparency details instructions. I face the students.

"Circle in pen any unfamiliar word or phrase. Highlight every line of dialogue spoken by Mr. Martin in yellow, and in blue for Ms. Barrows. At the bottom of each column, write a one-sentence summary . . . " My directions are enthusiastic and upbeat. The students sink a little in their seats.

After a minute of long-suffering sighs, they get started. I roam and read over shoulders, correcting errors and offering clarification. I could sing for joy. This is teaching. This is a good day. They may not like the story, but they are reading it, damn it. The notations and summaries, created while I watch in a silent room, are as close to real proof of actual reading as I am going to get.

If only, if only, we could have done this with *The Great Gatsby*.

In the deep-freeze of January, I begin getting my students ready for the PSSA (Pennsylvania System of State Assessment), a standardized test that, under No Child Left Behind, has become the most important test a public school in Pennsylvania can administer.

"So, we'll look at writing prompts released by the state, and you'll shape up your composition skills with a few essays before the writing component of the exam."

In my head, I am home with my toddler. We play pirate fort and veterinarian; we watercolor and discuss his favorite *Backyardigans* episode.

"The next part of the test is the big one: reading comprehension. To practice, we'll do some examples in these blue practice books. . . . "

In my head, after pirate fort, we play with the magnet letters on the fridge and make tomato soup for lunch.

"A certain percentage of your graduating class has to get a Proficient or Advanced score. Next year, the percentage will increase; three years later, it will begin increasing drastically every year."

This piques curiosity, finally. I see it bubble up around the classroom. And I haven't even explained to them the federal government's heavy-handed "answer" for school districts that consistently fail to meet the declared marks for graduation rates, attendance, test participation, and test scores: a progression of possible "corrective actions" that may lead to the eventual restructuring of the school through such means as replacement of staff and administration, reopening as a charter school, or relinquishing control to the state or a private company.

"That means some junior class a couple years from now will have to get the whole test right," Witty Dramatic Man says.

"Not quite," I tell him. "It means that by 2014, every eleventh-grade student must be Proficient or Advanced on the test. In other words, 100 percent of the kids in the grade have to pass."

"Yeah, right," says Quick to Have an Opinion. Girl Who Gets My Jokes looks at me with a half smile on her face, waiting for the punch line. None comes.

"Wait. For real?" Quick to Have an Opinion raises his eyebrows.

They are uncharacteristically quiet for a few seconds; then they briefly erupt.

"That's, like, *insane.*"

"No school could do that!"

"You know someone'll fail on purpose just to make it not be 100 percent."

I wait, letting my silence quiet them. I take a breath. "The only thing you need to be concerned with is getting a Proficient or Advanced score on the test. If you don't, you'll take a six-week tutorial at the start of senior year, then retake the PSSA. You probably don't want to do that—"

Scoffing, railing, muttering.

"—so let's get you guys ready for the test."

Back in my kitchen, my son and I line up the best laundry baskets for high-flying stuffed animals. Then I shake off the fantasy, almost entirely, and dig in.

My son loves books. We spend hours every week reading and talking about stories and pictures. At two weeks of age, his blue eyes stared with rapt curiosity at white-on-black and black-on-white board books. From six months, he was turning pages; from eight months, repeating sounds. It's been the cardinal rule in our house to drop what we are doing—even cooking supper, even paying bills—and read if he brings a book and asks.

He's two and a half now. One morning, I take him to Barnes & Noble for the first time. He sees the new world of the kids' section and whispers, "Oh my gosh." I get chills.

I match his excitement. "Look! There's the caterpillar book you have at home, only this one's so big, you need a handle to carry it. Here's a book with puzzles in it. And this is a little stage for story hour. Would you like to come back for story hour sometime?" He nods, swimmy-eyed and smiling. We buy one new book and spend the rest of the day enamored with it.

I choose this battle too; I will preempt this fight if I can. Keep him loving stories. Keep him interested. Keep him reading.

It's easy to get caught up in it: the rush to be ready for The Test. It strikes a chord in my competitive nature. I feel a need to prove myself; these are my students, after all, taking a test that every junior in the state will take, utilizing skills that I've taught them. Motivational charts and banners canvas the school. Every teacher in the building adapts lessons for "PSSA prep month." In Room 112, we open the blue practice books that model the PSSA. The students take a ten-second glance at the reading entry and look back at me.

"This is really hard," Girl Who Gets My Jokes says quietly. Nods of agreement ripple through the room.

"It's a challenging passage," I say, "but if you break it into pieces, and remember to preread the questions, and recall your literary terms . . . "

They try. They read, frown, scowl, read again. They note letter answers to the multiple-choice questions. When I reveal the answers, about half the class gets half the questions correct. Girl Who Should Have Taken Honors misses two. The rest get fewer than half.

After a review of the correct answers, they appear tired and defeated.

"Well," I say, "let's try another one."

At the end of class, Quick to Have an Opinion mouths off a smarmy "I don't care about the PSSA" to the student behind him. I move in for the quiet reprimand, but the bell rings and he dashes off. Alone in the room, I hear the echo of his comment in the empty space, and I suddenly realize that maybe I don't care about the test, either.

The deep freeze is never-ending. In early March, about a week and a half before the PSSA test, the temperature is still bottoming out in the single digits. At five thirty, I get up, get ready for school, load the car, and walk the dog—nearly impossible tasks once my toddler is awake. The moisture in the air promises snow again before the day is over.

I wake Aidan at six fifteen. He always needs some warm milk and bit of *Sesame Street* to get going, but even with these, I can tell this morning will be a difficult one. My husband travels for business, and sometimes—most times throughout the dark and cold of this endless winter—I have trouble getting Aidan and me out the door on time, especially when he resists getting dressed. I cannot figure how mothers who work full-time outside the home do this, and I pause for a few seconds in closed-eyed appreciation of my part-time, every other day teaching schedule. On my at-home days, I freelance when Aidan sleeps; challenging work, of course, but nothing akin to persuading a screaming toddler into a bulky winter coat at 6:45 AM. Time to go, and he's not budging.

"Aidan. I have to go to work today."

"We stay home, Mommy. I want to stay home today." At least I think this is what comes out; the decibel level of his words matches those of words screamed by frenzied fans at a rock concert, and they are enunciated just as clearly. In spite of my heart ripping neatly in two, I dredge up one last tablespoon of patience and try again.

"Aidan. I promise that we will play and read this afternoon. But right now I have to go to work. Now, you can pick your blue hat or your green hat—"

But his howls drown out my attempt to allow him some paltry control. The dog hangs her head and goes for a quiet corner. I cannot sacrifice any more time. I force his arms through the sleeves and grab for the zipper while he claws at the coat and stomps and screams. Once both mittens are shoved on—forget the thumbs, thank you very much—he can't pull them off or get the zipper down. As I yank my coat on and grab the keys, the howls get impossibly louder. Then there's a sudden, complete silence and a thud on our wood floor. I whirl.

"Oh my God! Aidan!"

He is just lying there, awake, tear-streaked, and unmoving.

"What's the matter? Did you hurt yourself?"

"No."

"Can you get up on your own?"

He makes a defeated little shrugging gesture and will not look at me. Bewildered, I haul him up; it's like lifting twenty-seven pounds of boneless Jell-O. He will not stand or walk, so I put him in the car seat, drive to the sitter's, beg a hug from him, and drive away trying not to cry.

I relate the whole sordid tale to another teacher that afternoon. "Do you think there's something wrong with him? He's never done anything like that!"

She smiles, not in a sage sort of way but more like a slightly sinister oracle. "His spirit was broken. That's what happened. You broke his spirit. He gave up."

I go to class feeling like I've been slapped. When the kids come in, after a review of literary techniques, I tell them to get out the blue PSSA practice books. There's a too-long hesitation; then they do it, and the look on their faces reminds me of Aidan's that morning when I scooped up his despirited form from the hardwood.

We begin the unit on *The Great Gatsby* as PSSA testing week wraps up. Teaching literature once the PSSA is over is renewing, like eucalyptus lotion on tired feet. I tell them *Gatsby* is a love story, that it's set in the 1920s Jazz Age, that the title character throws parties that rival the biggest bashes they've seen in print or on film.

Witty Dramatic Man raises his hand. "Has it got any adulterous affairs in it?"

This has been his usual question upon starting anything new, and it's a somewhat valid one, considering we've already covered *The Crucible* and *Ethan Frome*. "Actually, more than one."

We dig in. I teach the difficult introductory passage; I give them in-class guided reading time; we read a few tricky paragraphs of chapter one together. The rest of the chapter is assigned as homework, along with study guide questions.

The next time the class meets, most fail the reading quiz disastrously. Study guide questions are complete and correct, but, combined with failing quiz scores, it's clear that flagrant copying is occurring outside of class. We review, we find pertinent sections of the chapter, I read aloud. We do worksheets, character identifications, more review. I tell them bluntly that online summaries and friends' answers on study guides will not help them on reading quizzes and tests. We start chapter two.

Next class, most fail the second reading quiz, even more disastrously than they did the first. I face them. "Low scores now mean struggling to catch up over the next nine weeks. Some of you might not pass this class if you blow off this novel."

Can't Stay Awake looks at me. "If we would read it out loud in class, I'd get high scores on everything."

I have no patience left today, not even a tablespoon. "I'll continue to read aloud the first few pages of each chapter. The rest you'll be responsible for reading on your own."

This is the biggest battle: How can I teach effective and enthralling lessons on literary allusions, themes, and figurative language when the kids won't even read the story? I dig in. I try harder. Nothing works. I consider flinging a copy of the novel at the back wall in an effort to get their attention. I wonder if Fitzgerald is cursing the first teacher who placed his masterpiece in the hands of sixteen- and seventeen-year-olds.

At the end of six frustrating-as-hell weeks, knowing I can't spend even more time on this book and out of ideas to try, I give the test and hold my breath: one A, two Cs, one D, and ten Fs. Cringing, I write the grades in the book.

I want to dig in. I want to try harder. But gnats of doubt pester me all the time, even as the year begins to approach its blessed end. Between what the federal government is telling me I must do and what my heart and conscience—born again in me as a first-time mother—advise, my questions about my teaching career are vast, discouraging, and seemingly without end.

After more than ten years of serving in public school districts, I begin to have traitorous ideas. I desire to send my son to private or parochial school. The reasons swirl in my head when I stir them.

Counting forward from when Aidan is supposed to start kindergarten, I realize that he will hit third grade—the grade in which elementary school students in our state take their first PSSA—in the 2013–2014 school year, the year that every student in the nation must pass state-mandated assessment tests required by No Child Left Behind. I cannot fathom what I will tell my child when he boards the bus on exam morning, seven short years from now. "Good luck" doesn't seem like it's going to cut it. I worry about his sensitivity to high-stakes situations, already evident; I worry about what the consequences will be for kids who don't pass. I worry about my own two-facedness on that not-so-distant day: As a mother, I will think it's ludicrous, ethically demoralizing, and flat-out cruel to demand this kind of success of third graders; as a teacher, I may still be telling my students to open their blue books for one last PSSA exercise before the real test.

And what if he makes it through the early grade levels with his love of books intact? As a teacher, I recognize that the PSSA tests necessary skills, like reading comprehension and making inferences. But preparing students for the brief-passage, multiple-choice format of the PSSA doesn't inspire them to read more or better, or to tackle reading challenges like *The Great Gatsby*.

In the fight to keep my child reading, I don't want any interference with the traditional classroom encouragement toward a love of books. Private and parochial classroom environments are not obligated to follow the dictates of No Child Left Behind. To me, the complexity of this issue boils down to a simple matter of time: less time spent on PSSA prep and testing means more time for my child's reading and learning. To me, the administration of the PSSA and the actual teaching of reading and literature are mutually exclusive.

As I weigh my child's educational options, I wonder if I'm approaching the top of the Rising Action of my teaching career, if soon I'll be at the Moment of Crisis, the Turning Point, the Climactic Decision. Daily, I ask whether this job is worth the days away from Aidan, the hours I cannot devote to writing and freelancing, the stress and headache of the secondary school classroom; if I don't soon see some improvements in the system, some hope, some lessening of governmental "guidelines" so restrictive that almost certain failure is imminent, then perhaps my decision to leave teaching will become easy. Regardless, No Child Left Behind and the accompanying PSSA have left a taste in my mouth that may require several years away from public education to wash out.

For the last few years, I have tended secret red coals in my core on this issue; I burn, but it's been a quiet rebellion. I write study materials for high school students preparing for a national academic competition. I never see these mystery students; I know, though, that they are learning voluntarily, for the sheer fulfillment they find in it. Mine has been a silent activism, so far.

But sorting through these thoughts about Aidan's future school days gives me the urge to speak up and out. I am a mother; I am a teacher; I feel an unfamiliar obligation to share this crucial perspective.

I have never communicated with my senators and congressman. "Constituent"—who, me? But I'm burning hotter now, and I email them my thoughts on the use of high-stakes standardized tests like the PSSA. Each time I hit "Send," I feel a growing desire to let the fire roar.

Combing through computer files for my English final, I find a document named "ss#1 Responses." I open it; I'd forgotten. Before maternity leave, I taught a fiction-writing elective, and this file I stumble upon is a series of personalized, page-long, single-spaced critiques I wrote in response to each student's first story. I could never provide this kind of individual attention to my students now . . . not even for triple my salary.

I stare at the critiques, beginning to face the fact that the teacher I was before becoming a mother and before No Child Left Behind is not the teacher I am now. Now my devotion is focused on my son. Now an increasing amount of my time is utilized in preparing students for a dead-end test I don't believe in. And now I am realizing that any amount of time spent in this manner may be too much to ask.

In Euripedes' ancient Greek drama *Medea,* the playwright has written the title character into such an impossible plot bind that she can be saved only by the gods, played by actors who swoop down from the roof of the scene building in a crane-style machine. And— voilà!—the "god-in-the-machine" ending, the deus ex machina, was first employed. I am beginning to think that some plot twists cannot be recovered from; the plot line of my teaching career has been happily and beautifully interrupted by personal causes, and inexorably and oppressively complicated by political ones. Maybe the time has come to turn the final page on this plot line. Instead of waiting for the god in the machine, I am ready to begin a new story.

First-Grade Values

by Susie Bright

IN 1996, MY DAUGHTER ARETHA learned how to read and write. It was a miracle because I didn't understand how it happened and it seemed to appear all at once.

When Aretha graduated first grade, I sat with the other amazed parents in Room 7 at Longview Elementary, listening to the children chant, "And now I'm six, and I'm clever as clever, and I think I'll be six forever 'n' ever."

Just how clever were they?

Ordinarily, if my daughter called me a nasty name in public, I'd have had a swift punishment to deliver. But when she got angry with me over breakfast dishes and wrote "Mommy is a pig" in purple felt pen on her self-decorated bedroom walls, I was close to tears of joy. My baby expressing herself!—and her spelling is already better than that of many of her adult relatives. I had told Aretha she could draw on her walls, and now she filled them like pages of a diary. She was the living embodiment of the First Amendment.

Aretha learned more as a six-year-old than the strange rules of the English language—she got inculcated with the even stranger rules of American values. The things my daughter brought home her first-grade year on the subjects of sex, race, and religion made me want to wash out the entire mouth of our crazy world with the strongest soap I could find.

Take the last week of school, for instance. I picked her up on a Monday afternoon, with tears and snot running down her face.

"What happened?" I said, a phrase I repeated like a broken doll all school year long.

"We were playing the Power Game," Aretha sobbed—which, as she described it further, sounded like a sadistic cross between Jonestown and Simon Says, although it's one of those ephemeral games the kids make up at recess. "One person has 'the power,'" Aretha explained, "and they get to make all the other players do whatever they say."

The goal of the other players is to "take it" with as much stoicism as possible—not to crack. Aretha was in post-tournament pieces.

"Who plays this horrible game?" I asked, and Aretha paused her crying for a moment. "It's the *Power* Game," she said, as if that explained everything—and then, as if it were an afterthought—"No Mexicans can play, though."

I had to watch it when we had these conversations in the car, because I was wearing out my brakes. "It's a *Power* Game and no *Mexicans* can play?!" I plowed into a curb.

Our family lives in a beach town that's part university, part hippies, a lot of farmland, and a sprinkling of Silicon Valley interests. As in much of the state, the majority of the population is Latino, but an overwhelmingly white political and business elite runs the show. Her school is probably a quarter "American," and she can actually include herself as part of the majority; her birth father's family are native Californians and Mexicans.

When Aretha and I got home, we looked at a map of the world. I showed her where Mexico is, and reminded her that she is half Mexican Indian herself. I gave her a thumbnail history of Mexican and California Indian history, which I'm afraid she got a bit mixed up with the Disney *Pocahontas* script—but I'll take my antibigotry lessons where I can find them.

I told her that in fact, none of the kids in her class are "Mexican"—
that's just something idiots who don't know better say. I knew all the
students in her class, and except for one Yugoslav, all were born in
the United States. A handful lived with parents who were primarily
Spanish speakers, but they were not exclusively Mexican, either. Her
homeroom was bilingual. At the same time, the white and white-
passing kids—*las gueras,* like my daughter—were picking up all the
social cues that they were the real players in life.

The hardest part about these talks with my daughter was when
she asked me the hard questions—like why the Spanish treated
Indians like slaves and children, and why the Anglos went even further, exterminating tribes like vermin.

"Why did they treat them like that; how could they be so cruel?"
she asked.

"Yeah, well, why are you playing the Power Game?" I shot back.
"You all don't even have any money involved."

Another afternoon, another showdown. . . . "I'm going to clean
up after the boys today so that we can get ice cream," Aretha said
when I dropped her off at school in the morning. "Miss Rogers says if
we didn't clean up after our snack, then we won't get ice cream—and
the boys never do it, so I'm going to clean up theirs, too."

"I'll give you a double dip of *anything* you like if you promise me
you'll never clean up after a boy again," I said, in the first spontane-
ous bribe I ever made to her. "You start now and it never stops." She
was impressed and made the bargain with me.

I took her and her girlfriend Katie for double-dip chocolate cones
after their last class. They sat quietly in the car until Aretha spoke,
out of nowhere—"Mommy, all the girls at Longview giggle really
hard when someone says 'sex.'"

"Do *not* say that word!" Katie squealed, in perfect emphasis.

"Katie," I said, risking who knows what repercussions with her parents, "if it weren't for sex, you wouldn't be here, so maybe you should lighten up." I turned off my broken air-conditioning, so the car actually became hotter, but quiet. "Some girls get taught by their parents to be embarrassed about sex. But you don't have to be silly about sex; you know better."

"But sex is for when you get married," Katie insisted, and this prompted Aretha to jump in with some special school yard gossip on the subject. "Lorena is going to kill herself if she doesn't get to marry Rafael!"

I gathered that this was a direct quote from Lorena. "Does Rafael know about it?" I asked.

Aretha and Katie burst out laughing—of course not. The boys are clueless, playing kickball while the three princesses-in-training sit at a lunch table and formulate their wedding plans.

Aretha didn't yet have all these ideas strung in a row. She was in awe of wearing a wedding dress, but her favorite T-shirt was emblazoned with the slogan "GIRLS RULE." She had a mind to influence the masses, and the Room 7 recess crowd could thank your family for making the word "clitoris" as commonly understood as "penis" on the playground. During recess, those kids talked as much about sex as any crew of construction workers. But sometimes Aretha had her own entirely independent opinions, separate from me or her school, and those were the most provocative of all.

Another time, during the First Grade of a Million Questions, she asked, "How come Sandy and Jared don't take their clothes off when we go in the pond?"

"Because their family believes in a god that thinks the naked human body is shameful, and we don't," I answered.

"But do you believe in God, Mommy?"

Another one of those important questions! I never knew that one day I would feel shy answering a little girl. "I believe that there are big things I don't understand," I said, wanting to be tender. "I believe in being humble, but I don't believe in some god in the sky telling people how to live."

She looked sideways at me, uncharacteristically coy. "Don't you want to ask me? Don't you want to know who I believe in?"

I was a little fidgety. We were sitting on my bed underneath my gigantic five-foot hanging plastic rosary. A bronze Krishna figurine stood on the dresser next to my classic Barbie, and a book of Greek myths lay on the floor in a pile of dirty laundry.

"Okay, Aretha, do you believe in 'God'—what do you think?"

"I believe in *all* of them," she whispered, lifting her arms around her in a swirl. "And I pray to them, too." Her eyes shined, and I wondered what kind of prayers she'd write on those walls, next to the drawings of a pig.

How to Make a Democrat from Scratch

by Stephanie Losee

I STARTED BRAINWASHING my oldest daughter to be a Democrat in 2003, when she was eight years old. I could say it was a response to the appalling futility of my 2000 vote, which was cast in California, or to the perplexing decision of the DNC not to spend my donation on a media coach for poor Al Gore. But, to tell the truth, I figure it's my right and privilege to raise a bunch of little liberals. I have to live in the same house with them, after all. And why miss an opportunity to add to the number of people disposed to vote against anything and everything embraced by George W. Bush?

I thought my viewpoint was pretty standard until a Republican friend of mine said that—unlike me—she could never impose her political views on her children. My first reaction, after the shock, was to admire Heather's impulse control. But as impressive a feat as it is to stifle yourself in front of your kids, in this case the two of us are going to have to agree to disagree, just as we do about our chosen parties. I could no sooner leave my daughters unschooled about my political convictions than I could leave them in the lurch about my take on the Almighty. Maybe the reason is that politics *is* my religion. My husband is Jewish. I'm Democratish.

I don't belong to a church, so a good deal of my conduct and thinking find their expression in my political persuasion. The Democrats' Ten Commandments are as good a tool for teaching children values as the original, and they're certainly more modern. *Thou shalt feed the working poor. Thou shalt protect the environment. Thou shalt not limit women's reproductive choices. Thou shalt not wage war against people who had nothing to do with 9/11.* And so on.

So, in my quest to make Democrats from materials I found lying around the house, I began by explaining to my daughter Olivia that Daddy and I don't believe the same things that the president believes.

"What does he believe?" Olivia asked, all big eyes and trust.

"He thinks that science could be wrong about things like global warming and evolution," I said.

"What do you mean?" Olivia said. "If science is wrong, what does he think is right?"

"The Bible," I replied. "The Bible says that God created Adam and Eve, and that's where we all came from."

"But the Bible is just a bunch of *stories,*" Olivia said, rolling her eyes. My husband and I had actually taught her that the Bible was an important historical document, but clearly a detail or two in the message had been lost in translation.

"I know," I said, "but he thinks that's what actually happened."

"He's an idiot," Olivia said firmly.

Bingo. The world now had one more Democrat.

Within a couple of years, I had figured out how easy it was to weave moral lessons into the answers I gave to Olivia's questions about politics.

"What's the biggest difference between what Republicans and Democrats believe?" Olivia asked one day in the car on the way home from school.

"Oh, let me see," I said, overwhelmed by the possibilities. "I guess the role of the government. Democrats believe we should have a bigger government that helps to take care of the people in our country who are the poorest, and Republicans think we should have a smaller government and people should rely on themselves."

"Republicans don't care about *poor people?*" Olivia was practically shouting. Perhaps I had overstated the matter.

"No, no, of course Republicans care about poor people. It's just that the way Democrats think we should pay for it is to ask rich people to pay a lot more in taxes than people who have less money. And Republicans think that's not fair. They say it's like punishing the wealthy for doing well and earning money." It was a little adult for Olivia's level, but it was the best I could do to balance the argument while driving.

"What do Democrats say about that?"

"Well, we believe that a big part of the reason some people make a lot of money is that they've had more opportunities, so they should give more of the money back in taxes than people who make lots less." It was all I could do not to come right out and say *to whom much is given, much is required,* but I was trying to deliver the secular version.

"I hate Republicans," Olivia said flatly. "They're a bunch of jerks."

Maybe I needed to dial it back a bit.

"What are you talking about?" asked Greta, who was then five. On the ride home from school she often zoned out, exhausted from all the activity in kindergarten.

"We're talking about *Bush,*" Olivia sneered.

"He's horrible," Greta said from her booster seat.

So much for dialing it back.

As Olivia continued to ask questions about items in the news, I strove for objectivity, but since I lacked it myself I had trouble conveying it. When Olivia heard that no weapons of mass destruction were found in Iraq, she came home from school in a lather.

"Why did George Bush invade Iraq, then?" she demanded to know.

I took a big breath and delivered the following terrifically unobjective—not to mention blatantly reductive—explanation: "Because his father was president before he was, and his father invaded Iraq and tried to kill Saddam Hussein, and after he failed, Saddam Hussein tried to kill him back, and now the son decided to finish the job," I said. "Also, Iraq has a lot of oil, and Bush wanted to make sure we'd get to use it."

"And everybody just let him get away with it? How did that happen?"

Now I felt guilty. Wasn't I one of the everybodies who let him get away with it? Maybe I should go to a peace march or something. But people sometimes get hurt at those things, and with three daughters I couldn't take the chance. I mailed a check to MoveOn instead. They seemed a touch savvier than the DNC. Maybe *they'd* spend my donation on a media coach for the next candidate.

In 2004, when Olivia was in the fourth grade and the grown-ups were headed for the polls, her class scheduled a mock election between Kerry and Bush; each child would cast a vote. This would be interesting. I would have a rare opportunity to see how the other parents in the class were brainwashing *their* kids. Which meant I'd find out how these people—many of whom were exceptionally wealthy—were really voting behind their closed San Francisco doors.

"Kerry won," Olivia reported. "Twenty to two."

I was heartened. Then Olivia said, serious as a heart attack, "Sarah voted for Bush." Sarah was Olivia's best friend, and my husband and I were friendly with her parents. They were Republicans? Didn't see that one coming.

"No way," I said.

"Way," Olivia replied.

"Oh, don't worry about it. I don't think Sarah knows enough about Bush to really support him."

"But she does, Mom! She's in favor of the war and everything. She says Bush is doing a good job!"

A year later, Sarah's and Olivia's opposing party affiliations had become the source of daily friction that threatened to ruin their friendship.

"Sarah still loves The Shrub," Olivia said, using her preferred moniker for the president, dripping eleven-year-old condescension. "I don't want to be friends with anyone who loves The Shrub."

Then it hit me. I could hear myself back in college, telling my roommates that I could never have sex with a Republican on principle. I actually broke up with a perfectly nice and extremely intelligent—not to mention cute and athletic—junior I had just begun dating, after a rather ugly exchange in the library when he explained why he was a pro-lifer. Once I knew his position on the issue, I didn't want to spend another minute with him. I ignored a lovely letter he sent the next semester, asking if we could put politics aside to try to get to know each other better, which I later regretted.

I flushed with shame. Olivia wasn't just turning into a Democrat. She was turning into *me*.

"You know," I said earnestly, all big eyes and trust. "That's the great thing about the United States. We can disagree about things like who should be president and what the president should do, but we don't blow each other up over it. We just wait until another election and vote for our candidate the next time."

Olivia was sitting at her computer, where I saw from her email string that she was in the middle of an online fight with Sarah. They were sending angry messages back and forth about Bush's merits or lack of them, an eleven-year-old war of ideas.

"I know what," Olivia said, brightening. "I'll write back with a list of everything Bush thinks that makes no sense and convince Sarah that she shouldn't like him anymore. Then everything will be okay."

But before Olivia could finish pecking out her two-finger harangue, Sarah pinged again, asking Olivia to drop the subject once and for all. Olivia's shoulders fell, but I was relieved. It's one thing to have an agenda to populate the world with liberal progeny. It's quite another to see your progeny lose friends because of your little agenda.

Maybe my friend Heather was right; maybe it's wrong to teach your politics to your kids. But after she said that, I read that four out of five people vote the way their parents did, which means that I can't be the only one out there raising my children to vote like Mom and Dad. Of course, it's possible that most people are like Heather and try not to pass on their political beliefs. But I suspect that their kids can't help picking them up anyway. That's the reason I never blamed Heather for being a rare California Republican; I always figured it's not really her fault. Her parents were probably Republicans, too.

I still think these things. But I've stopped talking this way in front of Olivia. I couldn't pretend I'm not a rabid Democrat, of course; that ship has sailed. Instead, I gave her a version of my mother's old speech about Things We Discuss Outside the Home Versus Things We Don't, much as it galled me to do so. Nowadays, when I explain to her what Democrats think, I always try to give as unbiased a version of the opposing side as I can muster. But after 2016 all bets are off. That's the first presidential election Olivia will be old enough to vote in. As far as I'm concerned, it can't come fast enough.

Revolution on Your Skin

by Susan Ito

AT FOUR MONTHS, you helped take over a bank in Nicaragua.

In 1991, you were the official baby of the U.S.-Nicaragua Colloquium on Health. I was the staff organizer for the eighth week-long health workers' exchange that had begun in the first years of the Sandinista Revolution. North American physicians, nurses, psychologists, and midwives traveled to Nicaragua to meet with their counterparts, or *homologos,* to share clinical experience, to learn the toll of US foreign policy on Nicaraguans' health, and to deliver medical aid. Our first day in Managua, your suitcase was stolen from the trunk of our broken-down, borrowed Lada.

For the rest of our three-month stay in Nicaragua, it was disposable diapers from the *diplotienda* and hand-me-down clothes from Nicaraguan babies. No more OshKosh overalls or terry cloth giraffe or Pooh-bear sleeper. You had a *Salud y Paz* T-shirt that hung to your ankles like a pillowcase. You had a ragged little outfit whose snaps had long ago popped off, leaving your fat, white belly to tickle and kiss.

We took you with us everywhere, on the bouncing TurNica bus, to Huembes Market, to the Red Cross building where the dozen doctors and nurses lay on mattresses on the floor, one on a table with an IV in her arm. These *homologos* of ours were not in their hospitals or clinics, taking care of patients. They were on a hunger strike: fasting, protesting, starving for a living wage. The Sandinistas had been removed, and healthcare was no longer a national priority. The health workers' union, Fetsalud, said $2 a day was not enough.

They sat up when they saw you, Daughter, reached out their arms to touch the spiky porcupine fuzz on your head. They saw in your plump legs the potential for health and prayed that their own children would grow so fat.

We passed an envelope amongst us to contribute to their strike fund, and then climbed back on the tour bus. As the minibus swung through town, our handsome guide, Juan Carlos, stood up and announced that the National Bank had been taken over. *The bank workers have frozen the bank in solidarity with the health workers.*

We pleaded with the driver like children. Let's go, we said. Please, we want to go!

I don't know if we were fools to bring an infant into a building full of rifles, AK-47s, a demanding crowd. But we did. We brought you in, and the workers smiled and passed you around, from arm to arm, like a talisman.

I believed or hoped that by osmosis you'd grow up to be a justice-seeking activist. I never imagined that you'd spend your middle-school years longing for a Coach purse or filling your closets with more outfits than Huembes Market could ever hold. I admit I panicked a bit during that phase.

I hoped that you would remember, somehow. As it turned out, we didn't live the revolution like we thought we would. We made a life of contradictions instead, a life of antiwar protests and private school, designer jeans and sleepaway peace camp. That time in Nicaragua was just the beginning of it. I see now that the arc of your life is long. It is really only beginning now, as you enter adulthood, and the impact of these influences remains to be seen.

I hope that something in your skin, something in your body, will recognize the memory of justice fought for by the dozens who held you in the first springtime of your life, those who shook a plastic rattle in one hand, making you laugh and drool, and with the other hand held fast to their revolution, to their children, to *their* future.

I hope that their palms, so tender and fierce, left their invisible mark on you.

Because I'm Not Dead

by Ona Gritz

MY TWO-YEAR-OLD SON and I are sitting in a room with the other members of our "Baby and Me" exercise class. The session has ended, and I'm making small talk with the moms and caregivers while Ethan snacks on dry cereal mixed with peanut halves. We've been taking this class for over a year, and, while I don't count these women among my close friends, we have a rapport, our easy conversation centered on the children. I know about Emi's resistance to napping, but not what her mother did for a living before Emi was born. I'm privy to Ben's allergy to bananas, but I don't know the circumstances that brought his nanny to New Jersey from Trinidad. In turn, no one here knows that I'm a poet and children's author. In this circle, I'm simply Ethan's mom.

Ethan hands me the little plastic cup with the remnants of his snack in it.

"You've had enough, sweetie?" I dig in the bag at the back of his stroller for a sippy cup.

Hannah's babysitter, Lois, nods toward Ethan. "How long have you been watching him now?" she asks me.

I'm confused by the question but, before I can ask Lois what she means, Rose, Ben's nanny, breaks in.

"She's not the sitter. She's the mom!"

My throat tightens.

"But I thought . . . " Lois's sentence trails off, the ellipsis nearly visible in the air. I watch her face. She's more than surprised; it doesn't make sense to her that I could be Ethan's mother.

Here is what I want to believe. That Lois didn't think blond, blue-eyed Ethan and I were related because of my dark hair and eyes. Or that I look too young to be the mother of a two-year-old (even though I'm thirty-six). But there is another, more likely explanation, and I can feel myself trying to squelch it down. To Lois's mind, a disabled woman can't be a mother. The disabled are dependent and asexual. They are like children themselves.

I was born with cerebral palsy, a birth defect involving damage to the part of the brain that sends messages to the various muscles of the body. My case is mild. I walk with a slight limp. I also lack fine motor skills in one hand, but I'm adept at compensating for it, so few people know this about me. Nor can onlookers tell that the whole right side of my body is numb.

It's barely noticeable. I have been told this about my cerebral palsy all my life. It's meant to be a compliment, and I tend to take it as such. Yet, at the same time, I realize how self-deprecating it is to choose to pass as someone other than who I am. It reflects an internalized prejudice that is common among the disabled. After all, the very thing that marks us as different came to us as a result of something having gone awry. A birth defect. An accident. A disease. We pray to keep such misfortunes from afflicting our children. Rarely do we celebrate having been touched by them ourselves.

Instead of opening a dialogue with Lois by asking her why I seem such an unlikely candidate for Ethan's mother, I simply slink away, preferring not to know.

But, likely or not, I am his mother. This means it's up to me to figure out what I want to teach him about the world. And while I'm not always quick to claim my disability, it has shaped more than my body.

Disability has informed who I am, and I want my son, with his able body, not to mention his traditional good looks, to learn from it as I have. I want him to develop empathy and to value people for their differences.

Fortunately, thanks to the Americans with Disabilities Act, which passed five years before he was born, I get to raise Ethan in a society where it's common to see blind pedestrians crossing thoroughfares with the help of audible traffic lights, and wheelchair users maneuvering around the city. I imagine the talks we'll have when he's older, ones in which I'll describe the circumscribed life led by most people with disabilities when I was growing up, before curb cuts and wheelchair lifts opened up the world.

Meanwhile, our first conversations about disability, while Ethan is still a toddler, are practical, rather than ideological. I teach him that he can't run too far ahead of me on our strolls, since he's quicker than I, and insist that he not plow into me when I'm walking, because he can easily knock me down. Ethan also needs to understand why he has to hold my left hand when we cross streets.

"I don't feel things as well on my right," I explain. "So it's harder for me to know if you're safe."

"If I gave you a garbage can lid," he asks, "could you tell it wasn't my hand?"

"Definitely, but I wouldn't know what it was until I looked."

"What if I snuck you a sword?"

"I'd know that wasn't your hand, either."

"A lion's paw?"

"That would be tricky. Lions walk so nicely next to their mothers."

Ethan is in kindergarten when he tells me, for the first time, about a classmate who gets teased for being different.

"We were singing that 'Help' song, and when we got to the part 'and I do appreciate you being round,' everybody laughed because Greta's so fat."

I crouch down beside him on the kitchen floor, where he's piecing together a Lego spaceship.

"Did you laugh too?" I ask.

He shrugs and gives me a sheepish look. "Kinda."

"How do think Greta felt about being laughed at?"

Ethan concentrates on pulling apart a mismatched pair of Legos. "Bad," he mumbles.

"And if she's home right now talking about school, just like you are, what kind of day do you think she's telling her parents she had?"

"Bad," he says again.

I pick up a blue rectangle from the pile of Legos between us and poke at the holes with my pinky. "You know, there were a few times when I was made fun of at school because of the way I walk."

Ethan looks up from his project. "What did they say?"

"I remember one boy who imitated me and called me a mean word."

"What word?"

I take a deep breath, surprised to find it painful to say even now. "Spaz."

We have similar conversations periodically over the next few years. Most often when Ethan tells me about teasing that's going on at school, he says he stays out of it. There are even times when he stands up for the victim. I feel proud of him and pleased with myself for what I taught him. But I also know there is another, deeper lesson awaiting him in regard to disability, and that it's awaiting me too.

The truth is, I continue to try to pass as much as possible, convincing myself, in my effort to convince others, that I'm more able-bodied than I am. Rushing to work, I've even caught myself shrugging in commiseration with passengers who roll their eyes impatiently when our commute is slowed by wheelchair users boarding our bus. I startle and flush with embarrassment if the driver then noisily lowers the stair for me, bringing attention to my own awkward descent.

Another way I attempt to pass is through the men I choose. Richard, my ex-husband and Ethan's father, is handsome and athletic. In other words, he resembles the guys who wouldn't have considered dating a crippled girl in my high school.

My first relationship after our divorce was with a pin-up artist, Paul, who had no qualms telling me that we wouldn't be together if I weren't slim and pretty. As for my cerebral palsy, he found it barely noticeable.

Then I fell in love with Dan, a blind man I met in a poetry workshop. For the first time, I saw how I used my previous relationships to claim a place in the able-bodied world. Though our disabilities are vastly different, I can talk with Dan about my feelings and experiences, and I know he really gets it. I also begin to learn what life is like when disability can be neither hidden nor downplayed.

On our first outing together with Ethan, we go to see the children's movie *Madagascar*. Ethan is now eight. At the concession stand, we're juggling our bags of popcorn and bottles of water when a man runs toward us, calling out, "Excuse me! Excuse me!"

He speaks to me breathlessly. "I just have to ask. How does this man do it?"

I look at him, unsure of what he's asking. He continues.

"Does he follow the movie based on the soundtrack? Or do you explain it to him? I'm sorry, I just have to know."

Although Dan and I have been dating only a few months, this is not the first stranger to address me when he should be talking directly to him. I hang back and let Dan respond. He graciously explains to the man how he listens to the movie and has his friends fill him in on what's going on visually.

"Thank you. Thank you," the man enthuses. "I just had to know." He starts to leave but turns back around to add, "Congratulations!"

We walk toward the numbered door of our theater in silence. Then, using the exact words and inflection I hear in my head, Ethan says, "That was weird. . . . "

"Yes it was," Dan agrees.

"The strangest part," I put in, "was when he congratulated you."

"Yeah," Ethan says. "What was he congratulating you for?"

"Because I'm not dead."

Dan's timing is perfect and his tone is wonderfully wry. I burst out laughing. When I think of it again over the next few days, it still strikes me as funny. But after several more run-ins with people who seem surprised to encounter a disabled couple doing ordinary things, I begin to see the import of Dan's words. Many able-bodied people believe that if they lose their sight, or some of their mobility, their lives might as well end. Or, at the very least, they would shrink to such a degree that something as simple as going to a movie would constitute a feat.

As much as I take exception to being underestimated in this way, I've also discovered that, even with the Americans with Disabilities Act in place, there are still barriers that make getting around near impossible at times. Many taxi drivers disobey the law and refuse to pick us up once they see we have a guide dog with us. Dan has been denied service on a Greyhound bus because the driver claimed to be allergic to dogs. At my local train station, the only accessible turnstile is closed on weekends. I remember how I'd envisioned describing to Ethan how inaccessible the world was for the disabled before the ADA was passed. I've since done so, but he's seen for himself how far we've yet to go.

These experiences have been infuriating. Still, it's facing prejudice that stings the most. Because my disability calls less attention to itself, discrimination toward me has been subtler. I wasn't always even sure when it was happening. If it seemed to be, as it did when Lois assumed I wasn't Ethan's mother, I opted to explain it away in my mind, rather than having to confront it. I've begun to realize that in doing so, I'm being both unloving toward myself and a poor model for Ethan. I decide it's time for my life to be valued for what it is, rather than for what it can sometimes mask as.

All the while, I've been reading Dan's poetry, including several strong pieces on being blind. I also reread the work of Anne Finger and Lucy Grealy, two of my favorite disabled authors. Other than a couple of poems in graduate school, I have never addressed disability in my writing. I decide it's time to add my voice.

I approach *Literary Mama,* a well-regarded online journal that has published several of my poems, and propose a column that describes my experiences as a disabled woman raising an able-bodied son. They take me on.

I imagine this is what it must be like to come out as a lesbian. Shining a light directly on my disability feels freeing and also a little scary. I'm amazed to find I have so much to say, and I'm uncertain about how the work will be received.

The answer comes in the form of emails. Able-bodied readers tell me they identify with my feelings of vulnerability. People with disabilities share their own stories. A number of readers with hidden disabilities "come out" to me, their relief palpable in the messages they send.

I tell Ethan about the column, emphasizing how excited I am to be using my writing to talk about disability.

"Let's Google you," he suggests, sitting down at the computer. He finds links to poems and to online stores that carry my children's books. We also see a few mentions of the new column. There are a lot of repeats. Still, he's impressed by the overblown number.

"Mom, you're almost as famous as Helen Keller!" he says, making me smile.

It also makes me smile when Ethan stands up to the many people who address their questions for Dan to me. I usually stay silent, giving Dan the room to speak for himself, though occasionally I feel brave or annoyed enough to say, "Ask him." But Ethan has begun telling offenders, "Just because he's blind, it doesn't mean he's deaf too."

Dan and I continue to encounter those who assume that because we're disabled, we lead small, dependent lives. One night we go out to dinner. The waitress takes Dan's order and then asks me, as an afterthought, if I'm going to eat something, too. To her mind, I must be there as his aid since, being blind, he can't possibly be on a date. I'm never sure what to do in these situations; they always catch me off guard.

The following weekend, we go to a convention of the Pennsylvania Council of the Blind in Lancaster. Sunday morning, Dan attends a panel discussion. I opt to stay in our room, reading in a big cozy chair by the window. The chambermaid peeks in and asks whether I mind if she makes up the room.

"That's fine," I tell her.

She walks over to the bed and begins to pull the covers up, but then she stops and stares down at the sheet. "I have to change these," she says after a pause.

I'm mortified, knowing she's referring to the telltale signs of last night's lovemaking. But when she leaves to get new sheets, I wonder why she didn't bring them with her on her rounds. My guess is she figured that since the hotel was full of blind people this weekend, things were bound to remain clean and tame.

It's not without embarrassment that I relay the story to Dan.

"I think it's great," Dan says. "We're changing preconceptions, one chambermaid at a time."

Maybe he's right. Why couldn't we alter people's notions about disability simply by being who we are? Maybe we're just the people for the job. We're articulate, easygoing, and approachable. And we're out there, happy in ourselves and with each other.

For so long, I thought a life in which disability was held close to center would feel lesser, ghettoized. But it's turning out to feel expansive. This is what I hope to communicate to Ethan. When it comes to his mother and her people, I'd love for him to think, *Congratulations. You're very much alive.*

Making a *Minyan* in Vermont

by Nina Gaby

FALL 2004

I FIND MY WAY TO THE TEMPLE, on a dark side street in Montpelier, only after driving by it several times. There is nothing, really, to distinguish it from the other buildings in this ramshackle neighborhood. My thirteen-year-old daughter rubs the frosted window on the passenger side of the car and looks out doubtfully. I had wanted to find this place, to bring her here, sooner. But since moving to Vermont three years ago, I'd let other things take precedence, triaging emotional and financial survival over issues of faith and community.

We stand on the wheelchair ramp of the temple's porch, waiting for the doors to be opened. The cold tonight can make its way under even those coats stuffed with the highest level of powerfill.

"Let's go home," says my daughter.

I know what she's thinking. The few times we went to temple in New York were large, fashionable, and bright affairs. This place, with its peeling paint and shabby storm door, looks daunting. But we have driven twenty miles through the cold, and I am trying to be cheery and positive. I want to explain to her that we have come because it is the Friday night after the presidential elections, because I am heartbroken and overwhelmed with a sense of foreboding and I am seeking vindication. Because I heard there is a woman rabbi here and I have vowed never to make my daughter sit through a male-dominated religious service. Because I need to hear something that resonates with some authenticity from someone behind a pulpit—as antidote to the religious hypocrisy that has a stranglehold on our country tonight. Because I am homesick for better times. Because because.

But I keep it simple. "Oh, come on!" I say. "It's an experience! It's so *Vermonty.*"

She sighs and turns on her Game Boy.

There are fewer people in all of Vermont than lived in my hometown in New York. That makes for a very small percentage of Jews.

A middle-aged woman wearing a yarmulke pulls open the door. "*Erev tov,*" she says. "Good evening. Welcome." One of the first things I see is that the women of this little mishmashed congregation wear yarmulkes, the skullcaps usually reserved for males. I am impressed with this, although I won't wear one myself. They make your hair stick out. It is bad enough, as the mother of a thirteen-year-old, to have long, gray, sticking-out hair anyway. To place a round little cap in the center of it all would guarantee that my daughter would never, ever deign to come here again.

Not long after the service begins, the rabbi scans the room. She is supported by an aluminum crutch, and so tiny that she's dwarfed by her Great Dane assist. Her gray curls erupt from an embroidered yarmulke. She is lovely in her white dress and looks solid and wise, despite her small stature.

She tells us that tonight's piece will be about the Torah, about spiritual road maps other than those derived from the moral arrogance of the evangelical right. "But first—" she says warmly, seriously. She adjusts herself on her crutch, the dog attentive to her every move. "We must say the *kaddish* for Ellen's mother." The Mourner's Prayer.

I whisper to my daughter that this prayer can traditionally be done only with a quorum of ten males, a *minyan,* but she hisses at me, "Mom! We are supposed to be quiet!"

"I thought there would be more people here tonight," the rabbi says. She scans the handful of worshippers in the room. Ten of us and a baby.

Her eyes light on my daughter. "How old is she? Thirteen. Wonderful. A mitzvah! Because of your daughter, we have a *minyan.*"

Yes, a mitzvah, a blessing.

And in this moment, I find some of the vindication I have come here for.

FALL 1968

The *shul,* or synagogue, was in Zichron Ya'akov, a tiny village that neighbored the kibbutz where I was living while studying at an Israeli *ulpan*—a school for learning Hebrew. I was attending "the school of life," my grandfather said in blessing, forgiving me for not going to college. These were the first High Holy Days I was spending away from my family. I was too young and arrogant to be homesick; too innocent to recognize the frailty of these glory days in Israel, the beloved underdog of the Western world.

Tank-topped and sandaled, I walked from brilliant white sunlight into the dim *shul.* A gaggle of women guarding the dark vestibule threw a piece of cloth across my arms.

"*Mah zeh?*" What's this? I demanded, insolent, using one the few Hebrew phrases I had learned. Shoshana, my roommate at the kibbutz, explained. I needed to be covered up so I would not distract any man from his prayers. We were also to worship in a different space than the men—a chokingly hot, overstuffed balcony.

"What bullshit!" As an eighteen-year-old woman from America, I was not prepared for gender segregation. The vulnerability I felt as the women covered my bare arms only triggered some shame at being overweight. I knew no other shame at that time. I certainly did not know the shame of simply being female.

WINTER 1970

It is my second year of art school in Jerusalem. I am living in an old Jewish quarter in a small stone house on an alley, along with my friend Jane and the family who owns the building. The interior walls are painted blue, against the evil eye. A hot-water tank the size of an oxygen cylinder serves us all, spraying a drizzle of warm water over a standup tub two feet across and six inches high.

It is very cold in Jerusalem this winter. The ancient stones hold the chill, and the frost works its way into one's bones. Central heating in the old sections of town is unheard of. More than anything, more than television even, we miss bathtubs. Jane and I are dying for a good long soak.

We hear that there's a *mikveh,* a traditional ritual bathing pool, in a religious bathhouse a block away. We cross over to the back of the building where ritual baths are held; the windows are cranked open a bit, and steam is pouring out into the night. We giggle, fully aware of the audacity of what we are about to request. We pound on a heavy green iron door. A woman with a scarf on her head opens it a crack. Jane doesn't speak Hebrew, so it is up to me to convince this woman that she should let us rent tubs one night a week for payment in American dollars. *American dollars!* She opens the door a bit wider. She looks out into the alley, to the right and to the left. Come inside, quickly, she tells us.

The deep *mikveh* bathtubs were a luxury beyond imagination, becoming as much a ritual for us as for the Orthodox Jewish women who attended them for cleansing after their periods, so their husbands could resume marital relations. It was 1970, the height of the sexual revolution. For us, rules existed only to be deliciously broken. The contradictions made the experience only more extraordinary.

Over time, we developed a relationship with the proprietress. She told me that her daughter was studying English, and wondered whether I would give her daughter lessons, teach her conversational American, in barter for the baths. Could her daughter come to our room on Abulafia Street, where we could help her with her studies?

The daughter was an earnest, dark-haired young woman—unmarried, so her head was uncovered—and while her legs and arms were carefully covered, as required by the Orthodox, layered in grays and browns, her skirts were short and her shoes were modern. While sedate by our standards, her affect was alert, inquisitive. She made no overt notice of the decor in our student quarters: psychedelic posters taped to the crumbling plaster walls, emptied wine bottles turned into candlesticks, ashtrays full of the butts of cheap Israeli cigarettes and the detritus of cheap Israeli hashish.

She came to us two, maybe three times over the next few weeks. We made her tea and sandwiches with peanut butter sent from home. As is the case with many who learn English in foreign countries, her grammar was far better than ours. We dealt with syntax, slang, and dialect. She informed us that she would move to America and go to college soon. Maybe medical school. Her father was unaware of this intention.

One Tuesday evening, Jane and I laughed together as we swung our tote bags, making our way over the deep stones of the road to the *mikveh*. There was a dry chill to the air, and the stars overhead were bright between the crammed buildings. We gossiped about classes and complained about our boyfriends.

A milky light framed the *mikveh* windows. But tonight, the door wouldn't open. I yanked on the handle. I knocked quietly, then harder, the metal echoing each bang. We stood in silence, our chatter interrupted.

From inside I heard a hushed voice. I couldn't understand it. I knocked again, lightly. Politely.

"*Lech mi po,*" I thought I heard. Go from here.

In Hebrew I said, "Excuse me, I don't understand."

The door opened a crack, and the proprietress repeated herself with an urgent "acshav!" Now! From inside, I heard a man's voice raised in anger, but the door closed before I could understand what he was saying.

FALL 2004

I remember this as I sit among the unmatched folding chairs in the little temple. I ponder the fate of the proprietress's mutinous daughter.

I glance over at my own daughter, who is studiously trying to keep up in the prayer book, lips moving with the cadence of the Kaddish chant. *Good girl,* I think to myself. As mad as I am at my country, I have to acknowledge this fact: Tonight, in America, she counts—even as a girl.

Later, under the low ceiling of the recreation room, we share a plastic cordial glass of dark grape juice and a hunk of Sabbath *challah*. The rabbi approaches and thanks us for the mitzvah as the Great Dane brushes gently against us. "You don't know . . . " I start to say. She flashes a wise smile. My polite child thanks her as we zip up our parkas and make our way back out into the dark parking lot.

My daughter is not listening as I start the car. She waits for her Game Boy to boot up.

"I just want to tell you why it was so great that you were there tonight." I am determined to clarify the whole *minyan* point, maybe sneak in a bit about the *mikveh*.

"I get it, Mom." Her tone is verging on snotty.

We are both tired, and the car slips sideways on the icy road. I concentrate on my driving. You do what you can.

We are almost home, and the car is crawling through a sudden whiteout on our six-mile dirt road, when she mutters, "Kids should be able to vote."

I don't let her see how hard I am smiling.

SPRING 2007

My daughter, now sixteen, accompanied me to her last High Holy Day service before swearing off religion altogether, and for the time being she enjoys her status as the only atheist in her school. She has become wise enough to know it will all change again and again.

Despite this, she is selected to write and present an essay in the Rotary Club contest. I tell her I am surprised she was chosen, since it is a very conservative organization.

"Oh, I won't win," she assures me, and refuses to let my husband and me attend. All she says is that she chose the topic The Four-Way Test, a famous schema that the Rotarians employ to evaluate ethical decision making. I tell her I've never heard of it.

The day of the contest, she comes home and announces that she got second place, and that her friend Lauren won. "Lauren was really good," she conceded, although she also explained that Lauren and the other two kids chose the more neutral topic that was offered, and that Lauren won a bunch of money. My daughter seems genuinely happy for her.

My husband was really disappointed that she wouldn't let us go to the luncheon and hear her essay. I was relieved, as I get pretty uncomfortable around large groups of conservatives these days, no matter how humanitarian.

"I didn't want you to feel sorry for me when I didn't win," she explains.

"But why wouldn't you win?"

Her cell phone rings, and she drops her essay notes on the table before running off. My husband grabs the paper.

"Will you look at this?" He holds up her still-childish scrawl.

What if Bush Had Used the Four-Point Plan Before Invading Iraq?

It is the title of her essay. Below it are the points of the test:

Is it the TRUTH?
Is it FAIR to all concerned?
Will it build GOODWILL and BETTER FRIENDSHIPS?
Will it be BENEFICIAL to all concerned?

Her answers are scribbled in purple pencil below. My husband and I lock eyes. We share one of those perfect moments, and then we call after her to see if she wants to go out for Mexican to celebrate.

The Making of a Scholar

by Vera Landry

THIS PAST MARTIN LUTHER KING DAY, Pat and I took our two boys to San Francisco's Museum of the African Diaspora. We looked at photographs and charts detailing how the foods of Africa had migrated to cultures across the world. Oliver and Eric played with an interactive exhibit about the African roots of different styles of music. In a small screening room, we watched a short documentary about Howard Thurman, an influential thinker in the Civil Rights movement. The film included the familiar footage (familiar to me, if not yet my sons) of nonviolent civil rights demonstrators being beaten back and hosed down by Southern law enforcement. The image most striking to me and, judging from the look on his face, to my older son, Oliver, was the footage of a slowly circling picket line of young black men in suits and hats, with placards around their necks that read I AM A MAN.

On the way to school the following Wednesday morning, I reminded Oliver that he had Mad Science after school, an enrichment class I'd chosen for him.

"Why'd you sign me up for that?" Oliver protested, stopping in his tracks. "There are only white kids in that class. I don't want to be the only black kid. I'm not going. Science is for white kids."

"Oliver," I said gently, "science is for anyone who wants to learn it." I paused, seeing *You can't make me* written all over his face, and tried a different tack. "Remember that movie we saw at the museum? Remember the men in suits and hats, walking around with the signs saying, I AM A MAN? Those men you saw in that movie were marching for themselves and for you. They fought for your place in that science class, and you belong there. Science isn't just for white kids. It's for you too."

He softened. "It better be a good class."

I felt like I'd won a small victory.

Oliver's third-grade class had nineteen kids: the same number, give or take a few, as every other third grade in the Berkeley Unified School District. The class composition was also about the same: a wide distribution of skills and scholarly motivation, and a pretty even mix of kids of different races. It had eight African American students, five white students, two Asian American kids, two biracial kids of Asian and white heritage, one Chicano child, and one girl who had just moved to the United States from Yemen.

I'd already heard from the teachers that Oliver's class was a "difficult" one compared with the other third-grade classes—lots of kids behaving badly, talking out of turn, needing reminders to pay attention, talking back to the teacher, practically begging to be corralled. This particular third-grade cohort had been a "challenging" group ever since they'd entered as kindergartners, the teachers told me, and each year it had been hard for the school to divide them up in a pattern conducive to creating smoothly running classes. This year's assignments didn't seem to have worked out well, for Oliver's class at least. His teacher, Mr. Simon, welcomed parent volunteers, admitting he needed the help.

On this morning, the class was involved in an activity called "literacy centers." Mr. Simon assigned me the job of working at the writing center, where the students had to write a letter to the drama teacher explaining the meaning of their class play.

I worked first with a group of three kids. The first didn't know how to put a sentence together and didn't seem to care whether she ever learned to. She hung over her neighbor's shoulder, asking her what she was writing. She whined over and over, loudly, "I don't know what we're doing," demanding that the other two tell her what to write. She put her head down on the table and sprawled her arms across it, crowding the boy across from her. When I asked her to sit up, she scowled. "I'm thinking," she said.

The second girl was smart. She immediately understood the task, and in response to my question rattled off a quick, clear summary of what she was supposed to do. She then spent the next twenty minutes having to be coaxed, chided, and urged to write her ideas down. The third child, a boy, had more difficulty pulling the meaning of the play out of the facts of the story, but when he wasn't succumbing to distractions from the first girl, he tried. He had an acceptable letter written by the end of the session.

The morning's work continued that way, with me working my way through four different groups, each made up of kids with varying attitudes and abilities. There was a girl who did her work calmly and quickly, and within the allotted twenty minutes came up with a good description of the play, though she didn't have much to say about the point it was trying to make. Then there was my son. Oliver stared off into space, sighing, and needed to be nudged to write anything. He kept saying, "What else do I have to write? Am I done?" As he returned to his desk, I felt frustrated. I knew he was capable of more.

The largest group, made up of nine kids, included six who were very self-directed and literate, as third-graders go. They worked with almost no guidance. I was grateful for the competence of those six, because the remaining three were a boy who threw balls of paper across the room, a girl who spoke very little English, and another boy who couldn't tell me what happened in the play, let alone its underlying meaning.

None of the eight black kids in the class, nor the sole Latino child, were in the group of students that performed well—not even Oliver, my very intelligent son, a boy whose state test results had ranked him above the 90th percentile in reading and math.

What I saw in the classroom numbed the feeling of victory I'd had earlier that morning, the feeling that I could soften, maybe erase, the effects that everyday racism has on my son. I saw that my son's teacher was not there for him as I wanted him to be. He simply couldn't be. He was there for a class of nineteen students of varying abilities, many with needs much bigger than Oliver's. It wouldn't be his job to unearth whatever it was that prevented Oliver from diving eagerly into his writing assignment, to take the time to draw Oliver out, and to help him create a sparkling piece of work. There was too much else there for him to do.

I kept returning to the striking fact that not one of the star students in that class was black. When I later asked Mr. Simon about the racial composition of the groups, he became a bit flustered. "I grouped them by ability, not race," he said.

But the fact that not one of the black kids—who made up almost half of the class—was in that group did not seem to be a simple coincidence. What was going on?

There is a label for the differences in school performance between black and white kids: "the achievement gap." Ever since standardized testing began in the early part of the twentieth century, black kids have consistently done worse on achievement tests and other markers of school success than white kids. It's a phenomenon that exists nationwide, not just in the Berkeley schools. The gap narrowed after World War II and through the Civil Rights years, but since the late 1980s, it has been widening again.

Over the decades, scores of articles and books have been written in an attempt to understand the causes of the achievement gap. Conservative writer Charles Murray, in his notorious and discredited 1994 book, *The Bell Curve,* raised the old canard of genetics, claiming black people just don't have the same abilities as whites. John Ogbu, an anthropologist at the University of California, Berkeley, proposed that the legacy of slavery is at fault: Blacks, as an "involuntary minority" in this country, adopt an "oppositional identity" to the dominant culture, setting themselves apart from American culture at large by rejecting the things it values, including academic achievement. Smith College professor Ann Ferguson points to the effects of institutional racism on the performance of black students, suggesting that the harsher discipline meted out to black boys, and lower expectations for African American students in general, produce lower performance. A *New York Times* article in November 2006 ("What It Takes to Make a Student," by Paul Tough) detailed how other scholars have focused on investigating exactly how socioeconomic status and parents' education skills can affect children's school performance. No one theory, it seems, is universally accepted.

Here in Berkeley—a place known for its progressive stance on just about every issue—the problem is no less pronounced than it is nationwide. Pat and I were initially pleased that we were in the Berkeley school district: good test scores, a student community that was rich in diversity (family structure, economic status, race and ethnicity), creative teachers, a sensitivity to the social issues that kids bring to school. It sounded like just what we were looking for. But I began to hear disturbing things from other parents of color. The experience in the schools was not the same for black kids as it was for white ones, they said.

Particularly upsetting was a 2001 article in *Salon* by Meredith Maran. It described a tracking system at Berkeley High that crowds kids of color into the "low achievement track." Then I read Ann Ferguson's *Bad Boys: Public Schools in the Making of Black Masculinity,* which details how the racial attitudes of teachers and school administrators shape black boys' perceptions of themselves as students. As the title of the book suggests, many of the boys did not come to see themselves in a positive light. While Ferguson disguised the school she used for her case study in order to generalize it as any American urban school, a friend who is also an education professor told me that Ferguson's research had been done at a Berkeley public school.

But Oliver is only nine. Was it possible that he was caught up in the achievement gap already? Through kindergarten and first and second grades, he had done well. His teachers saw him as one of the bright students in the class. Second grade was the first year of achievement testing, and his scores were high. I had begun to think that he would be able to do just fine in school, despite the statistics. But this year, his first report card was the worst he'd brought home. His second-grade teacher had warned me that third grade was a demarcation point, an age when many kids decided to opt out of school. It was nothing so dramatic as dropping out, but a more subtle event—settling on a self-image as someone who just doesn't do well at school. I worried that Oliver was beginning to lean in that direction.

When Oliver was in the first grade, he told me that his friend Sean had accused him of "acting white." *Oh no,* I thought then. *Not already. He's too young!*

I kept my voice casual as I asked, "Why do you think he said that?"

"Because I was doing what the teacher told me. He said I shouldn't. Why is that acting white?"

I struggled to put the concept of "internalized racism" into words that made sense to a six-year-old. I wanted him to understand, right then, in that moment, that "black" does not equal "bad."

"Sometimes people think that black people just don't know how to behave, that black people don't do the right thing," I started. "I don't agree. I know a lot of black people, a whole lot, who did what they were supposed to do in school. They listened to their teachers; they got good grades. You know them too. There's Coach Chad and his son Donnie, there's Auntie Emily, there's your Uncle Bill—actually, all your aunts and uncles—there's Andrew . . . "

I tried to tell him about all the black people in his life, in his world, in history, who tried their best and succeeded. I drowned him in the flow of a lecture.

Oliver's two best friends, both black boys, are not put off by his doing well in school. Robert is an athletic kid who also wants to go to college. He sees it as a step to the NFL. He plans to get there by honing his athletic skills, not his academic talent. The other boy, Sam, is very bright; he was already reading when he entered kindergarten. Sam's mother tells me that he, too, struggles with being a smart kid, wants to just be one of the guys, doesn't want to be accused of "acting white."

Oliver, Robert, and Sam are friends in large part because they share a love of sports. Their guiding star is UC Berkeley tailback Marshawn Lynch. On the one hand, this is understandable. How many third-grade boys *don't* worship a sports star or two? On the other hand, it's more complicated for black kids. These three boys and their larger group of friends at school take their cue for what it means to be a successful black man from the culture at large. Black men are valued as entertainers: ballplayers, rappers or soul singers, maybe actors. Being a student or a scholar—or even excelling at something other than entertainment—is not something the culture expects of black men.

American culture as a whole is not known for valuing intellectual achievement, of course. We are all obsessed with celebrity. But according to a 2000 study by scholars Robert Entman and Andrew Rojecki, called *The Black Image in the White Mind: Media and Race in America,* the problem is starker for African Americans. American culture, they propose, offers an extremely limited view of who black people are. The three most prevalent media images of African Americans are the athlete, the entertainer, and the criminal. Given those cultural cues, Oliver, Robert, and Sam are limited to two positive choices.

In fact, Oliver's personality and talents operate to push him toward the stereotype. He *is* a good athlete, better than almost all of the boys at school. Success at sports comes easily to him; classroom success requires work. And his social nature makes him want to fit in with his friends. He is not a rugged individualist who relishes swimming upstream. If his friends buy into the prevailing cultural myth about black men being good entertainers and athletes—and mostly, they do (eight-, nine-, and ten-year-olds are not generally known for their ability to engage in cultural deconstruction)—he's happy to go along.

The channeling of black boys onto that narrow life path starts very young. When Oliver was a baby, I was shocked at how many times some well-meaning person would look at the infant in my arms and say something like, "So, you've got a basketball player there." They'd say it smiling, looking at me for confirmation. The first few times I heard it, I just smiled and took it in the spirit it was offered in—an offhand remark, a conversational gambit, the male equivalent of "What a pretty little girl she is!" But as I heard it over and over and over again from complete strangers who knew nothing about my child other than what they saw when they looked at him, it began to make me bristle. The comment started coming far before he could walk, let alone demonstrate any athletic ability. He was not a particularly big baby. As far as I could see, there wasn't any reason that he should be assigned the life goal of "athlete" when he was less than a year old. But as he moved into toddlerhood, I'd heard it so many times that I'd developed a stock response: "No, he's going to be a Supreme Court justice." I don't remember anyone who knew quite what to make of that.

As Oliver has grown older, I've done what I can to connect him to men whose lives are much richer than the stereotypes. Family men, business owners, teachers. I've been conscious to name what they do, and to point out the black men he knows—his grandfather, an uncle— who are engineers. And I make myself present at school so that I have some chance of understanding what images he is picking up there.

But at the end of this particular morning with the third-grade class, my regular volunteering over the past four years suddenly seemed a very small effort. My presence there in the classroom was a help, but not much. I had little real power over the culture outside of the classroom. Whatever would spur Oliver to excel in school in the face of evidence that "black boys don't" would need to come from him, from some internal motivation or self-confidence that would make it comfortable for him to stand out, apart from his friends. I had a visceral feeling of his moving away from me, out of my sphere of influence, away from my protection. He will be who he will be, have the experiences he will have, approach them with whatever enthusiasm or disdain he chooses, regardless of me. I can be there to witness, to whisper in his ear, to point things out, to cajole, but I can't do much more. He is beginning to define himself as a black student in a world that only recently began to see black men as men, let alone as scholars. The process is already in motion.

Chubby Cheeks, Dimpled Chin

by Margaret McConnell

THE THREE-WHEELED auto rickshaw bumps along the road and a warm breeze flowing through the open sides blows my hair. My daughter and I sit facing each other, her knees between mine. It's our little attempt at vehicle safety. Any abrupt stops pitching her forward, and she will land in my arms. I will cushion the fall. My head might bump against the metalwork behind me, but that's okay.

Aside from this small plan, we are relaxed. She sits up straight with her arms spread wide, holding the bar behind her. She appears open and confident, ready for anything. This is generally true of our life in India. She is pitched forward into new ideas and surprising conflicts that exceed a five-year-old's understanding. But I am here, enveloping some part of her within me. She is smart and demands to understand everything, and I am watching, producing explanations, hoping to cushion the impact.

At the moment, we are riding home from school. Her lips move silently, and a wisp of hair is caught in her eyelashes. I give her knees a squeeze with mine to get her attention.

"Whatcha thinkin' about?"

"Oh," she says, pulling the hair from her face. "I was thinking of that poem we learned in school called 'Chubby Cheeks.' Do you remember it?"

"I think so. Say it for me now."

"It goes like this: *Chubby cheeks, dimpled chin, rosy lips, teeth within, curly hair, very fair, eyes are blue, lovely too. . . .* " She pauses, scrunches up her face. "It sounds like *me.*"

I laugh a little. "Yeah, I guess it does."

"Except for the dimpled chin," she says. "I'm not sure what that is, but I don't think I've got it."

"You don't." I touch my chin. "It's like a little dent."

"A dent. Well," she starts to sound chatty and slangy beyond her years, "*all* the kids have, you know, 'teeth within.'" She sort of rolls her eyes here. "And Bhavia and Sanjuna, and even Sai Krishna, have curly hair. But I'm the only one with all the other stuff. I don't think they knew I was going to come live here or anything, so why do you think they have a poem that's not about anyone at that school?" She shrugs her shoulders. "It's kind of strange, don't you think?"

Yes, it is strange, I think.

Even as a visitor to India, it's not hard to see that complexion matters here. "Fair and Lovely" skin cream is a top seller, and television shows are peppered with ads showing how much your life will improve with lighter skin—you'll get the guy, the job, whatever you desire. Most matrimonial listings request a bride that is "fair," and young Indian women on mopeds wear elbow-length gloves and baseball caps, along with traditional *salwar kameez* outfits, to avoid tanning. Beauty salons, suffocated with the aroma of bleach, fill their seats with women covered in greenish-blue "lightening" cream.

If I had only these examples, I might think of "fair skin" as a beauty trend, equivalent to something like leg and underarm waxing in my own culture. Worthy of a few feminist and cultural debates, but not the weightiest issue in the pile. However, my long-term stay has left me with the impression that "fairness" is not a secondary issue in India. It is a status symbol. And in India, status is essential. The legacy of the caste makes it so.

Outlawed in 1950, the caste system previously assigned socio-economic status, line of work, and honor or degradation along hereditary lines. The system was recorded and formalized by British colonialists to align Indians with their own class system. The notion of caste was separate from, but supported by, the Hindu belief in four *varnas,* each of which sprang from Purusha, a primeval giant and creator of the universe. The Brahmins (teachers, scholars, and priests) sprang from Purusha's face, Kshatriyas (kings and warriors) from his arms. From his thighs came the Vaisyas (traders and merchants), and from his feet the Sudras (farmers, craftsmen, and service providers). The higher and lower parts of the body correlate to the higher and lower degrees of wealth and honor allowed to each group.

Those people not accounted for were without caste, considered untouchable, and lived in the greatest poverty, shunned by society. These were laundry men, barbers, toilet cleaners, and cremators.

Today, in my own town, most farmers and service providers, like the laundry man, are a darker shade of brown. The one lost soul wandering half-naked and bewildered down the road is ebony black with wild, wavy hair, and the corporate employees who pass him with unseeing eyes are often more fair and sport straight, shiny hair.

Sadly, on not one but two different occasions, a gorgeous dark woman holding a beautiful dark child has leaned in and told me quietly, "I wish my baby looked like yours."

Is it a confession? A compliment? Perhaps it's not meant to be an insult when they tell me, "It's not your skin we like, it's hers." And it's true, my daughter does have different skin—creamy white, like milk, and rosy cheeks too, because so often she is flushed from the heat.

In my own childhood I didn't stand out.

Although I was surrounded by my share of political issues.

I ate dinner while the Vietnam War flashed by on a black-and-white television. I watched Patty Hearst wearing a cute beret while wielding a rather large machine gun. I listened to reports on feminist Angela Davis, associated with the Black Panther Party and, at that time, one of the FBI's ten most wanted fugitives.

These things weren't explained to me. Looking back, I don't even remember asking questions. By then I'd learned not to bother my parents with questions, because, really, they were *that* kind of parents—*children should be seen and not heard*. And a quick smack would serve to remind if you forgot the rule.

At that time, the word "feminist" really caught my attention. Without any explanation on offer, I assumed it meant you were committed to all things girly, like pink flowers and curly-cue handwriting. Sitting there in my Levi's cutoffs, with various bruises and scrapes from tree climbing, I thought, *Yuck! I'd never want to be a feminist!*

I was wrong about the meaning of the word, right about what kind of woman I wanted to be.

Despite the wishes of my conservative, old-world, "I'm gonna smack you," Irish Catholic parents, I grew up strong and independent, interested in education, and politically left of center. Why this happened I do not know.

Perhaps the swinging '70s beach community where I was raised trumped the East Coast, Depression-era sensibilities my parents provided inside the house.

Perhaps it's all down to me and what I was to become, no matter what.

Either way, I wandered through my twenties and thirties, through different jobs and different countries, soaking up as much information as I could and forming my own explanations for the world around me. I partnered late, had my child even later, and became the kind of forty-year-old who thought a work-related move to India was the perfect next adventure in life.

Up to that point, my daughter had been raised in touchy-feely, education-based childcare by day, and by a new-generation mom and dad by night. She'd never been hit and, I think, not yelled at either. As for parenting, all duties were split fifty-fifty, according to personality, interests, and availability. Gender notions were left aside as we figured out who would cook, clean, or mow the lawn each week. As we packed up our blossoming three-year-old for a move abroad, we were in for a change.

Our hearts remain the same, but our current arrangement resembles . . . well, my own childhood. Dad goes to work; Mom is the caretaker. There's a fair share of shouting (from schoolteachers, not parents). Worst of all, my kid now knows the smack of an angry hand, delivered—once—by a corpulent school authoritarian who reminded me of my own mother.

Ironic, isn't it?

A series of painful meetings ensured that the hitting would be a one-time event for my girl—but this is the system in India. And now it is no longer just appearance that sets her apart from classmates. I fear she will be seen as the little princess in the classroom—or, worse, that she will see herself that way.

As I watch her, across from me in the auto, my mom eyes see a delicate flower.

They also see a badass intelligent mind.

She is soaking it all up and sorting every day.

She is asking questions.

And we are explaining, explaining, explaining.

It's time for bed.

She is cuddled up in a Winnie the Pooh sleeping bag—it's where she wants to sleep tonight. There's a favorite doll in her arms, and the air-conditioning rattles quietly.

It's that time of day, the twenty minutes before she falls asleep, when things bubble up from her mind: questions, observations, from today or from the past. It can be anything, like:

> "Teacher's pronouncement is sooo different from mine. She says tamarind is *saaah* instead of *soww-errrr.*"

> "*Luna, luna.* I know it means 'moon,' but I can't remember 'sun.'"

> "How old do you think Mulan is?"

I'm resting on the wood floor, a pillow under my head, wondering what it will be tonight. And when she speaks, it catches me off guard, freaks me out a little.

"Mama, am I really the most beautiful girl in the world?"

If we were living within our own culture, this might be a sweet question, answered with a simple glowing *yes*—nothing more than a chance to express love. But I know there is more to this. My mind shifts and sorts quickly . . . my love for her, her self-esteem, issues of social justice. *How to balance it all?*

I reach out and hold her hand. We both stare through the dark at the shiny ceiling fan that spins slowly. I clear my throat. "Well, I'm your mama, so, you know, to *my* eyes you will always be the most beautiful."

She laughs, "I know *that,* but I mean *really.*"

"Oh."

"Teacher is always saying I am the *most* beautiful girl in the world, and today in the elevator that lady with the bump on her face said the same thing, and she pinched my cheek, which hurt, and there were other kids there. And she didn't say anything to the other kids. And everyone wants to take my photo, every day—and they say stuff that's kinda the same. Why do people say that?"

After a quiet moment, I start carefully with, "Well, there's a simple way to think about it, and a more complicated way too."

"What's the simple way?" she asks.

"Well, you look very different from people here, and you are very young. Lots of folks we pass want to meet you for a moment. When they pinch your cheek and shake your hand, and say that you are pretty, in a way, they are just saying, 'Hi. You're a visitor here, and I hope you feel welcome!'"

She turns her head toward me. "What's the complicated way?"

We've talked about this before. I don't think she understands it, but it seems important to say. I don't know if *I* understand it or if I'm getting it right, touching on the right line of logic to explain why things are the way they are, right now, in this one place in the world. But I try.

"Do you remember how, a long time ago, people from Europe started sailing around the world to see what they could find?"

"Mmm-hmm."

"A lot of the people sailing happened to have white skin, and when they started finding other bits of land, a lot of the time the people living there had brown skin."

"Okay. . . . "

"Okay. And a lot of the sailing people thought they might be smarter or better than the new people they were meeting because they had big ships, and science for getting around the world, and because they had thought up the idea to go looking for other stuff. And then—because they looked different from the new people they were meeting, they thought maybe that was the explanation for why they were better."

She falls into synch, like this is a favorite bedtime story. "But they weren't better. They were just different. Right?"

"Right. So then, the sailing people wanted to be the boss of the new people—by setting up governments. Anyway, the colonial period began, and England set up a government in India."

"So England was being the boss."

"Right. And the Indian people could see that the English people had enough food to eat, and money, and that they were treated as if they were very important. And then—this is the most complicated part—over time, I think that some Indian people thought it would be good to be like the people who had enough money—so they might have changed the way they dressed, or spoke, or they might have carried parasols to have lighter skin."

"And tell about the fighting."

"Well, the Indian people decided they would like to be the boss of their own country, and they came up with ways to fight that took a lot of courage and intelligence and patience, and eventually they won the fight."

"Mahatma Gandhi—G-a-n-d-h-i-j-i. Gandhiji. That was on our last exam."

"Right. And this is the last complicated bit. . . . Even though they got the English people to go home, they might have hung on to some of the funny ideas about what makes a person important or powerful."

"Or pretty," she says through a yawn.

And then, it comes almost as a surprise, I feel her hand twitch in mine.

Our friend Gowri has come to babysit, and we are standing in the kitchen. The three of us will go to a baby-naming ceremony in a few days. A silk sari will be draped from the ceiling like a sling, and the little girl will be placed inside. Each visitor will lean in, whisper her newly given name, and sprinkle rice on her head.

Gowri lifts her hand and flips it back and forth in a valuing gesture. "The first baby no good, madam. Dark skin and rough hair." Then she gives a big thumbs-up. "But new baby good, madam, skin more white, and soft soft hair."

I look to my daughter, who says in almost comical exasperation, "How can a baby be not good? That sounds kinda, I don't know, *crazy* or something." And as she says "crazy," she raises her eyebrows and wiggles her eyes around.

Gowri frowns at what must have been some verbal misunderstanding. "No, madam. First baby dark, madam. Second baby good."

"I'm really looking forward to the ceremony," I say. Then I look to my daughter again, who seems to be waiting for me, and she rolls her eyes in conspiracy.

The funny thing is, I know she's doing this for me. I don't approve, and she is giving the eye roll *for my benefit*.

She is only five. It will be so long before she really knows what has happened here and where *she* stands on these issues. She will walk through life and experience so much. What will influence her more? The world inside our home, or the one outside? Will it just be down to her, how she is made, and what she is meant to become?

And when she looks back at our life in India, will she think it helped or hurt her? Will she feel I cushioned the impact as much as I could?

We're starting to pack up our furniture—it's time to move home. Soon she'll be running on a playground with so many types of children— just one dab of color in an impressionist painting. The only screaming she hears will be that of her friends as they run by her side.

I know she'll encounter skin-color issues at home, too, but I am optimistic.

At times, when she's not out to please me, I can see her developing color-blind eyes.

"Mama," she says, holding out her two arms and inspecting them. "You know whose skin is most like mine?"

"Who?"

"It's not you, it's Nita."

Now, one of those color specialists who drapes fabric over your shoulder and tells you what to wear might say my daughter and I are different "seasons," but we are both Caucasian. Nita, on the other hand, is my best friend in town, and Indian.

"You're more like Nita than me?" I ask.

"Well," she frowns with a moment of doubt, then regains her confidence, "she doesn't have *frankles* like I do," and here she points to four small dots, "but . . . well . . . yeah. I think I am most like her."

She holds her arms in my direction, lifts her face. "Can you see what I mean?"

"Well . . . "

I stare at her delicate bone structure, the soft, creamy white skin. I don't really get it. But I like it.

"Yep," I finally admit with a shrug of my shoulders, "you guys are pretty much the same."

Mothering in Real Time

by Jane Hammons

"IF HILLARY CAN FORGIVE BILL, why can't you forgive Dad?" my seven-year-old son wails one night as I put him to bed.

It is 1998, and his father and I are in the first year of a difficult divorce. My son's familiarity with the president and first lady is the result of the constant reportage on Bill Clinton's affair with Monica Lewinsky. I do monitor my sons' TV watching, but I'm also a news junkie. I listen to and watch a variety of news programs and subscribe to several newspapers and news magazines. The transcript of President Clinton's testimony has been published in the *San Francisco Chronicle*. Jokes about cigars and blue dresses abound on the playground. We have come to know Hillary and Bill and Monica as if they were characters in a sitcom. Except I'm not laughing. Okay, sometimes I'm laughing. But when my son compares my capacity for forgiveness to Hillary Clinton's, and I come up short, I resent her.

"We don't really know if Hillary has forgiven Bill," I explain to him, falling into the familiar address he began. "Just because she is staying with him doesn't mean he is forgiven."

Despite Hillary Clinton's 1992 proclamation on *60 Minutes* that she was "no Tammy Wynette, standing by her man," in 1998, she is still standing by her man. The accurate part of that statement is that she is "no Tammy Wynette," who was married five times and perhaps understood something Hillary Clinton does not: Standby is one way to fly. But it's pretty clear that Hillary is not going to fly—not first class, not standby. She's going to remain by Bill's side.

"Why would she stay with him if she isn't going to forgive him?" my nine-year-old son chimes in from his bed on the other side of the room. A conversation about how Hillary Clinton gains and maintains power, in part, from her marriage to Bill Clinton isn't one I particularly want to have with my young sons. There is very little about this conversation that I *do* want to have with them.

"People make all kinds of choices about how they want to live," I try to explain. "I can forgive your father and still not want to be married to him." Having stayed in my own dysfunctional marriage for far too long, I have vowed to be honest with my children, who have witnessed their father's decline into alcoholism, drug addiction, and delusion. He is violent and unpredictable: flying into rages at the park, threatening my sons' classmates and their parents. He has stumbled into walls, knocking himself unconscious. We have found him in pools of his own blood and urine on more than one occasion. He is often prevented by restraining orders from seeing our sons. I would be lying if I told my children I had forgiven their father at this point. And they would know it.

We don't have much use for euphemism in our lives. When they ask questions, I do my best to respond in what I hope are age-appropriate but concrete ways. More often than not, their inquiries lead to what I think of as cultural exchanges between the worlds of adult and child, women and men—thus, issues of power are often at the core.

I was a junior in high school in 1970, when I declared myself a feminist. I understood little more than the basic concept that feminism was a movement concerned with the rights and equality of women, but that was enough for me. Historically speaking, this makes me a second-wave feminist, though I'm not much interested in parsing the waves of feminism. As early as 1975, Robin Morgan celebrated feminism's diffuse strands in a *Ms.* magazine article. When I use the word "feminist" to describe myself to my sons, I do not affix any adjective or prefix—radical, global, Marxist, Amazon, post-, etc.— nor do I discuss historical waves, unless it comes up in a specific context, such as suffrage or *Roe v. Wade.* My sons are too young to have been aware of riot grrrls at the height of their movement. But they did come of age in the era of government-sponsored Girl Power, launched in 1996 by the Department of Health and Human Services. It is most often represented—or misrepresented—by slogans on their female classmates' T-shirts: GIRLS KICK ASS; BOYS ARE STUPID.

My sons are smart enough to know that real ideas are seldom represented by slogans on T-shirts; nonetheless, some of these messages, like a lot of public discourse, must be mediated. I've found the best way to do that is to try to keep a discussion going when they raise an issue or when we observe an event together. A few years ago, I was teaching a unit on gender with my first-year composition students at UC Berkeley. I had assigned excerpts from two books popular at the time: *Reviving Ophelia: Saving the Selves of Adolescent Girls* and *Raising Cain: Protecting the Emotional Life of Boys.* When he was ten, my youngest son saw the books on our dining room table. He was not yet familiar with the reference to Ophelia but understood the significance of Cain.

"Do people think boys are all bad like Cain? That we don't understand our emotions?" he demanded to know.

This was in the wake of the Columbine shootings, and suddenly everyone was focused on the emotional well-being of boys. But my son had it exactly right. In large part, the point of entry to this concern was fear: that all boys, because of repressed anger and violent tendencies, were potential Harris and Klebold clones. I talk to him about the fact that the authors of these books were drawing on familiar cultural icons—Ophelia, a girl who drowns in her emotions; Cain, a boy whose weapon is anger—to draw attention to the positive guidance they offer in their books—that the words "reviving" and "raising" suggested ways of taking action against common self-destructive trends in both boys and girls.

Years later, while watching the breaking news of the Virginia Tech massacre, my older son checked the clock and wondered how long it would take to blame Seung-Hui Cho's rampage on a taste for violent video games. In the span of a few hours, reporters began to posit—with no basis whatsoever—that, like Harris and Klebold, Cho was addicted to violent video games. Thus far, no evidence supporting that claim has been found. On the contrary, what his computer holds is evidence that, violent and disturbed as he was, words—drama and poetry—were his chosen forms of expression until he ultimately communicated his madness with easily obtained guns and ammunition.

As consumers of products (video games, books, music, and movies) containing violent images and themes, and the often attendant sexism, my sons are sensitive to the common claims (some more well founded than others) that people who share their tastes are prone to violence. So if you were concerned that my children were being constantly subjected to academic lectures and feminist dogma, let me assure you, there is a fairly even exchange in our household—after all, there are two of them, and only one of me. I was persuaded by my sons (fifteen and sixteen at the time) to take them to see Frank Miller's R-rated *Sin City,* which I watched, eyes averted as I slunk farther and farther down into my chair, in both discomfort at watching sexploitation, dismemberment, and torture with my children and embarrassment about having exercised such poor judgment.

But if I tried to ban everything that contained sexism or violence from their realm of choices, I would miss out on a lot of interesting cultural phenomena, and anyway, I believe it would be a losing battle. And the truth is that I share a lot of their tastes. As a child I was probably more addicted to superhero comic books than my sons are now, so I read and enjoy those they recommend to me, especially updated versions of Marvel superheroes in series such as *The Ultimates* and, from DC Comics, the Justice League of America in graphic novels such as *Divided We Fall*. And I've read more Neil Gaiman than I care to admit. I am genuinely interested in and often amazed at what they have learned about genre and graphic arts. I find the Cold War mentality of the PlayStation video game *Metal Gear Solid* intriguing, and often watch the "cinemas"—the short movies that advance the narrative of the game—with my sons while they play. I have always been a fan of war movies and westerns and don't shy away from movie violence, having cut my teeth on Arthur Penn's *Bonnie and Clyde* and developed a taste for Sam Pekinpah's movies as a teenager. So when they want to see a movie like *Sin City,* having already read the graphic novel as I stood in the aisles of Barnes & Noble, I express my concerns but trust their judgment. Sometimes I make mistakes.

Without this open exchange, however, my younger son might not have introduced me to Marjane Satrapi's first graphic novel, *Persepolis.* More than reports in the news about headscarf girls in Turkey or France, this book raised for him the issue of human rights for Muslim girls and women. Recently my sons and I watched in rapt attention a report on the *Lehrer News Hour* about Dr. Sunitha Krishnan, the founder of the Prajwala School in India, a school for girls infected with AIDS as a result of rape, incest, or prostitution. Dr. Krishnan became infected with AIDS when she was gang-raped, and subsequently found that there were few resources for her in India. Both of my sons were deeply moved by her story and voiced their admiration for the incredible strength she demonstrates in continually fighting off not only criticism for providing shelter and education for these girls, but also physical attack. She has been physically assaulted fourteen times since opening the school in 1995.

Our household is full of talk—politics, the arts, ethics, and values—but not every moment leads to analysis or debate. Shortly before his death from a stroke in 2004, my sons' father, chronically unemployed and on the verge of becoming homeless, told them that he wished the Catholic Church had a job opening for a hit man to kill all the women who'd had abortions. That was a job he'd like to have. When my older son tells me this, I am literally speechless.

"That's crazy talk, isn't it?" he says.

"Yes," I answer quietly and draw him near. "It is." This is a moment not for a discussion of abortion rights, but merely for consolation.

When we watched Nancy Pelosi pound that gavel as the first woman to be elected Speaker of the House, I saw her in that way: the first woman. And while my sons recognize the significance of that fact, the event was equally meaningful to them, because when Pelosi invited children to the podium, for the first time, they saw people like themselves in the picture as well. At ages sixteen and seventeen, my sons now have a far deeper and more global understanding of the lives of women and children than I did at their age. I feel certain that they would not use the word "feminist" to describe themselves; nonetheless, they have a growing awareness of the fact that the welfare of children is often tied to the political power of women.

It has been almost a decade since our first discussion of Hillary Clinton when my older son asks, "Are you going to vote for Hillary Clinton because she's a woman?"

"No," I answer honestly. "I haven't decided who I'll vote for or why. I wouldn't vote for her *just* because she's a woman." But I do confess to him that the first time I was eligible to cast a vote was in the primary election of 1972. And that I did vote for Linda Jenness, of the Socialist Workers Party, precisely because she was a woman.

And I still feel a certain amount of pride, while also acknowledging my naiveté, for voting this way.

Impressed by John Edwards's appearance at a labor rally for workers at UC Berkeley, my son has decided to cast his first vote, in the 2008 primary, for this candidate, who represents to my son the ideas he considers to be at the core of differences between the Democratic and Republican Parties: a commitment to the working class and improving the lives of the poor and disenfranchised. My younger son, several years from voting age, is a fan of Barack Obama. As an actor, my son finds Obama's presence impressive and believes that Obama represents a new direction; he tells me that Baby Boomers are responsible for what is wrong with the world. We have a lot of heated discussions about this. Just as second-wave feminists did not make the world a perfect place for women and children, Baby Boomers did not rid the world of all the problems they pledged, as young idealistic people, to address.

Much work remains to be done. I would be lying if I said I wasn't looking for women to lead the way as the work continues. Who those women will be remains to be seen.

All-Consumed: The Restoration of One Family's Values

by Alisa Gordaneer

MY EIGHT-YEAR-OLD SON looks up from the kitchen table, where he's trucking his Hot Wheels "solar concept" car back and forth over the oilcloth.

"Mama? When I grow up, will there still be cars?"

I shrug. "Probably not. That's why we're going to bike to school from now on."

"But it's a long way! I want to drive!"

"Do you want to save the planet or not?"

He coughs repeatedly, a nervous twitch he's developed since I started coming on heavy about peak oil, climate change, global warming. He's gripped with anxiety, that boy. And it's all my fault.

Oh, I know it is. No kid of eight should be privy to adult concerns like the future of the planet. But I can't hide my worries under a veneer of "everything's fine," and I don't think I should have to. The first words I spoke to him, seconds after he was born, were "What a strange world you've come into."

And he says he remembers everything about being born.

It *is* a strange world.

I watch him putter his car over the tablecloth, biting my tongue when I'm gripped with the urge to point out that eating oranges like the ones decorating it could one day be an unthinkable luxury—one day, when we are surviving off the Jerusalem artichokes and kale from the garden, and the eggs from our flock of chickens. There's no need to scare him further, is there?

I suspect I've come on a bit strong about the whole global warming thing, have emphasized one too many times the way our role in the global economy is contributing to climate change that could turn the world into a monsoon-swept desert by the time he's an adult. Never mind telling him there's probably no reason for him to ever learn to drive. By the time he's old enough, oil will be so expensive, he'd be better off if he starts learning to ride a horse now.

No wonder his eight-year-old mind is fraught with anxiety.

Is there a problem here?

I don't think so.

It's a strange world he's come into. A strange one indeed.

And no, it wasn't always like this. Not at all.

My son was born in America, embraced within the bosom of consumerism even before he entered the world. I remember waddling in a pregnant daze through the endless aisles of a baby-gear superstore, astounded at the variety of cribs, mobiles, bedding, slings, strollers, swings, snugglies, bouncy chairs, bathtime equipment, and feeding equipment.

"Do we really need all this for a tiny baby?" I asked my equally amazed and dazed husband.

"Uhhhhhhh," he replied. "Um, maybe?"

A store employee helpfully provided us with a list and gave us an electronic scanner to automatically record the items we wanted to receive from loving friends and relatives.

"What friends and relatives of ours would dare shop here?" I whispered.

"Uhhhhhh . . . "

In the end, we settled on nothing, really, besides a required car seat, a stroller that seemed more complicated than our car, and a crib that gathered dust and dirty laundry for the next three years until we gave it away.

At the time our son was born, however, it seemed as though we'd made all the wrong choices. Where would we put him? How would we entertain him? We had no clue how to be parents. But, thanks to living in America, we *did* know how to shop.

Off we went, back to the baby superstore, delighted to be able to define the needs we knew it could fulfill. And back home we came, carrying even more gear than was on the store clerk's list.

Thus began what I like to think of as our "consumerist phase." Oh, it was a dark time. Sure, it was filled with cheerful objects made of brightly colored plastic and toys adorned with enormous eyes and even bigger smiles, but it was also a sinkhole of endless shopping hours, money wasted on things that provided, at best, a few hours of child entertainment. At a time when we should have been bonding with our baby, we were instead packing him into his high-tech stroller for miles and miles of mall walking. Our happy new family, living the suburban American Dream.

And we were not even wondering how we'd gotten to this point. We'd been swept up in the tide of the mainstream, washed into the same ocean as everyone else in America: the endless sea of consumer desire.

And our son was the beneficiary of it all.

He didn't mind one blinking bit.

And then the astounding happened.

One day, when he was about two, we visited a toy store. We looked around, we admired, we left. And we hadn't bought a thing.

I could call it a radical act, but truthfully, it was probably just an oversight. Maybe we figured our son wouldn't notice. But after we were back in the car, with him safely strapped into his car seat, he gave us a confused look. "My package?" he said. "My package?"

"What do you mean?" I asked.

"My package!" he wailed. "My package! My little package!"

Somewhere along the tantrum-filled drive home, it dawned on us. He'd become so conditioned to getting a package—the bag containing whatever toy we'd just purchased—that the lack of it came as a tremendous surprise. The proper order of things had been disrupted. The world had turned on its axis. He was in shock. His position as a consumer of goods was in doubt, and he didn't like it one bit. We felt like the worst parents in the world. Or at least the worst parents in America.

Back at home, as I waded through the ankle-deep piles of fast-food toys, plastic objects, and character-related items we'd fallen victim to, a message and a meaning became clear. This was not how I wanted my son to learn about the world. And this plastic object–filled house was not the home in which I wanted to live.

I thought of my grandmother, who, as a child growing up in Finland, had only one doll, made from scraps of wool her mother couldn't spin into something useful. She'd follow her mother through the potato fields, making toy sheep for her doll to tend from twigs and the green berries of potato plants. She was an adult before she learned that toys could be made in factories. She doesn't, as far as I can tell, feel as though she missed out. That was less than a century ago. How far we've come.

How, then, to reverse the damage before rampant consumerism became even more ingrained in my son than the desire for a post-shopping package?

You'd think it would have come naturally for us. That escaping the consumerist world of parenting would have been a no-brainer. It wasn't like my husband or I had learned at our mothers' knees the joys of brand comparison or shopping therapy. Not at all.

My husband was raised by radical communists who were too busy planning the revolution to bother with shopping—and when they did shop, it was for thrift-store clothes purchased just so they wouldn't have to waste time doing laundry. I was raised by beatnik artists whose credo had seemingly been to make everything themselves, from clothing to crockery to cabinets. I grew up knowing how to cobble together almost anything out of anything, but I had no clue that you could actually shop for furniture. Both my husband and I are incorrigible trash pickers, "free box" gatherers, and gleaners of all sorts. And our politics—well, it's not like they fit with consumerism, either. Call me feminist, and you'd be getting close, especially if you threw in a dose of anarchic individualism. Call my husband a communist, and he'll reply with, "No, Trotskyist."

Fortunately for us, our recognition of our need to change coincided with two things. One was a move from America to Canada, where I took a massive pay cut in order to live in an expensive city doing a job I knew could help change the world. The other was the growing awareness of peak oil, a sea change in the world economy that I could see threatened the status quo beyond anything I could have previously imagined.

To begin, we chucked out, gave away, and otherwise disposed of as many toys as we could. Strangely enough, our son never even noticed. We moved into a relatively small house in a city where rent was so high that shopping was done by necessity only, a carefully considered activity rather than a casual afternoon's pastime. And when our kids asked for things, we pulled no punches in explaining why they weren't going to get them.

Recently, our family went to a department store for a much overdue pair of shoes for my husband.

"Do we really need to be here?" I ask loudly in the toy section, which the kids insisted we walk through. "Why would we want any of this plastic in our lives?"

"We don't want plastic," my daughter, now five, declares. She goes to an alternative environmental school that matches our restored life philosophy of anticonsumerism and environmental responsibility. "Plastic hurts the earth."

"What's our shopping mantra?" I ask.

The kids dutifully look and me and chant in unison: "We're here to admire, not acquire."

"Right."

And I don't care who thinks I'm a bad mom because of this.

We cruise the rows of plastic-packaged plastic objects. "Look," I say. "Made in China. Remember that movie about the environmental damage caused by factories there?" We've watched a lot of documentaries lately, ones that demonstrate the principles we want to remember. The kids prefer them now to Disney, prefer them to pretty much anything.

"Do they make those toys there, really?"

"Somewhere around there. There are kids breathing pollution-filled air just so kids in North America can have a few hours of pleasure playing with a piece of plastic that's likely to break the first day they have it."

"You're right. I don't want that."

Some purchases are all right. Scooters, for example, because they allow kid-powered mobility. Bikes, for the same reason. Books, of course. And pretty much anything from thrift stores, with certain conditions. Nothing military. Nothing needing batteries. And nothing, absolutely nothing, themed with a corporate character. Strangely enough, the kids don't want this kind of thing anymore anyway. Somewhere along the line, they figured it out.

"Mama, is this CPC?" My son holds up a plastic bow and arrow that I know he covets.

"It's totally CPC," I say. Cheap Plastic Crap. "Remember that toy helicopter you got last spring? You were really disappointed when it broke right away."

He nods. It had been a major trauma.

"And didn't you say you'd rather have toys that last than toys that fall apart, even if it means waiting a bit longer for them?"

"All right then," he says, knowing he's getting a real recurve bow for his birthday in a few months. In the absence of commercial toys, he's discovered he loves archery, and he excels at it. And, I figure wryly, someone's going to need to be our family's hunter if it comes down to peak-oil food shortages.

It's been only a few short years since the end of our consumerist period, and already it's receding into my memory. It'll be like this, I suspect, for many others in the future, especially when we see global economies change and collapse under new crises. Kids will be back to making their own toys, like my grandmother did. I knew we were making small steps toward that the other day, when the kids made their own iPhones out of cardboard. They'd rummaged through the recycling bin for materials. Next, they fashioned their own playsets, modeled after the plastic ones at the store.

I now feel more grounded, more down to earth, for having made choices that support a sustainable lifestyle. Just as our son was brought into the wallow of consumerism, our daughter was brought into the asceticism of anticonsumerism. But they're both committed to the new way now.

My son looks up again from his solar-powered toy car. "Mama? Oil? Will it all get used up one day?"

"Probably," I say.

"What then?"

"I don't know," I say, gathering kitchen scraps for our flock of chickens, another move toward sustainability we've decided to make.

"Will someone invent a way to fix the world?"

"Honey," I say, "that's up to you."

"All right," he says. He points to his sister. "You too."

"I know," she replies. "We need to help the earth."

And I breathe a sigh of relief. We're on our way.

Playground Prophets

by Carolyn Alessio

THE DESIRE TO PASS ON political allegiance, parent to child, is a natural thing.

I inherited my own hardcore Democratic leanings from my mother and father, Joan and Sergio. Children of Irish and Italian immigrants, they swore allegiance to their childhood memories of FDR and the New Deal. My mother even fondly remembered how workers from the Civilian Conservation Corps once lifted her up over a Chicago sidewalk they were repairing.

My parents were firm in their beliefs but balanced their political ardor with humor. Not long after the Watergate hearings, they went to a Halloween party dressed as John Dean and his wife. My mother wore a blond wig and flat button earrings; my father carried a borrowed tape recorder in his briefcase.

In 1976, when I was eight years old, my parents had high hopes for Carter, and so did I. He was smart, I had heard, and an engineer, just like my father. At the mock presidential election at my grade school in Elmhurst, Illinois, I dutifully deposited my vote. Later that day, the sixth graders counted the votes: Gerald Ford had nearly shut out Carter in our school election! Nationally, of course, Carter won—but this was almost irrelevant in my suburban microcosm. I walked the playground aimlessly, stunned and chagrined.

With voting comes not only hope, but also heartbreak—even for young children. This became even more clear to my husband and me when we had to inform Charlotte, our young daughter, of John Kerry's loss.

"No! No! No!" she cried when we broke it to her. Later that day, once she'd had time to reflect, she tried, "Maybe he'll win next time?"

I couldn't blame her for having such a strong reaction—not after my husband and I had spent months instructing her in the oh-so-clear virtues of the Democrats, and in the warmongering naughtiness of the Republicans. I knew I wasn't doing politics justice by merely turning it into a story of good and evil. But when explaining Washington to a three-year-old, cartoony battles are so much easier to convey than the intricate and complicated reality.

In the fall of 2007, I attended the first parent-teacher conference of the year at Charlotte's public school in Chicago. Unlike my suburban, ranch-style alma mater, her school building dated back to the 1920s. Its warped stone steps reminded me of an old Venetian cathedral's. I had been eager to offer my daughter the diverse environment I never had as a child. But this meeting made me realize that "being different" isn't exactly smiled upon, even in big-city public schools.

"We call her the Little Old Woman," Mrs. M began.

The assistant piped up. "All her stories start out, 'Well, actually . . . '"

I smiled, though I was not sure whether they thought the affectation was cute.

We went over Charlotte's report: "Exceeds Expectations" in most of the language arts categories, but pure "Beginner" in working puzzles and physical education.

It sounded great to me.

But then the teacher added, with some irritation, that my daughter often disrupted story time by giving away the ends of some of the books, like *Caps for Sale* and *Frog and Toad*.

The meeting had taken place just after midterm congressional elections, and at one point, I happened to mention that the night before, my husband and I had been trying to explain to Charlotte about voting.

They stared.

"Voting?" Mrs. M peered at me over her half-bifocals. "Why'd you talk to her about that?"

"Well, you know, she hears us talking about it and sees the signs."

This conversation effectively ended the conference. The teacher had me sign the report card and motioned to the next parent in the hall. Meeting with me, it seemed, had quickly explained to the teacher why my daughter was the way she was: Interested in Literature + Outspoken = Liberal.

For the next few weeks and months, I brooded over that exchange. By settling in the city and sending our child to a public school, my husband and I believed we were committing to our politics, living our ideals and our hopes. But I was becoming increasingly concerned that our style of debate was overly influencing our daughter. Had we made her into one of those annoyingly precocious kids dreaded by meat-and-potatoes teachers?

During the rest of the school year, my husband and I backed off from talking about the 2008 presidential candidates when Charlotte was around, limiting those discussions to late at night or early in the morning.

But as the candidates began to campaign harder, my abstinence from hearty political talk at home felt increasingly phony.

Several weeks later, while working on an article about child and adolescent morality, I had the good fortune to interview Dr. Robert

Coles, the Harvard child psychologist and author of *The Moral Imagination of Children* and *The Political Life of Children.* He also wrote a children's book about one of the first African American children to be part of school desegregation in 1960s New Orleans. It's called *The Story of Ruby Bridges,* and my daughter and I often read it together.

In our conversation, Dr. Coles spoke at length about his experience counseling young Ruby Bridges. In general, our conversation centered on children, and how they develop a sense of concern for others by connecting with both their families and communities.

Toward the end of the interview, I decided to slip in a question of personal relevance.

"Dr. Coles," I blurted out, "what do you think about talking politics with kids—I mean, with actual names?"

Coles answered emphatically. "Children need to understand our political judgments basically are our moral judgments," he said. "It's very helpful for children to be brought into that in a very specific way—for the parents to say, 'Here is why I'd like to see Hillary Clinton or Barack Obama president, or Rudolph Giuliani. . . . '" He added that when parents discuss their politics with their children, the children learn not only about their parents' values, but also about themselves and what their future may hold.

Since then, I've felt more like myself around my daughter. When there's a political debate on TV, my husband and I talk about who is speaking and whether we support the candidate. I point out occasional bumper stickers and signs, and I even talk at dinner about feeling divided over Obama and Clinton.

Not long ago, at dinner, we were discussing the war in Iraq when Charlotte leaned over her soup and said, "George Bush tries to stop all these good things that happen in life. If I was someone like president, then I would make the world wonderful, much better—with no wars."

"Well," I said, "I agree with you about wars being bad. I don't think they come to any good. But," I said, steeling myself, "I don't think that everything can be the president's fault."

She looked at my husband, who nodded.

"And at school," I said, "you probably know kids whose parents like George Bush."

Charlotte considered this carefully. "Well, not Cameron," she said. "Cameron's parents would go for Obama for sure."

I shook my head. "Just because they're African American doesn't mean they'll vote for another African American," I said. "You know, even *I* agree with George Bush on *some* things, like immigration," I said. "And there are people your father and I like who support him."

"You've got to be *kidding!*" my little redhead yelped.

Despite some tricky conversations and that uncomfortable parent-teacher conference, I have never been truly repentant about having broached the subject of politics with my daughter. I believe in talking to children about the way our country is operating, and about the fact that we're all a part of it—for better or worse.

By the time I became a parent, there was plenty in the world of politics to be cynical about, but also some hope. I know I mumble about President George W. Bush getting "crowned" by the Supreme Court, and that I cheer at the TV when Barack Obama is speaking. But what really matters are not the individual politicians and their shenanigans. What matters most is making our country, and the world, a better place.

This is the message I am hoping to convey to my daughter.

Girl-Shy

by Kris Malone Grossman

I'VE WEPT AT DR. CHRISTIANE NORTHRUP public television specials. I've dreamed of marching on Washington with my little girl. So the second my tummy popped last winter, all my friends greeted me with a hug. "Going for a daughter," they'd wink—I already have two sons—and I'd crack a joke about finally getting to gorge on miniature tutus and matching hair accessories. Then the sonogram flashed me another full-frontal boy, and I started to cry. But not because I had to kiss those tutu dreams *so long,* because I'd have to stomach another bris, or even because nature had just issued a de facto death warrant for my mitochondrial DNA. I cried because I was profoundly relieved: I wouldn't have to bring a girl into this man's world.

I know, I know, it's not a man's world anymore. Except that it is. Why else would I feel the nagging urge to hang my diplomas with the linens in the laundry room? Sure, on the better days, they'd serve as a reminder—to me *and* my kids—that I once excelled at something besides slinging waterproof sheets in my extended stay-at-home gig.

Then again, they might also bring to mind my former students' reaction to Judy Syfer's '70s essay "I Want a Wife": outrage and ridicule. "She should keep her place," a steamed female reader said. "Sexism's a thing of the past," a male student added, and the whole class, save a young woman from the Bronx, nodded in assent. This was the same group that proclaimed, much as Norman Mailer once asserted, that one can identify a woman's writing by its inferior, emotional tone—plenty to turn me emotional. Where, and from whom, had they learned this? It was the new millennium, and still the dawning of the Age of Aquarius, for goodness' sake, but Mother Earth remained unfit for any daughter of mine. Granted, at the next class meeting I did distribute a stack of blind reads to illustrate that one *cannot* determine a writer's gender (or anything else) by "sniffing," in Mailer's tradition, his or her ink—an exercise that devolved into an enlightening, if discouraging, class debate about women's work ("not so bad"), the ERA ("quaint"), and Britney Spears ("liberated").

A more effective lesson may or may not have been a stroll through the university's writing department, headed by men and staffed with a fleet of part-time female instructors effectively derailed from the tenure track (and health insurance) because they wished to cobble together a schedule that allowed them to breastfeed *and* earn. Or maybe (as was my case BC—Before Children) they wanted to work as a freelance writer *and* earn a regular paycheck, even if it was a pittance, even if it included grading papers at home among other "hidden" work (not, come to think of it, so unlike housework)—a desire the school exploited simply because it could. *The dean wants a wife, too,* I almost told my students—*multiple wives*—and consoled myself: At least the restrooms in our country's institutions of higher learning didn't read "women" and "professors" anymore.

The world of book publishing, where I had also been employed BC, was no different: Men occupied the hotshot positions, while a gaggle of women, jacked on caffeine, toiled after hours like Santa's elves on the nether floors, a custom that made me long to stage a *Free to Be You and Me* revival—and made me shudder for the girl I might someday bear. Fresh out of grad school, I'd managed to fast-talk HR into bumping my starting pay from twenty two to twenty-four thousand a year because of my advanced degree, a feat I considered no small coup until I discovered that a male colleague in an adjacent cube leapt from the low forties to three figures in a matter of months. That, plus the fact that many publishing houses were pushing novels whose male authors regularly scored higher advances than female writers (because, as Mailer might have argued, their prose had "balls"), chagrined me as a writer. It also compounded my recent shock, as mother and woman, at a full-time mom who was quoted in *The New York Times* as deliberately declining to purchase books about the female experience because doing so "protected" her sanity. So much for pumping up those advances. I couldn't help but remember the physician husband in the 1800s short story "The Yellow Wallpaper," issuing his struggling, postpartum wife a companion prescription: No writing; it will only upset you.

Thankfully, no women I know have taken such an outmoded cure, and a host of recent articles has stirred up serious food for twenty-first-century thought. Such as how the majority of today's parents, while they assure their girls they can grow up to inhabit any role they aspire to, rarely mention in detail the unique choices they might have to face as women. Choices that, because of the way our country's work culture is structured, have yet to affect men in the same, often detrimental manner. Take, for example, statistics underscoring the innumerable perks (promotions, raises) corporate men are afforded for having families, while women are penalized or, at best, marginalized for the same. "Hey, baby girl! Bet you can't wait to be pushed out of the office—for pushing out a baby! And should you stay, you just might earn unequal pay!"

Or zero pay. For the past six years, I myself have so-called "opted out" of the (paid) workforce—by opting *into* the domestic sphere to raise my children, a sphere to which I have yet to acclimate without assistance from a patchwork of sitters and various SSRIs that soften the edges around incessant wiping and diapering, spit-up scrubbing, and, in a Friedan-esque nod, peanut butter sandwich scarfing. My earning power having all but flagged, or even reversed course, I am rendered economically dependent for the first time in my adult life, while my husband amasses ever more raises and desirable titles and actually gets to do things like commute—thirty minutes of silence, not once but *twice* a day—and travel to such places as Parisian boutique hotels, sojourns that hara-kiri me with envy. Oh, to be served a meal, even airline grub; to recline, unmolested, in a comalike state anyplace apart from the aforementioned laundry room! Eerie to consider that my mom and her peers regarded their husbands' travel in much the same way thirty-five years ago.

Eerier still is the bizarre refrain I often employ to justify my having relinquished, however temporarily, my previous professional pursuits: *Good thing I was never driven to be a CEO.* If I had been, I'd undoubtedly experience *authentic* ambivalence about my current title as homemaker, as if my vocation as teacher and writer, becoming the very "anything" my parents always assured me I could be, clearly doesn't count because of—like mommyhood—its unremarkable pay. As I did when my students protested Syfer's essay, I have to ask: Where, and from whom, did I learn this? Certainly not my parents or husband or peers, all of whom concur: Mothering is a respectable job. A good job. The most important job in the world (along with fathering, of course). It's just not always that fulfilling.

Don't get me wrong, I love my kids. And I *do* manage to eke out writing time between slicing bananas and reading *Curious George;* enough, anyway, to cover our annual diaper bill. And yes, my husband and I religiously refer to his salary as "ours." We even regularly dare to break those precious email chains referring to a mommy's paycheck as "sunshine, smiles, and hugs." Yet something on the home front still rings disingenuous whenever I remind my kids (and anyone who hopes to eat in my kitchen) that "mommy" is synonymous with "privilege" and "super-important job." If this were true, wouldn't the hospital have sequestered me in the lush maternity ward for a civilized fortnight, rather than turning me out while I was still waddling and beholden to the Bermuda Triangle of pain (mammaries, loins) after a pitiful two days? No man on the planet, in such condition, would allow himself to be discharged from round-the-clock coddling, especially not to weeks of *unpaid* leave. And by the way, if mothering really were the most important occupation in society's eyes, wouldn't the government be paying moms for vacation time and, providing us with our own health insurance, 401(k)s, Social Security—anything for our daily grind, which entails raising future laborers, stay-at-home or no, who will someday fuel the economic pool?

An economic pool, by the way, ensconced in a democracy that elects a disproportionately high number of men into office, then slaps their mugs on all of our currency, relegating Sacagawea and Susan B. Anthony to rare stamp-machine peep shows at the local post office. I was shocked, at age six, when my own mom picked up a bookshelf globe and pointed to various locales she claimed not only revered women, but actually featured female figures and forms not just on money, but in public places and all significant art. Not so enlightened a land in which government stiffs long to drape Justice's breasts in the name of decency, or where priggish administrators suspend girls for using the word "vagina" in suburban high schools (where, for the record, a walloping double standard persists to this day, as my sweet-sixteen sitter can attest). Note to self: Determine just how to explain to a child—girl *or* boy—that while our country champions family values, it can't muster the guts to meaningfully support the notion or, by extension, truly value children. Truth is, if my husband were to expire tomorrow, there's no way that this government, which scarcely supports its war veterans and their families, would truly assist me and my kids, the very kids our leaders claim we should be making number one.

And let's not forget another, equally daughter-dampening helping of cultural schizophrenia, or what I like to call the Victoria's Secretization of America: the sexed-up status quo encompassing everything from thong underwear for elementary school–aged girls to peewee princess manicures to the grocery store checkout rags touting women whittled to prepubescent frames. Women waxed bald from the neck down and adorned with exaggerated, otherworldly, yet somehow virginal breasts, a.k.a. giant pacifiers for even balder men: mothering, sunk to its creepiest form, while real-mom images languish in backwater websites and indie photo shoots. Bad enough I recently had to try to explain to my four-year-old just why it is that he sees our town's coiffed and Botoxed female population swill mondo black coffees rather than eat, while the daddies huff doughnut holes; I can hardly imagine trying to convince a daughter—straight-faced, as I have my sons—that I and the spandex mamas hamstering on the treadmills in the gym adjacent to the town preschool do so solely to stay "healthy." And earlier this year, when a relative competed in the Miss USA pageant (is it possible this prime-time, soft-porn parade actually still exists?), I was eternally grateful that I had no daughter to contemplate our beauty queen's post-loss comment: "No cocktails! I want pancakes—I haven't eaten for a year."

Eating disorders, of course, while perpetuated by society, are also genetically to blame, and my genes are packing a hearty helping of anorexia, which gathered me to its bony bosom at the age of twelve, courted me through college, and has yet to entirely loosen its grip. How could I, even after years of recovery, ever presume to teach a daughter that it's far from normal to converse with a carrot—or to shed so much poundage that you're virtually erasing yourself, becoming invisible, the very antithesis of feminism? One could, of course, mount an argument against procreation by conjuring any number of genetic ailments—addiction or mental illness, both of which, like eating diseases, run in my husband's and my families, and both of which could be passed along to either a boy *or* a girl. At this rate, why reproduce at all?

To raise more feminists, of course. And as a feminist—and mother, woman, human being—I *do* mourn the might-have-beens a daughter may have brought. Like simply nurturing a girl. Or marching on the Capitol for women's lives, as my own mom and I did. Or throwing an all-night fest when she gets her first period, dishing about the first stack of texts she buys at college, helping her navigate her own set of choices someday—choices that, for better or worse, won't be so different from mine—and even observing her interacting with and learning from my husband, who considers mothering a hardcore feminist pursuit. Which, in the end, reminds me that even with three boys, we'll have our work cut out for us. That now more than ever, it falls to us to teach them: It's only through their participation that this man's world will ever change enough to deserve its daughters. And, for that matter, its sons.

A Letter to My Daughter at Thirteen

by Barbara Kingsolver

HERE'S A SECRET you should know about mothers: We spy. Yes, on our kids. It starts at birth. In those first months we spend twenty-three hours a day trying to get you to sleep, grateful you aren't yet verbal because at some point we run out of lyrics to the lullabies and start singing, "Hush little baby, don't be contrary / Mama's gonna have a coro-nary." And then you finally doze off, and what do you think we do? Go read a book? No, we stand over your cradle and stare, thinking, God, those little fingernails. Those eyelashes. Where did this perfect creature come from?

As you grow older, we attain higher orders of sneakiness. You're playing dolls with your friend, and we just pause outside the door of your room, *hmm-mm,* pretending to fiddle with the thermostat but really listening to you say, "Oh, my dear, here is your tea," as you hand her a recycled plastic Valvoline cap of pretend tea, and our hearts crack, we are such fools for love. We love you like an alcoholic loves gin—it makes our teeth hurt, it's the first thing we think about before we open our eyes in the morning—and like that, we take little swigs when nobody's looking.

These days I watch you while you're sitting at the table, concentrating on algebra, running your hand through the blond curtain of your hair. Or after I've dropped you off at school and you've caught up to your friends, laughing, talking with your hands while your shoulders and hips rest totally at ease in the clothes and style you've made your own. I stare, wondering, How did I wind up with this totally cool person for a daughter?

You have confidence and wisdom beyond anything I found at your age. I thought of myself, at thirteen, as a collection of all the wrong things: too tall and shy to be interesting to boys. Too bookish. I had close friends, but I believed if I were a better person I would have more. At exactly your age I wrote in my diary, "Starting tomorrow I'm really going to try to be a better person. I have to change. I hope somebody notices." My diaries, whose first pages threatened dire punishment for anyone who snooped into them, would actually have slain any trespasser with pure boredom: I resolved with stupefying regularity to be good enough, better loved, happier. I looked high and low for the causes of my failure. I wrote poems and songs, then tore them up after unfavorable comparison with the work of Robert Frost or Paul Simon. My journal entries were full of a weirdly cheerful brand of self-loathing. "Dumb me" was how I christened any failure, regardless of its source. In a few years the perkiness would wane as I began to exhibit a genuine depression, beginning each day with desperate complaints about how hard it was to wake up, how I longed for nothing but sleep. I despaired of my ability to be liked by others or to accomplish anything significant, and I was stunned whenever anyone took any special interest in me.

Turning page after page in those old cardboard-bound diaries now, reading the faint penciled entries (I lacked even the confidence to use a pen), I dimly grasp in my memory the bleakness of that time. I feel such sadness now for that girl. This superachiever who started high school by winning a state essay contest and finished as valedictorian—why on earth did she fill her diary with the word "stupid?" What could any adult have said that would have helped? When I look at my yearbook photos, I'm surprised to see that I was pretty, for I certainly had no sense of it then. I put on the agreeable show I thought was required of a good girl, but I felt less valuable than everyone around me. I took small setbacks very hard. Every time I took a test, I predicted in my diary that I'd flunked it. I was like the anorexic girls who stare at their bony selves in a mirror and chant, "I'm fat," except the ugliness was my very self. I chanted, "Worthless me" while facing daily evidence to the contrary. I've always considered this to be the standard currency of adolescence. So it takes me by surprise when we're discussing some hassle and I sigh and say, "Adolescence is a pain," and you grin and reply, "Actually, it's not that bad." As your maturity dawns over our relationship, I think hour by hour about how I was mothered and how I do the job myself. It doesn't explain the differences between my thirteen-year-old self and yours; I take no credit for your triumphs, nor was it my mother's fault that I was depressed. She did her best with a daughter who was surely frustrating. I remember her arguing with me, insisting almost angrily that I was pretty and talented and refused to see it. She must have rained steady compliments over my scholastic and artistic efforts. But compliments help only if one believes them. At some point before age thirteen, many girls stop believing in all praise, even when it comes straight from a mirror. For you it's different. I watch you talking with your friends, or combing your little sister's hair, or standing at the back of your orchestra and elegantly bowing the strong bass line that holds everything else in place, and I see a quiet pride that's just part of your complexion. When you were little I used to declare you beautiful, and you'd smile and say, "I know." Now you're too savvy for that. But in the kitchen after school when you've reported something tough you dealt with well, and I say to you, "You have such good judgment about stuff like that," you'll look off to the side, and it'll be written all over your face: *I know*. It's your prize possession. I'd do anything to see you keep it.

When I was pregnant with you, I read every book I could find on how to handle all things from diaper rash to warning lectures on sexually transmitted diseases. I became so appalled by the size of the task that I put my hands on my belly and thought, *Oh Lord, can we just back up?* But the minute you were born I looked at your hungry, squinched little face and *got* it: We do this thing one minute at a time. We'll never have to handle diaper rash and the sex lecture in the same day. My most important work will change from year to year, and I'll have time to figure it out. At first I was just Milk Central, then tiptoe-walking coach and tea-party referee. Eventually I began to see that the common denominator, especially as mother of a girl child, was to protect and value every part of your personality and will, even when it differed from mine.

In this department I don't think girls of my generation got such a good shake from the guardians of our adolescence. The guide-book for parents then was organized around a whole different the-sis; spanking was mandatory, and the word "self-esteem" had not been invented. The supervisors of my youth loved my accomplish-ments until I started campaigning against things they believed in. They thought I was beautiful, but they bluntly disparaged the getup required for *my* idea of beautiful. I wasn't even allowed to say I dis-liked a particular food. I made almost no significant decisions about my own life: I ate what I was fed, washed dishes but never planned meals, participated in school-sanctioned activities but virtually never hung out unsupervised with my friends. The parents of my time and place worried about pregnancy, drinking, and car accidents—as well they should have, since these shadows would fall sooner or later across the lives of most of my peers. I participated in a mind-boggling number of school-sanctioned activities but lacked time to be *me,* away from adults, just with peers. That must have looked too dangerous. As a child I'd spent endless hours poking around in the woods or playing disorganized games with other kids in the fields around our house, but once I grew breasts, my unchaperoned days were over. I felt increasingly scrutinized and failed to develop a natural ease or confidence with my peers. I was convinced that my parents would never let me grow up, so I railed against them internally but then felt guilty after, fearing they would mind-read my rebellious thoughts.

At age fifteen I was allowed to go on a trip with the high school English classes to see a performance of *Measure for Measure* in a nearby city. It was my first experience of Shakespeare (my first real play at all), and I felt elated afterward by this exposure to mature ideas and drama. But discussing it with my parents that night at dinner, I grew tense. There had been some implied sexuality in the play; my brother and I had made a pact not to mention it, but I feared somehow they knew anyway, and I was too nervous to eat. I felt sick inside, as if by watching this wonderful work and loving it so much I'd betrayed my parents' trust in me and my own goodness.

When I went off to college at eighteen, I promptly went straight off the deep end of the social/recreational pool. It frightens me to look back on that reckless period of my life, but I also understand it perfectly. I'd been well under control up to that point, but I had no practice in *self*-control. I was extremely lucky not to damage myself in the process of learning moderation.

As penance for this close shave, I vowed early on to give you more choices than I had, so you could learn self-control in a safer laboratory than I did. The dance of letting go the reins is never easy—two steps forward, one step back. I've spent so much of my life stitching together the answers to the hard questions that it's natural for me to want to hand them down like a glove, one that will fit neatly onto an outstretched little clone hand. I try sometimes. But that glove won't fit. The world has changed, and even if it hasn't (drinking, drugs, and pregnancy are still at the top of the immediate-worry agenda), the answers will work for you only when you've stitched them together yourself.

People say it's because parents *love* their kids so much that they want to tell them how to live. But I'm afraid that's only half love, and the other half selfishness. Kids who turn out like their parents kind of validate their world. That was my first real lesson as a mother—realizing that you could be different from me, and it wouldn't make me less of a person. When you were three, in spite of all the toy socket wrenches and trucks I'd provided in my program of teaching you that women can be as capable and handy as men, you basically wanted to be the Princess Fairy Bride. You'd have given every one of your baby teeth for a Barbie doll. I tried to explain how this doll was an awful role model, she didn't look the way healthy women should, she was obsessed with clothes, blah blah. Translation: My worldview doesn't have room for Barbie in it, and I'd be embarrassed to have her as a houseguest. I wouldn't give in on Barbie.

Then, one day you and your friend Kate were playing in your room, and I was spying just outside the door (yep, fiddling with the thermostat again), when I heard you say, "My mom won't let me have Barbies. But you know what? When I grow up I'm going to have *all the Barbie dolls I want!*"

Yikes, I thought to myself. Soon afterward, Barbie joined our family.

That was a stunner for me. Believe it or not, it was the first time I really pictured you as a someday-grownup, completely in charge of yourself (and your menagerie of dolls). Eventually I'd have zero power over you, I realized, so this might be a good time to start preparing for it by shifting from 100 percent to 99 percent control. Let the Barbies come, and let you handle the Social Impact. You did, and along the way you probably learned a thing or two about physics: What happens when you shoot Barbie from a paper-towel tube? Also about disabilities: When the puppy found your abandoned Barbie party and left it looking like the Plane-Crash Barbie Close-Out Sale,

I made you keep most of the Barbies, asking, "If your friend lost a leg or a hand, would you throw her away?" (The headless ones we laid to rest.) And I learned to say, when you dressed yourself in bridal veil, roller skates, rouge, and a tutu, "Wow, you have a really creative sense of style." I've never lied to you. I didn't say I thought you looked *good*, just creative. Maybe that's why you believe in my compliments now.

Every mom has to set limits, but that's never been so difficult with you. When you want something that I truly think will do you harm, I explain my reasons, and then usually let you have a *little* of it (except if it's illegal, or skydiving) or give you permission to abide by your friends' mothers' rules when you're at their houses (case in point: watching TV). Though you may not notice it, I'm keeping an eye out to see how long it takes you to decide you've had enough. Except for that one time when you put your whole face in the birthday cake, your judgment has proven exceptional.

All your life you've been apprenticing for adulthood. I recognized that when you were in preschool, learning how to be social: having feuds with girlfriends, then forgiving or sometimes moving on. One week they'd shun you, the next week you were queen bee while somebody else suffered. It tore me to pieces to watch, but I knew I couldn't save you. You were saving yourself, slowly. In fifth grade, it suddenly got harder: A boy started picking on you, mostly trying to embarrass you with sexual innuendo. Oh, man, did I want to walk into that classroom and knock some heads together. But I took a deep breath, knowing that even this—*especially* this—you had to learn to do for yourself. I was scared. It was my hardest mom event so far, and I didn't want to screw it up.

And it is *so* easy to screw this one up. When I was a teenager, the story I got from the world around me on how to behave with boys was a real song and dance, which boiled down to this: Boys want only one thing, which is to have sex with you, which is too nasty even to talk about, and it's your job to prevent it. They're also stronger than you and likely can do what they want, but if they succeed in raping you it's your fault, actually, because it was your job to avoid getting yourself into a position where you couldn't stop it. Also males are more important, they run the world, and if you want any kind of happiness or power, you're going to have to win their favor. Got it? Ready, set, go.

The day I sat down with you on your bed to talk about the grade five boy problem, I felt as if I were jumping out of a speeding car, blindfolded, into a snake pit. I took a breath and said, "This is a good time for you to start learning how to handle inappropriate male attention." I told you three things: First, if you ever got truly scared, I would intervene. Second, it was fine to get really pissed off at this boy, because everybody deserved the right to go about her business without being harassed; the creepy feeling you had was *not* your fault, it was his. Third, boys are just people like us, and if they behave sensibly they can be very cool to be around—even in a physical way if that is your inclination, when you eventually feel the confidence and fondness to be with a guy like that.

Finally, I told you that unfortunately there would always be some guys who feel it's their gift to behave as irritants and scoundrels. You'd run into this many times in your life, and a classroom was a safer place to learn to defend yourself than, say, a college bar or a workplace.

Then we practiced role-playing. I wanted you to say, "No, I hate that, you make me sick, go away." You found it hard; your tendency was to be polite, even coy. I realized, with agony, that the world had already begun teaching you that girls should be pleased with, or at least politely tolerant of, male attention of any type. I tried not to hyperventilate. We practiced some more, you learned to take a very firm tone, and you made it through fifth grade. *I* learned what you were up against. It was not too early for me to begin thinking of you, and talking with you, as a transitional woman, with important disputed ground to claim for yourself on the map of equality. You've kept me posted on the main events in the boy-girl arena, and so far I've been impressed with how you've handled them.

I didn't do nearly so well myself, as a teenager. My first kiss happened the summer after I turned fourteen, at band camp—a school-sanctioned activity during which I was theoretically chaperoned every minute of the day. I met a cute boy named Dave who showed a flattering interest in me, and one evening when we were meant to be washing dishes he asked me to go outside instead, and mess around behind the so-called mess hall. I was scared to death; I went. Our kissing was nowhere near as graceful as in the movies, with an icky dampness factor that seemed categorically not too different from washing dishes, but I felt thrilled to have been chosen. After camp ended I never heard from him again because, of course, we'd had no friendship, and I felt creepy about my tryst. I'm lucky he didn't expect me to go beyond kissing. I hope I'd have resisted (I'm pretty sure terror would have helped me out), but I'm sad to admit I can't say for certain. It took me years to get over being flattered and flattened by any kind of male approval. My first relationships in high school and early college were stunted by my inability to separate my interests from my boyfriend's. The guys who did time in that capacity during those years were invariably sweet; it wasn't as if they *meant* to ignore or malign me. It was just that I felt such pressure to remain coupled that I swallowed my own will to keep from rocking the boat. *Like* what he *likes, do* what he *wants:* I couldn't imagine just acting like myself in the company of a guy.

I see a lot of girls your age who are just the way I was then. I remember hearing one of your friends declare helplessly, "I can't say no to boys"—in the sixth grade! I feared for her future reproductive life. But not yours. I can see very well that if a male friend didn't take an interest in the things you care about, or wasn't respectful, you would use your remarkable charm and wit to lose him, fast. Or at least tell him that, as I heard you recently say, "he's not *all that* and a bag of potato chips." It's a huge relief to me. I look forward to meeting the guys you'll date.

You already know a lot of the things I had to teach myself in my late teens and early twenties. What saved me was nothing short of a complete transformation, the kind of soul-shattering revelation that some people find in religious salvation. *I* found it in the novels of Doris Lessing, Maxine Hong Kingston, Margaret Drabble, and Marilyn French, along with the words of Betty Friedan, Germaine Greer, Gloria Steinem, Robin Morgan, and lots of others. I began to find these books my last year of high school and then really sank into them in college, reading the way a drowning person breathes air when she finally breaks the surface. I stayed up late reading; I sat all day in the library on Saturdays reading. Every word made sense to me, every claim brought me closer to being a friend to myself. These writers put names to the kinds of pain I'd been feeling for so long, the ways I felt useless in a culture in which women could be stewardesses but the pilots were all men. They helped me understand why I'd been so driven by the opinions of men. I was not stupid; in pandering to male favor I'd been pursuing what would be the smartest possible route to power in, say, Jane Austen's day, when women couldn't own property or vote. But these writers allowed me to imagine other possibilities. There are still many countries where women have to go the Jane Austen route: Muslim extremists stone women to death if they show their faces and declare their opinions in public, but here you'll only get some hate mail for it. The worst that was likely to happen to me, if I began standing up for myself at age nineteen, was that some guys who handled me with less deep concern than their auto transmissions would probably cut bait and run. This loss could be endured; that was all I needed to know. When my despair finally crystallized as anger, my conversion was rapid and absolute: I cut off my long hair, I began to dress for function rather than sexiness, I got mad at whosoever tried to bully me by virtue of unearned privilege—and I discovered there were guys who actually *liked* me this way. I joined a women's group on campus, then found a church that was more forgiving of personal lapses of judgment than of larger, social ones, such as war and hunger. I began working with migrant farm workers in central Indiana whose problems were larger than mine: They had no clean water or shelter. I learned more about the Vietnam War than I'd previously gleaned from *Reader's Digest.* By concentrating on what I could do to make things better for people who were worse off than I, I taught myself to feel significant. Word by word, day by day, I revised the word "stupid" out of my journal.

The premises of feminism—that women are entitled to do any kind of work men do, for the same pay, and to be accorded an equal measure of social respect—must seem obvious to you. But in 1973 these items were just barely on the agenda. The first time I suggested to my father that a woman could be president, he got a pained expression on his face just thinking about a woman having to go through that mess. He asked me, as delicately as he could, to consider what a disaster it would be if we had a war and the president was on her menses. Both of us were acutely embarrassed, and that was the end of that. (It didn't occur to me until years later that most presidents are elected well past the age when menses would be an issue.) When I told my parents about an older college friend I admired who intended to keep her name after she got married, my mother offered sadly, "Any woman who'd do that doesn't love her husband."

My parents, in telling me of these and a thousand other limitations on my gender, weren't trying to hold me in contempt. They were merely advising me of the ways of the world—which, in 1973, held me in contempt. Since then they've changed their minds about many things, including my keeping my last name, which is now also yours. (And if you ever run for president, I'm positive Dad will vote for you.) But the persistence of misogyny in the world outside our family is not forgivable, and it makes me crazy. Why is it, for instance, that on the popular teen radio station, all the women are singing about guys who treat them like dirt (or, on a more optimistic note, declaring the jerk must go), while the men are chanting, sometimes literally, "Die, bitch, die"? It scares me that boys listen to this stuff; it scares me more that *girls* do. I can't tell you what to listen to, I know. To this day I get a buzz when I hear the first notes of "Lay Down Sally," probably from all the warnings I received against its morals and grammar. But if you're going to listen to these guys, *listen*. Eric Clapton was singing to me, "You are *so* the best, I can't stand for you to leave the room." I'd just once like to hear that from some rapper. One of the best gifts you ever gave me was when you turned off Eminem and started listening more to Sheryl Crow and Alanis Morissette on your CD player. I think—I hope—you did it not for me but for you. Because you didn't need "Die, bitch" as bedtime music.

I know that some girls of your acquaintance worship Eminem. Some are already doing drugs and having sex with guys because they need male approval that badly. I understand that perfectly, because of how *I* was in my teens. I wish I could tell them it's not too late yet: If they can just yank it back for a minute and find some little island of pride, there's hope. But it takes believing in some larger space for women in the world than they can presently see. For me, that belief came from the right books, because I happened to revere the printed word. Even more, it was finding and joining a huge, heady current that allowed me to believe I could change things a little—that I could fight back against what made me angry, in some way that was real and grown-up. Piercing and branding one's flesh or getting pregnant or getting AIDS is *not* fighting back, even though it may feel like it from the inside. From the outsider's point of view, these things make a display of self-loathing, which is the opposite of fighting back—it's a score for the opposition. I know, because I used to hate myself, and now I don't.

You never did, it seems. You like who you are, you work hard at whatever you do, you're kind to your friends, you show compassion for the world. You're a person I'd choose as a friend even if we weren't related. I actually like the ways you're turning out different from me; your confidence and smart-aleck wit inspire me. I was impressed, the day we were listening to the presidential campaign and the one guy started pandering to the audience, when you rolled your eyes and said, "What a suck-up!"

If I'd said that about a presidential candidate when I was your age, I would have gotten it for disrespecting authority. So I had to ask myself, *Am I allowed to laugh at what she just said?* Answer: yes. I agreed with you totally; he was groveling for the vote. I can't insist to you that all authority is worthy of your respect, because much of it is not. In five years you'll have to see through all the sucking-up and vote for your own president. Why *shouldn't* you start practicing now?

Every authority has its limits. I find myself defusing the menace of maleness by viewing it as a source of fascination. I study it constantly, not trying to learn how to *be* that, just trying to understand it. To say they run the world just doesn't cover it, because we do, too, in our less material way. Not in terms of real power, of course; it's impossible to imagine a reverse Saudi Arabia, in which we walked around doing whatever we pleased while forcing our entire male population to vacate themselves from public life and wear black cloth sacks with sideways slits for their eyes. We could never get them to do it; they're devoted to being in charge of things, and we seem unable to whip up any zeal for treating people like that. It's hard even to imagine a tradition of fine art in which naked men would recline on picnic blankets while fully clothed women looked on. Recently an artist in Colorado tried to communicate (especially to men, presumably) how it feels to have our sex so constantly and casually appropriated: She created a display of colorful penises pinned to a clothesline. The surfeit of masculine heebie-jeebies wrought by this little demonstration made national news, and lasted only days before a man broke in and destroyed the installation. I hope the artist has sense of humor enough to see that she made her point perfectly. Men rule, but in general seem to lack our fortitude.

And yet in some way or other their whole lives long, heterosexual guys are knocking themselves senseless to get our attention, and you can't help being charmed by the parade of nonsense. One of the most absurd, sexiest, most entrancing things I've ever seen took place right outside my study window. I was trying to think of a metaphor or something, staring out there into the mesquite woods, when suddenly my eyes snapped to focus on some movement: two rattlesnakes rising up together, face to face, as if they were being noodled up out of two snake charmers' baskets. Moving slowly with muscular, sinuous strength, they levitated nearly the entire front halves of their bodies, twisted themselves together, tussled a little, and finally slammed to the ground. It resembled arm wrestling. I ran to get everyone else in the house, and we all watched this thing go on for nearly an hour, the two snakes rearing up again and again, silently entwining and then throwing themselves to the ground. We called our friend Cecil, the Arizona reptile expert, who informed us that arm wrestling wasn't such a bad analogy: These were two male snakes doing a dance of combat to win the favor of a female that was surely watching from somewhere nearby. We scanned the brush carefully from behind my window—these snakes were not even thirty feet away—and there she was, sure enough, stretched out languidly under a bush.

Then all at once, after innumerable tussles, according to some scoring system invisible to human eyes but unmistakable to the contestants, one guy won. The other slunk quickly away, and Sheba came sliding out into the open, with no eyelashes to bat but with love clearly on her mind, for off she slithered with her he-snake into the sunset. The greatest show on Earth.

When you, my dear, were about two and a half, I carefully and honestly answered all the questions you'd started asking about reproductive organs. For several months thereafter, every time we met someone new, the unsuspecting adult would tousle your adorable blond head, and you'd look up earnestly and ask, "Do you have a penis or a vagina?"

If you are *ever* tempted to think my presence is an embarrassment to you, please recall that I stood by you during the "penis or vagina" months, July to September 1989. I wasn't sure I'd live through them or have any social life left afterward. I gave you a crash course in what we call "polite company" and harbored some doubts about whether honesty had really been the best policy.

What I see now, though, is that honesty *was*. Manners arrive in time; most girls are gifted enough at social savvy to learn the degree of polite evasion that will protect their safety and other people's dignity. But before anything else, you've got to be able to get the facts. Penis or vagina? I couldn't possibly tell you it wasn't to be discussed, or didn't matter. It matters, boy howdy, does it ever. Barbie or Ken, Adam or Eve, pilot or stewardess, knuckle sandwich or mea culpa, scissors, paper, rock, War and Peace. It's a very reasonable starting point. So begins the longest, scariest, sexiest, funniest, smartest, most extraordinary conversation we know. Cross your fingers, ready, set. Go.

ACT

Action is the antidote to despair.

—*Joan Baez*

The Maternal Is Sustainable

by Rebecca Walker

WHEN I WAS PREGNANT, I was constantly bewildered by the volume and velocity of the questions elicited by my impending motherhood.

Should I plan for the epidural that supported the man-as-God medical paradigm, or restore the power of birth to the feminine by laboring without drugs at home? Should I eat a steak from a cow that had been raised on steroids and brutally slaughtered by exploited immigrants, or down two jars of molasses for the same amount of iron?

What about vaccinations? Was I willing to roll the dice on my kid's potentially developing autism?

Scanning the Internet for answers to my ever-evolving concerns about pregnancy, I wondered about women without computers or Internet access. *Is there an outreach project that provides reliable answers to pregnant women without computers?* I wondered. And then: *Why am I talking to anonymous others through a machine, rather than gleaning wisdom from real live human beings?*

I bought organic eggs, free-range chicken, and a basket of blueberries, then muttered as I walked back to my car. *Who can afford to be pregnant in America?* And: *Where is the article in Fit Pregnancy Magazine called "Social Engineering 21st Century Style: Procreation Only For the Rich?"*

My partner, later the same night, added: Is organic food really the beginning and end of a child's health? Are the millions of children who don't have organic food inherently deficient and destined for failure?

Housing was another trip to Questionville. When I broke up with the person I was with before I met the father of my son, I lost a fortune on a house we bought together. I was now living in a small apartment on the sixth floor of an old building with a sporadically operational elevator and paper-thin walls. It did have a lovely view of a lake and the perfect retro-chic gas stove, but the whole time I was pregnant I dreamt I was going to have to use the bathtub as a crib.

I was working with a pitch-perfect Berkeley real estate agent at the time, a woman who drove me around in her white Volvo wagon to look at what she called "substandard housing" that started at $500K. After looking at houses I wouldn't want my worst enemy to live in, I would throw open the door of what I then understood to be Shangri-La, and let myself drop backward onto the bed. "Do I have to move to the Netherlands to live in a decent house in a decent school district?" I asked the ceiling. "Am I going to have to sell a kidney?"

I wasn't living in rural poverty in India. I wasn't living in an urban battleground in East Saint Louis. I wasn't living "on the Res." I wasn't alone. I hadn't been sexually abused. I wasn't dealing with right-wing zealots trying to deny me the right to start a family with another woman. And yet the string of political realities disguised as simple, unrelated questions was never-ending.

And I hadn't even given birth yet.

Is there one single aspect of motherhood that isn't political? From conception to graduation, from your kid's first apartment until you die, it's basically one political decision after another.

Do you choose a mate from the culturally, economically, and aesthetically acceptable gene pool, or do you make a decision that makes possible outcasts of you and your baby? Can you afford the secondary schools that prepare your kid for a top college, or do you secede from the great triumvirate of Montessori, college prep, and Ivy League?

Do you write the letter keeping your son or daughter's name off the military recruitment lists, do you schedule meetings with the principal to discuss whether teaching gender is a stated part of the school curriculum? Do you invest limited hours in working to keep food on the table, or in spending time with your kid to keep the sexual predators, drug dealers, and gangs at bay?

Did you even want your baby?

My son is three years old now, and I wish I could say the questions are less charged, but that would be a lie. My coping mechanism is a bit more honed. I get that I can't bring home the bacon, fry it up in a pan, and put an end to greed, tyranny, and sexual exploitation before I put the baby to bed. But that doesn't mean that the politics of being a mama aren't the running subtext to all my days.

Yesterday morning, I realized I couldn't tell a client my kid was sick without it being held against me. Last week, my partner stopped me midmorning to ask if I had any idea how difficult it is for him to sublimate traditional ideas of masculinity in order to be a fully present father and partner.

And then, day before yesterday, my son was outside playing in the grass. We are living in Hawaii this year (partly because we're concerned about the political climate on the mainland) in a quasi-suburban development with perfectly manicured lawns and peekaboo views of the ocean. Really, I can't complain, but as I watched my son roll around on the bright green grass, it occurred to me that in the six months we've been here, I've never seen so much as a weed or inappropriate insect anywhere.

With horror, I looked around at all the other lawns and thought, *Huh!* Our grass looks just like our neighbor's grass, and their neighbor's grass and their neighbor's grass. Could this be the rollout turf environmentalists refer to as genetically altered, chemically treated, and pesticide-laden? Do I live on a lawn that pollutes every aspect of my environment, from my son's neurological system to the community's access to nontoxic drinking water?

Huh. Wow. What do you know?

Until I could deem my assessment inaccurate, I made my son come inside and get in the bathtub—the one filled with heavily chlorinated water I have to pay for by the gallon.

When he was dry, I had him sit at his sustainably harvested bamboo table as I sprayed fruit and vegetable wash over pears and tomatoes. I washed my hands with Ecover dishwashing soap and looked out again at the grass, asking myself yet another question: *What if even my efforts to "go green" make no difference whatsoever in my son's life and health?*

My friend Coco, who supports my crusade to eliminate all things inorganic from my house but mocks me, too, says that green is the hottest product on the market. It's even more insidious because no one can argue against saving the host planet. "You've got to admit," she says, flashing her *AdBusters* credentials, "a lot of people are making shitloads of money on all of these Priuses and bottles of Kombucha. Ethanol is the biggest boon for corn farmers in a hundred years."

"This is the beginning of a global transformation that will impact human systems at every level," I say. "Al Gore just won the Nobel Prize, for Chrissakes!"

But Coco just rolls her eyes at how hopelessly bourgeois-bohemian I sound. She buys lavender soap at Whole Foods, too, but when she walks out of the store she calls me on her cell.

"Whole Foods is a cult," she says. Or, "What have they done to all of the *real* health-food stores—remember those, the ones that were cheaper than the chain supermarkets?" Or, simply, "Whole Foods broke my heart."

That day, after I brought my son in from playing in the grass, I looked down at him, surrounded by all the cancer-fighting, eco-sensitive objects I've bought for him, and I sighed.

Even as I shook my head in momentary defeat, I bent down to wipe my son's table with a paper towel: a miracle, a wondrous moment of modernity!

At that moment, a ten-year-old I know and love happened to be standing in the kitchen with me, and asked a simple question.

"Paper towels are bad for the environment," he said. "Why don't you use an old T-shirt to clean the table?"

It was as if the sky opened up and God herself appeared, or at least Buddha. I shouted (a little too loudly, I realize in retrospect), "Exactly right, you smart fabulous boy! Where did you learn that? Have I taught you how to compost?"

He, of course, being ten, looked at me as if a giant organic cabbage had sprouted from the side of my head, but I didn't care. Because I suddenly got that the kids of today—my son included—will someday look at Styrofoam and 409 as the crazy, suicidal petroleum products that they are.

What's really going on, I plan to tell Coco the next time I see her, is that I'm slowly, consciously giving my son the smell, taste, and feel of unadulterated food and honest, sustainable materials, and this is the way it happens: One day he will grow up and tell me that I should use old T-shirts to clean the counter.

And even if the so-called developing world is producing more toxins and pollutants every day, I'm going to tell her—and the West's backing off may not matter one iota—no one will be able to take away my son's intuitive gravitation to the real, planet-saving thing.

And even though there are women being sold into sexual slavery, and most women in America can't afford to have children because of the state of our health and education systems, I still value this shift

I'm making with my kid, because in a world where enduring values are hard to come by, this love for a poison-free world at least has a chance.

It isn't the answer to everything, but it is *an* answer. And for the moment, I can live with that.

Politics of the Heart

by Jennifer Graf Groneberg

MY FOUR-YEAR-OLD SON Avery sits at the wooden dining table, tracing letters in an alphabet book. He can count to five, he can say the alphabet up to G, and he knows the signs for more than fifty words. I watch him as he works—he has hair the color of ripe wheat and blue eyes, like his brothers, and he holds his colored pencil with careful seriousness. The scene playing out before me, ordinary in so many ways, is a small miracle, something that for a while I was too scared to hope for. Avery is my middle child, a fraternal twin, and at five days old, he was diagnosed with Down syndrome.

The fact of Avery studying his letters, of his articulation of numbers and words, of his success in learning sign language, these things are happy and joyful, and even a bit surprising to me, but what really causes me to catch my breath is that this small moment at our dining room table, this triumph born of a mother's intuition about how best to teach her child, almost didn't happen.

Avery has an eight-year-old brother, Carter, and a twin, younger by two minutes, Bennett. On Carter's first day of kindergarten, he did not get on the school bus with the other children. Instead, we set up a wall of books and school supplies next to the dining room table and became a homeschooling family. It fits us like a well-worn shoe.

Then, in early 2005, SB291, a bill introduced by Senator Don Ryan (D—Great Falls) made its way to the Education Committee floor. The bill was the biggest single attack on a parent's right to home educate in recent Montana history, calling for restrictions on all homeschooling families. Hidden within the pages of legal language was a single sentence that applied directly to me: If passed, the bill would forbid me from teaching Avery with his brothers, simply because Avery has Down syndrome. The bill's hearing date was set for February 14, Valentine's Day.

I'm not a political person by nature. I'm a peacemaker, a smoother-over, a find-the-middle-ground kind of woman. But reading the language of SB291, particularly section 8, part 3, which stated that any child with developmental delays must be educated in a classroom, caused something within me to shift. I recalled the Constitution, which until now seemed like nothing more than a dusty old document I'd read in a history book, and its guarantees in the preamble to "secure the Blessings of Liberty to ourselves and our Posterity." The words came alive for me: I was a citizen; I had rights—and if I didn't exercise them, my sons would pay for my apathy.

The twins were still tiny babies then. I found myself writing emails to each of the members of the Education Committee in the still of the night, while my children were sleeping. I helped other homeschoolers do the same, organizing our efforts through email chains conducted early in the morning, before Carter's little feet pattered down the hall. I made phone calls during naptime—in between loads of laundry, or while emptying the dishwasher—politely urging a "no" vote on SB291.

And one evening, after tucking each baby into his crib, after turning the knob on the music box that plays "Lullaby" and shines circus figures on the ceiling, after whispering three "I love yous" and gently pulling the door shut, I left my husband, Tom, in charge and drove through the dark night to the library. There I prepared a written statement, photocopied it twelve times, as required, and dropped it off to a family who planned to hand-deliver it at the hearing.

Valentine's Day arrived, cold and snowy in the heart of winter. I woke early with the babies and fed them in the early morning light, the three of us rocking together in the big green chair in their room while Carter slept. We couldn't risk the six-hour drive over the mountain pass in bad weather, so I waited, and rocked, and watched the light shift and change from dawn to day.

The homeschool community in Montana is a far-flung, eclectic mix of Amish, Mennonites, Christians, Constitutional Reformists, Unschoolers, and liberal Democrats with one thing in common—a desire to educate our children at home. Like me, others felt compelled to activism over the language of SB291. They'd scrambled to arrange speakers, and to spread the word to families across the state so that they could be informed and ready. And while I couldn't be there in person, I felt as if I were there in spirit, the twelve copies of my statement there to speak for me and my family.

Carter woke just as email updates from the Montana Committee of Home Education (MCHE) started coming to those of us who couldn't make the trip. Hundreds of people had attended the prehearing planning meeting at a local church, an email told us. As the space filled with supporters, extra rooms had to be opened to accommodate the turnout.

At my house, the snow continued to fall. From the big picture window in front of the dining room table, I watched the flakes drift to the ground. Avery played on a quilt below the window. Bennett slept in the Pack 'n Play. Carter sat across from me, eating a breakfast of wheat toast with peanut butter and orange juice.

When Carter finished eating, I cleared away the breakfast things, and he began work in his reading primer, tracing the letter C with a crayon called Azure. Carter's lips pressed together in concentration; his forehead wrinkled. Then he smiled, proud of his accomplishment. I looked from Carter to Avery, who'd fallen asleep on the quilt beneath the window. Avery's diagnosis was still fresh. There was so much that I didn't know about Down syndrome—I wasn't sure if Avery would ever read. But I wanted the chance to find out—I wanted to do what I felt was best for my son; I wanted the chance to try.

At noon, another email update from MCHE arrived, explaining that the crowd had moved to the Capitol. I fed Carter a grilled cheese sandwich, and I fed the babies pears and green beans and bits of Ritz crackers in their high chairs, thinking about how flimsy my position felt—I was fighting for the right to educate my son, but I had nothing to go on but a mother's intuition, a mother's love. I had no experience teaching children with learning disabilities. I'd taken education classes in college, and I'd recently completed an Early Childhood Development class with the thought of getting my teaching certificate, but special needs was a new world to me.

And yet. Who would try more, who would push hardest, who cared the most? So much rested on this hearing, and it felt so fragile, as vulnerable as the bodies of the two little babies I worked daily to nurture and grow.

At the Capitol, I learned, more than 1,100 people had gathered. Capitol security informed the crowd that the passageways needed to remain clear. The staff set up TVs in multiple locations for the overflow. These stations became packed, too, and there was standing room only on all floors.

At 3:15 PM, the hearing on SB291 was called to order. Senator Ryan introduced the bill, and its five proponents made their arguments: Homeschoolers should be subject to the same forms of testing and requirements as public schools.

Then it was time for the parents to speak. A mother from a small community south of Great Falls, Senator Ryan's constituency, took the podium. Prior to the hearing, Senator Ryan had often quoted the story of a young woman in his district who had tried to enter nursing school after being homeschooled, but couldn't because her academic skills were below those of other students her age.

The woman at the podium was the mother of this girl. She explained to the committee that her daughter had been born with cerebral palsy and was also deaf. The mother had been told that it was unlikely that her daughter would ever be able to read, so she decided to homeschool her daughter, whose dream was to become a nurse. Despite problems in the beginning, the young woman had eventually become a second-year nursing student.

My eyes filled with tears. This mother was telling my story, I hoped—a story of love and hard work and triumph, one that takes a leap of faith to believe. She concluded her testimony by thanking the committee for allowing her to speak and set the record straight about her daughter, of whom she was very proud.

I put the babies down for their naps; I let Carter take out a stack of clean, white paper and a handful of markers. Parent after parent took the podium until time expired, and those with typed testimonies were asked to come forward and deliver them to the secretary. One of those testimonies was mine: a simple statement about my life, in which I pleaded for the chance to continue teaching my children at home. It was the first time I put my hopes and dreams for Avery in writing: He would learn to read, and I would be the one to show him how.

The committee immediately called for a vote. The result—a ten-to-one decision to table SB291—was unprecedented: Never before in the Montana Senate had a bill been killed without a period of deliberation. The halls of the Capitol erupted in cheers.

At home, I took in the news quietly, uncapping the brown marker, the blue, the green, the yellow. Carter began drawing a brown box, a blue triangle on top—a house. Next, a yellow circle, sunshine in the sky. A big stick person, then another. A medium-size stick person. And finally, two tiny ones. He smiled proudly and I marveled at it: our family, whole.

Campaign Confidential

by Ann Douglas

It's Nomination Day and I'm holed up in the campaign war room, doing battle with the telephone system. The phone refuses to speak the language of laptops until it dawns on me: *This is a "dial 9" kind of motel room.*

Problem solved, I head to the bathroom while my laptop and the hotel phone make a connection. My sudden movement causes a wall-size campaign tracking sheet to tumble to the floor. The tape that has held it in place all day has nothing left to give.

The bathroom is definitely this motel room's best feature, although it's admittedly lean and mean when it comes to amenities. The proprietors toss in a tiny square of white hand soap, but you're on your own when it comes to shampoo. Still, the intricate black-diamond pattern in the glossy salmon-colored tiles harkens back to a time when even a "no-tell motel" had a sense of style—the golden age of the value-priced strip motel.

I pour myself a glass of warm juice—anything but coffee tastes great at this point—and wonder what the brand new national party leader would think if he knew the nomination campaign for this riding was being mounted from a pay-by-the-hour motel. I can't say for sure, but the "Girls! Girls! Girls!" poster hanging outside the strip club in the back parking lot, while highly effective, might not contain the precise messages the leader has been trying to convey to prospective female candidates nationwide, let alone in this political jurisdiction. Throughout the day, a steady stream of party members turned into the parking lot, heeding the frantic calls from campaign shepherds urging them to head down to the banquet hall to vote. The shepherds worked the phones from motel rooms turned war rooms, occasionally spilling out into the parking lot to flip open a cell phone and get away from the noise and the crowd.

I hadn't intended to become involved with anyone's political nomination campaign. I hadn't intended to become political at all.

But early in the fall of 2006, the nine-month-old Conservative government in Canada (a government that can best be described as "Bush lite") began slashing funding to, and redefining the mandate of, the federal department in charge of women's issues. The rationale? Women were already equal (or "equal enough," as some people were putting it). I followed the dialogue online at grassroots websites that sprang up to challenge the cuts. I looked at my eighteen-year-old daughter and thought how very unequal her generation of young women remained, and said to myself, *I don't think so*. Then I discovered that my local Member of Parliament had refused to carry forward a petition to the House of Commons, signed by local constituents, protesting these very changes. I took note, using an angry red pen.

Meanwhile, on the other side of the border, Al Gore was spreading the very inconvenient truth about the environmental action that would be necessary to prevent catastrophic climactic repercussions, action very different from the ridiculous environmental plan that the Conservative government had recently tabled in Ottawa: a plan that wouldn't see any meaningful changes implemented until my daughter was sixty-two. And then I did some enviro-sleuthing and discovered that my local Member of Parliament had been a member of the governmental committee involved in drafting this plan of nonaction. I took note, using my favorite green pen.

Around this same time, the same-sex-marriage debate hit the floor of the Canadian House of Commons. The tone of the debate was heated and ugly. "Ultimately, faith influences how this House makes law," one Member of Parliament declared. "The separation of church and state was set up to protect the church from the state, not the state from the church." That Member of Parliament was my Member of Parliament. I took note—in my blog—and officially joined the ranks of the politically charged, the politically freaked out, the politically obsessed.

Turns out I was in good company. Increasing numbers of Canadians were becoming politically engaged and politically enraged. All you had to do was read the newspaper in the morning, listen to the radio on the way home from work, or tune in to the late-evening news, and you couldn't help but turn to a like-minded friend and ask, "What the hell is happening to our country?"

I knew I had to try to do something to get Canada back on track, because Canada didn't feel like Canada anymore. I became involved with the nomination campaign for a woman in my riding who was seeking the opportunity to go head-to-head with my local Member of Parliament in the next election. She had two things going for her: She had outstanding credentials in her own right, and she was running for the nomination for the federal political party that had just elected an outstanding new leader—a leader who had recently brought me to tears with his vision for what Canada could be again.

Becoming involved with the campaign seemed like the perfect way to turn my political anxiety into political energy: I'd work with a team of other highly enthusiastic volunteers to help make the case for a candidate who had so much to offer.

Then we'd simply let word of mouth take over from there.

I figured it was a total no-brainer.

The more idealistic you are about anything—love, motherhood, politics, you name it—the greater the opportunity for disillusionment.

The early days of the campaign were heady, intoxicating. I felt like some sort of born-again politico—except there was no "again" about it; this was my first time showing any sort of interest in politics at all.

The political birth was great. It was the postpartum that really sucked. My candidate clearly had a lot to offer—so much so that she ended up being the target of a nasty smear campaign. It didn't matter that many of these rumors were ridiculous (she and another fiftysomething female candidate were written off as "too old," while a male opponent just a few years their junior was being pitched as "the youth candidate") or untrue (she was unfairly and inaccurately described as a "parachute candidate" who had been dropped into the riding by the party elite). These falsehoods took on a life of their own. From up close, I saw that campaigns are becoming less about the caliber of the candidate and more about survival of the fittest in the most Machiavellian sense of the word—who can weather the smear campaigns or fight back with even more vicious tactics. The three-moves-out chessboard strategizing that goes on among the political old boys makes the much-lambasted mean girls look like pussycats—declawed kitties on choker chains. On some level, the public knows this, which is why the majority of those who actually bother to vote also bother to tune in to campaign coverage in only the most superficial and cursory way. Everyone else tunes out.

I started to understand why so few women—and even fewer mothers—go into (and remain in) politics, and why so few women—and even fewer mothers—are politically aware. If your time is maxed out—if you have to pick and choose where you invest your energies, as most of us mothers do—return on investment becomes a critical factor. How many mothers with young children can invest the time required to play the political game the way those in charge of the game insist it should be played? And if you know at the outset that you can't play to win, why would you want to bother to play at all?

As the campaign continued and the tally of injustices continued to mount, I told my friends I had developed political depression: a condition that occurs when you get a peek behind the black curtain and find out how the system really works. I wanted to scream in outrage, "Why didn't anyone tell me that politics was so political?" But I realized how crazy that sounded.

One night when we were out for dinner, my husband asked me what was wrong—if it was the campaign. I had been terrible company all evening, communicating more with sighs than with words.

"It's not just the campaign. It's everything. Politics. Democracy. I feel deceived—like the person who pitched me the concept of 'anyone can run for office' democracy back when I was in high school lied. Or that they left out a lot of important details: like the fact that most people who run for office have money and connections. We don't have a democracy. We have the *illusion* of a democracy, and I want to tell everyone who will listen, so that they won't get sucked in and have their hearts broken like I did."

"I'm sorry you're so upset, but really, what did you expect? We're talking politics here, after all."

At this point I was crying, and I didn't care how many people in the restaurant were staring, mistaking our passionate discussion about democracy's future—and whether it had one—for a marital meltdown.

"Well, of course, you always hear that the system is corrupt, and politics is terribly political, but I thought that was just cynical people talking. *And now I've become one of those cynical people.* There are so many problems with the way things work. And now that I've seen what really goes on, I've lost my faith in so many people who used to be my heroes. I don't know what to do to try to fix the system, or if it can even *be* fixed, it's so messed up. And yet most people just blissfully go about their lives, trusting that democracy is working just the way it should, or not really caring at all. I don't know which is worse."

"You know what they say: 'Ignorance is bliss.'"

"Okay. In my next life, I'm choosing ignorance."

The rules that are in place on voting day are light-years away from what I witnessed on nomination day. So much for that law that says you can't have campaign signs within so many feet of the entrance to a voting location. Vehicles are tarted up with political bling; campaign posters, stickers, and banners compete for space on either side of the front doors of the voting hall. For a moment, I wonder whether I've stumbled onto the set of the political edition of *Pimp My Ride*.

Inside, the hall has been arranged in classic wedding formation, with segregated seating for friends of the bride and the groom. It's a fabulous idea except for one minor glitch: There are two banks of seats and three candidates. That leads to some forced intermingling between members of the three political "families."

Today will be the first time that the candidates have shared the same stage, and they have just two minutes to sell themselves. There will be no all-candidate debate today, just as there was no debate during the campaign—a source of continual frustration to my candidate and her supporters. She is the least known of the three candidates and likely the strongest of the three potential debaters. But the other two candidates are unwilling to play verbal volleyball.

The first candidate, the incumbent, knows what issues really matter to those in attendance—healthcare, the environment, poverty, the aging population, and education—but she isn't able to deliver her points in a moving or meaningful way. By the time she is finished speaking, it is obvious that the audience has written her off as a contender.

The next candidate—my candidate—speaks from the heart. Her passion goes over well with the audience, but she may not have enough nuts-and-bolts policy points to take her over the top. She focuses on all the things that Canada once was and could be again: a country known for social liberalism and multiculturalism; a just and peace-building society. "Today, I don't recognize my Canada," she laments.

The final candidate to speak is the heir apparent: a middle-aged golden boy whose candidacy has been endorsed by the riding's much-loved former Member of Parliament. Those hours spent hammering in lawn signs and working the phones on behalf of political old boys can really pay off. This candidate's message is simple and direct. "I grew up in this area. I can get things done for the people in this area. I understand how the system works."

The atmosphere is tense during the speeches, with members of one political family drowning out the closing remarks of an opposing candidate by launching into singsongy chants of their own candidate's name. And so respect and decorum become the first casualties of the day—frail political canaries. Having an ambulance and a team of paramedics on-site for the day no longer seems like overkill.

On their way to the polling booths, 1,500 voters pass through a wedding-style receiving line that is manned by three nervous couples: the three candidates and their three campaign managers, shaking hands in a last-ditch effort to solidify or swing the nomination vote. Then the voting begins—a process that takes the better part of four hours.

When the voting results are announced, the people in the room start acting crazy—or crazier than usual.

A few disgruntled members of the other camps storm out, cursing the "instant Liberals" who had supported the successful candidate and vowing to vote Conservative in the next election.

Members of our team are jumping, screaming, hugging one another, and swarming our candidate, who looks just as stunned by the results as we are. This is the kind of feel-good, Cinderella happy ending that has the potential to restore your faith in the political process, even when you swear there's no faith to be had.

But it ain't over yet.

One of the other candidates challenges the results.

A few days later, our candidate's victory is upheld.

Cinderella gets to keep her crown.

I finish updating the campaign blog back in the campaign war room—Room 5 in the strip of seen-better-days motel rooms. Then I grab the room key and head off to join the rest of the campaign team at the victory party in the lounge above the strip club. This was going to be my political swansong—the night I was going to announce I was leaving the campaign, that I was going to get my life back—but the emotions of the day have short-circuited my ability to think logically. I agree to stick around for Phase II: the down-and-dirty fight that is expected when my candidate goes head-to-head with the current Member of Parliament during the next federal election.

I make like Scarlett O'Hara and decide I'll think about that tomorrow. For tonight, it's all about savoring this hard-won victory—a victory made all the sweeter because this time, the backroom boys didn't have their way.

The party winds up, and I say my goodnights. There is still a smattering of vehicles decked out in all their campaign finery, but other remnants of the day's activities have disappeared, most notably the campaign signs along the boulevard that lead your eye past the front doors of the motel and convention center and toward the "Hot Girls!" sign at the far end of the property.

A couple is pressed up against an unpainted wall in an alcove outside the side entrance to the strip club. It's nice to have company—just about any kind of company—when you're crossing a dark parking lot at night. If I run into trouble in the back parking lot, they might hear me if I scream.

As I round the corner and enter the lot, I spot a young woman, roughly the same age as my daughter. She is crouched down, sitting on the curb next to the entrance to the strip club. She is dressed in a slinky blue top and an almost-not-there black skirt. Her outfit screams sexual liberation, but it's a synthetic kind of freedom.

She flicks some ashes from her cigarette. Her movements are tentative and weary, like those of a pet that has memorized the boundaries of the invisible fences marking its world.

"How are you?" I ask.

"I'm alive."

"That's good."

I keep walking, wondering if there is a better answer to that question or a better question to be asked; if I should get my vehicle and swing back this way or just drive off into the night. I feel like I should ask her if she needs something, if there's anything I can do, but I sense that would be risky. Risky for her. Risky for me. The last thing I see as I turn out onto the street is the "Hot Girls!" sign.

For months afterward, I can't get that young woman out of my head. She becomes an important player in the day's events—someone who helps me to make sense of the dark side of politics and the way that politics plays out in women's lives.

It's all about power and control: favors granted and favors owed; and being asked to play by someone else's rules. The difference between the types of deals that were made in the parking lot behind the strip club, made on the campaign trail, and everyday inequality is the credit terms: payment in advance versus payment down the road versus hey, you owe me. Party girls; party politics; what did you expect, a party? Same game.

One Hundred and Twenty-Five Miles

by Amy L. Jenkins

My daughter invited two friends to the Packers game. I knew one, a longtime friend from her old Girl Scout troop. The other was a nice-looking guy, about twenty-three, who said his father was a pastor.

While we drove from Milwaukee to Green Bay, we started talking sports. Taking a dominant role in the conversation, my daughter's guy friend said he was liberal in his views, but he didn't agree with women playing sports with men. He thought they should have their own teams. "It's not just that the men are stronger," he said. "It's that it would be humiliating for a man to be beaten by a woman in front of other people."

He went on to remind us—the women in the car—that "man is the head of the household." He quoted Second Peter, the part where Peter tells wives to submit themselves to their husbands. My daughter's guest reminded us that *we cannot dispute the word of God.* He told us that in his father's church, the men are supposed to discuss matters with their wives and then consider their input before making a final decision. "So," he said, "women do have power, even if they can't hold any positions of authority or vote on church matters." In his world, God intended that a woman be kept in the background, where she could quietly and obediently respect her husband's power and his position as her true spiritual leader. "This is God's way," he said.

He pointed out that his own views were liberal compared with his father's, because the son would let his wife work. He spoke in a

lyrical manner, telling us with his singsong voice that he was conveying God's true message for eternal happiness. If women made peace
with their role, he told us, they could be protected and cared for by
the men in their lives.

Now, this was my daughter's friend, a guest in our van as we
drove the 125 miles to Green Bay for the game. I didn't want to
cause a fuss. I didn't think I should tell him that, no matter how
he tried to sugarcoat oppression, everything he said was a twisted,
ugly distortion. I thought my daughter would be uncomfortable if I
brought up the fact that 70 percent of the children born in the city of
Milwaukee are born to unwed mothers. And that 65 percent of those
single mothers are working for poverty wages.

I didn't think I should tell him that being raised to believe a
man will take care of her leaves a woman unprepared to face the
abandonment that is all too common; that even though women share
the responsibility, almost half of all children live in homes without
a father.

I didn't think I should tell him that I, too, am a Christian and
believe, as Christ taught, that scripture is read through faith. Since he
took the Bible literally, I wondered whether he believed that all cir-
cumcised men in prison grew back their foreskin because, in Romans
2:25, Paul says, "If you are a breaker of the law, your circumcision
has become uncircumcision."

I wondered whether the girls would be uncomfortable if I ham-
mered on about the fact that the book of Second Peter also instructs
slaves to be submissive to their masters. Would it be impolite to ask
him if his church kept their slaves chained to the wall in the basement
of the rectory, or whether the people he owned were happy to remain
in servitude without physical restraint? Would it be too personal of
me, I wondered, to tell him that because we lived in a society built
on his premise, when my daughters' father left, we lived in poverty

because the traditional female jobs available offered low pay and no benefits?

I didn't think it would be polite to tell our guest, a preacher's son, that the Christ that I know is filled with love, not law, and that First John says that *everyone* who loves is born of God and knows God. Now that educated women have begun translating scripture, it has come to light that the story of Eve being taken from Adam's rib could be translated to reveal that Eve was created from a side, a half. Man and woman evolved equally, from the same source.

I especially didn't think it would go over well if I told him that to feel shame in being beaten by a woman is an intense form of bigotry and self-idealization, that he will be beaten by many women in his life, and that if I weren't a Christian woman who was trying to understand and love him, I'd have pulled the van over right then and beaten the crap out of him.

I didn't think I should tell him all these things. But I had two young women in the van, and it is 125 miles to Green Bay.

So I did.

He was polite, seemed to listen. I told him there were many others who believed as I did, and that men and women working together were more likely to fulfill the commission of God and serve the world than were men working alone while subverting the talents of women.

He said he would think about it but not mention this conversation to his dad. His dad would never have listened.

I wonder whether the young man did consider my words.

I wonder how he will treat his wife and raise his children.

I wonder how far we went in 125 miles.

The Mean Moms

by Helaine Olen

WHEN MY OLDER SON, Jake, was an infant, I joined a local mother-baby group. I hoped to make some friends who had children.

Lord knows, I needed the help. After Jake was born, I didn't gain automatic admission to the sorority of fellow moms I always imagined existed. Instead, I found myself wheeling my newborn in a stroller up and down the semideserted streets near my Los Angeles home for what seemed like hours every day. Conversation with other moms I met at the park or in my wanderings felt forced. Many ignored my friendly overtures entirely, seemingly wrapped up in their own work or cliques. After a few months, I was so desperate that I was willing to pay an organization several hundred dollars in the hope that maybe, just maybe, I would make a mommy friend.

As we new mothers sat in a circle at the first meeting, introducing ourselves to one another, our children played in front of us. I watched idly as Jake slowly inched his body toward a nearby rattle. Just as he was getting within striking distance, the mom sitting next to me reached out, grabbed the toy and placed it in front of her own son.

Jake wailed.

I waited till the woman's attention was turned elsewhere and snatched the rattle back.

The Toy Incident was a harbinger of things to come. As the weeks passed in the new-mothers' group, alliances formed and collapsed with a ruthless rapidity that would have put the contestants on

Survivor to shame. Women who had the misfortune to miss one of our Friday morning sessions could count on being discussed in unflattering terms behind their backs. "Overgrown hippie," they whispered about one mother with a proclivity for granny dresses. Another was deemed "pathological" for deciding to attend medical school while her daughter was an infant. A third was subjected to ridicule for feeding an underweight child hot dogs ("Not even organic!") in an effort to fatten him up. Women who revealed any unhappiness or vulnerability immediately became the subject of rumors claiming that they were suffering from postpartum depression.

And then, suddenly, I was on the outs.

A private group within the group formed, ostensibly for infant music lessons. Jake and I were not invited to join. I was hurt and baffled. Then one afternoon, at one of the group's semiregular lunches, the mother who had taken Jake's toy at the first meeting—and who was also a main organizer of the private music group—sat and stared at me angrily, refusing to say a word. It became increasingly uncomfortable, and I tried to remember what I possibly could have done to fall afoul of her.

As the waitress cleaned the plates, Toy Mom spoke.

"My husband says you're beautiful."

Now, we had all met each other's spouses exactly once, at a group picnic. Toy Mom's husband, I had heard, had announced his opinions of other women in the group at the time, saying, for example, that Medical School Mom was "brilliant," and referring to another group member as "outgoing." Now he thought a lonely, sleep-deprived, and slightly overweight mom was good looking? In my embarrassment, I turned red. I might have said something like "Oh." This, for the record, was the wrong response. Toy Mom never spoke another word to me again, nor did her chosen best pals.

I wish I could report I rose above the common behavior. Instead, I learned to be as cruel as the others in my group, moving in for the kill with an effectiveness straight out of my teenage past. When a mother who drove a Lexus and carried a Louis Vuitton purse flipped out at group one day, crying about how she was the only person present who could not afford even a half day of babysitter help, I—a former personal-finance writer—did not gently point out to her that we all make choices about how we spend our money. Nor did I recall that, like me, she lived across the country from the rest of her family and had talked in group about how much she missed them. Instead, I remembered that she was a close friend of Toy Mom and had played no small role in my shunning.

I gleefully turned to the phones, calling the few moms in the group with whom I enjoyed friendly relations.

"She can't pay her babysitter bill!" I gasped with faux shock. "If she took the bag to a consignment shop, she could pay for a week of full-time help." And then the coup de grâce: "Do you think she's suffering from postpartum depression?"

Lexus Mom was never seen in group again.

So began my introduction to the world of contemporary motherhood. It would take me years to understand that my group's dynamics were not unusual. The mothering world I would continue to encounter combined the worst of the 1950s and the modern age. It was as harsh and judgmental as anything Betty Friedan condemned, yet it didn't offer that earlier world's compensations. I never received the practical support that my mother—along with most women of her generation—took for granted: effortless socialization with neighbors, easy access to other children, nearby friends who came over and pitched in when things went wrong.

Instead, I found the mean moms.

I could fill page after page recounting the mother-against-mother nastiness I have experienced or witnessed since becoming a parent. There are the Selective Inviters: women who plan birthday parties and Moms' Nights Out that seem designed to cause the maximum amount of dissension. There are the mothers who spread false rumors about other mothers; the women who comment on one's breastfeeding or stroller choices; and the PTA moms who hoard information about class assignments or school administration goings-on, to the detriment of all the children.

And, of course, there is the famous stay-at-home versus working mother battle. I wish I could agree with the commentators who say the mommy wars are a figment of the media's imagination, dreamed up by producers desperate to goose their ratings. Like most women, I've been in and out of the workforce since having my children, and I've experienced the anger from both sides. I'm not arguing that it is from all—or even a majority of—mothers. But it definitely has been enough to make an impact.

The most memorable encounter came at the hands of the mother of one of Jake's friends. One year at summer camp, Jake became friendly with a girl, Ava, whose mom worked near the facility and would often break from her job to pick her up. I wasn't working at the time, and I was in awe of Ava's mother, who was always perfectly made up and turned out, dressing in outfits that would not have looked out of place on Julianne Moore in *Far from Heaven*. I, needless to say, was regularly dressed in battered shorts, dirt-stained after spending the day with my younger son, a rambunctious toddler.

One afternoon, when we were waiting for the counselors to let the children go, I summoned up my courage and suggested we get Jake and Ava together for a playdate.

"Oh, I'd love to," said Ava's mom with a bright smile.

Then she laughed—a high, tinny sound.

"Oh, wait, I forgot. I work."

She turned away and began to speak with another mom, one wearing a suit. At the time, I wanted to cry. This mom hadn't said that she simply didn't have time for playdates during the week—that, I would be able to understand. But her response seemed intended to cause hurt. Why else emphasize our different statuses, vis-à-vis work and motherhood, in such a pointed way?

For years, I thought it was just me. I'd never done well in cliques before, and motherhood, it appeared, was one vast network of former teenage girls. In my high school days, I wore the wrong jeans; these days I was more likely to fall afoul of the parenting police by feeding my sons formula in public, but the resulting shame and isolation were the same.

I can't say I ever had an "aha" moment, a split second in which I realized my motherhood problem was much greater than just a few moms who were convinced that the playground is a version of high school. It was, rather, an accumulation of stories, hearing the same ones over and over again: mothers "fired" from infant playgroups, playground chitchat of such incredible viciousness, I can recall the tales years later. (My personal favorite: a mother accused of hiring a wet nurse to feed her infant daughter. It sounds ridiculous, but sophisticated urbanites repeated it as though it were gospel.)

I remember early in my motherhood career talking to my own mother about her first years as a parent. "I was friends with everyone who lived in our building who had children," she recalled. "The way you live now—this is craziness."

I tried to explain. I talked about how working mothers didn't seem to want to give the time of day to their nonworking counterparts, and vice versa. I talked about how hard it was to have playdates with someone if you were, say, organic, and the other mom thought anything goes when it comes to food. My mom cut me off.

"You need common interests? We all had babies. That's common interest."

That, I've since realized, is exactly the problem. Despite all the talk, despite all the lip service of unity and sisterhood, we moms don't believe we have anything in common.

We're wrong.

The fact remains that the decision to become a mother almost always moves women several rungs down on both the economic and social ladders. At work, our salaries fail to keep pace with those of men and our childless peers. At home, we often pick up the second shift. But our reaction, for the most part, is not to protest our new second-class status. Instead, we internalize our oppression and see our fellow mothers, not to mention any other women we perceive as being somehow more successful than we are (Hillary Clinton, I'm looking at you) as the enemy. We take a problem that is political in nature and make it a personal one. In our desperation to get a leg up, we moms bring one another down. Letty Cottin Pogrebin could have been describing my original mother's group—and the mothering world I would continue to encounter—when she wrote on the topic of women and competitiveness in the inaugural issue of *Ms.* magazine, "If you feel depressed, don't examine your discontent—find a woman who's worse off than you."

The solution is within all of us. It *is* possible to tolerate each other's differences and revel in the fact that more than one type of parenting can lead to good results. It *is* possible to refrain from engaging in petty behavior, even when provoked, and to keep from bickering with one another over problems that cry out for societal solutions—like the need for and appropriateness of daycare and flexible work schedules. When mothers fight, we don't unify. We continue on, isolated, friendless, and alone. Our children are the ultimate losers.

We can change. We can start with something as simple as small gestures of support for fellow moms. It can be done. I know. I was recently the recipient of such largesse. I found myself working almost full-time over a holiday break to meet a deadline. I was feeling fairly guilty and panicked about it, and mentioned the situation to one or two parents in Jake's class.

Over the next several days, I began to field calls from several of my fellow moms that went something like this:

"We're taking a day trip to the aquarium/natural history museum/other fun activity. Would Jake like to come with us? I hear you are writing a book. . . . "

After the third such call, I began to cry. I couldn't believe I—and my child—were the recipients of such generosity. It was no organized effort. Rather, several of my fellow moms had heard I needed help and reached out. Alone, they could offer me only a few hours of respite here and there. Together, they had solved my childcare problem.

Jake, I'm happy to report, had a terrific week, and so did I—and it was courtesy of my fellow moms. You know, the nice moms.

One Day

by Benazir Bhutto

JUNE 17, 1997

WHEN I GRADUATED FROM university in the '70s, I was thrilled. My education was over. A life of exams, grades, waiting for results was part of the past.

I was wrong.

Life is one big exam.

And whether it is an election, a speech, a court decision, or a domestic matter, I am always wondering whether I am going to pass or fail, whether I am going to make the grade or not.

Some days are good. Some days are not. As Lady Thatcher once said to me, "In politics, always expect the unexpected." I would only add, *In life, always expect the unexpected.*

As leader of the opposition in the National Assembly of Pakistan, I have to open the debate on the budget proposal tomorrow.

I get up today and head straight for the big bundle of budget documents, which the finance minister has placed on the floor of the National Assembly. I finish the first reading of the budget documents by lunchtime. I find that the Intelligence Bureau of Pakistan spent one-third over its allocation.

Was this huge expenditure to rig the general elections held this February, to fund my opponents, to bribe witnesses into giving false statements, or to bribe journalists into writing negative stories? These questions whirl in my mind.

Last November, my government was dismissed by presidential decree on the eve of our signing an agreement with the International Monetary Fund.

A witchhunt was launched. It still continues. That night of November 4, 1996, my husband was kidnapped by security agents. He was produced forty-eight hours later after we raised a hue and cry. For eight months, he has languished in a prison cell in solitary confinement, with temperatures soaring to forty-eight degrees Celsius. He has not been indicted in a single case so far, despite the government's tall claims that he was "The King of Corruption."

Later in the afternoon, my cousin Fakhri comes to our house along with her three grandchildren. I send them, along with my own three kids, to have pizza and chocolate cake. They shout with delight. Children are so easy to please. What happens to us when we become adults?

Mummy, Fakhri, and I have lunch. The cook has made *Karri*. It is made with yogurt and gram flour. Mummy says it is delicious, so her cook must have made it.

Mummy has just returned from a religious pilgrimage. She says she prayed really hard for me and our party workers, and things are going to get better. Let us hope so.

After lunch, we sip green tea and chat until the sound of shouts and screams heralds the return of the children. The kids now demand to see a cartoon.

I do not like my children watching cartoons. But I am feeling guilty. I have to catch a flight to Islamabad, where the Parliament is based. So I cave in.

As I come down the stairs to leave for the airport, my seven-year-old daughter, Bakhtwar, looks up. Casually waving, she says, "Bye, it was nice seeing you. Come back soon."

"What do you mean?" I say. "I am your mother. I am stuck to you like that arm of yours for life."

"But Mama, my arm keeps going away," she complains.

"But it always comes back," I reply.

"Yes, it does, it does," says my eight-year-old son, Bilawal, as he gives me a hug.

On the flight, I see my mother-in-law. We say hello. She says the regime is still bothering my father-in-law. He is in Lahore, meeting lawyers in connection with politically motivated allegations made against him.

I write my speech by hand during the two-hour plane journey from Karachi to Islamabad. I rush home and into my study to complete the speech. Once the draft is finished, I call my party leaders to vet the draft. While they are doing that, I binge on pizza and chocolate cake.

It is four in the morning by the time we finish. We leave the speech for typing, translation, and copying, and call it a day.

Trying Out

by Gayle Brandeis

AMAZING THINGS HAPPEN when I take my daughter to auditions.

Last year I brought Hannah, then twelve, to an audition for a local production of *Annie Get Your Gun*. As I sat on a bench, ready to watch the tryouts from the sidelines, the assistant director walked up to me. "As long as you're here," he said, "why don't you audition too?"

I resisted at first—I was just there to support my performer girl. While I have performed as a dancer throughout my life—jazz and ballet and figure skating as a child; from high school on, modern dance along with some belly dance, Balinese dance, and *folklórico*— I had never sung or acted in front of an audience, at least not as an adult.

Sure, when I was ten my sister and I staged *Annie* on roller skates in front of our building, and we briefly put together a traveling theater troupe that involved knocking on neighbors' doors and asking them if they wanted to see a production of *Hansel and Gretel* right in their very own living room.

But those were flukes in my life as a shy, quiet girl. I've never been comfortable with my singing voice, and I've always felt incredibly self-conscious singing around other people—even "Happy Birthday" at parties makes my heart pound. But the assistant director was persistent, and Hannah chimed in with her own encouragement, so I decided to go for it. I told myself that if I ever wrote a story that involved a character auditioning for something, at least I'd understand the experience from the inside out. Writing often gives me a good excuse to go outside my comfort zone, to be braver than I normally would allow myself to be.

I threw myself into the audition process. I danced up a storm (lots of Charleston-type boogying and some spirited square dance–style partnering). I read lines like "Ah don't shoot like a girl, ah shoot like a man!" in a hammy Western accent. I dug deep into myself to belt out "Happy Birthday" louder than I ever had in my life. And, much to my shock, I ended up with the lead role. Never in a million years would this gun-abhorring peace activist imagine she'd have a chance to swagger around as sharpshooter Annie Oakley. But life, I keep learning again and again, is full of surprises.

Hannah was cast as my sister Minnie. Not only did the show become a mother-daughter experience, it also became a sister-sister experience, putting us, for once, on a kind of equal ground. In sharp contrast with those times when I had to needle her to do her homework, we learned lines together, worked on choreography together, commiserated about frustrating rehearsals together, shared excitement and nerves about the upcoming show. Best of all, the show provided an opportunity for me to remind her how important it is to use our voices—not just our singing voices, but our voices as citizens of the world. This is something I've tried to impart to Hannah throughout her life, but the play offered up a real example of how to translate these ideals into action.

Written in 1942, *Annie Get Your Gun* is full of horrendous stereotypes of Native Americans as cartoonish, ignorant savages. A revised script for the 1999 Broadway revival did away with the most offensive references, but we were working from the original, and it made me uncomfortable. I spoke to the director about my concerns and shared my suggestions for revision; to my relief and delight, she incorporated most of them into the show. In the first line in the script, for example, a little girl freaks out about Indians coming to town; we had her holler about the "show people" descending upon the inn instead. We changed lyrics throughout the script, turning fearsome, "cut-your-throatable Indians" into "bandits" and the like. We completely took out one song, "I'm an Indian Too," which seemed beyond redemption, riddled as it was with names like Big Chief Hole-in-the-Ground and its drum-heavy tune—a cheesy, sarcastic interpretation of native music to which I just wasn't comfortable hopping around.

Looking on the whole time, as I voiced my concerns, was my daughter. I was glad that Hannah had the chance to witness this process, to see firsthand, while her idealism was still fresh, that people truly can work together to right wrongs, to stamp out injustice—and have a lot of fun in the process. At times she felt embarrassed by my activist interjections during rehearsal (at twelve years old, how could she not?), but she understood where I was coming from, and one day, as we chatted and sang in the car, she said, "I'm proud of you, Mom"—something every mother wants to hear. (Of course, I was just as proud of her.)

During those months, I found that acting was actually a lot like writing fiction—I needed to get out of my own way so I could become Annie without any of Gayle's hang-ups; I had to let my own edges disappear, let the character roar through in all her feisty glory. I needed to let go of fear, let the energy of the moment buoy me. *We're all alive for just a short time on this planet, so why not enter into this experience fully and freely?* I told myself. *Who knows if this chance will ever come around again?* If I hadn't experienced the liberation and empowerment of finding my way as Annie Oakley, it's unlikely I would have had the courage, a few months later, to further find my way as me—to stand up, dressed in hot pink, during a congresswoman's speech and ask her to not buy Bush's war.

Just like my stint as Annie Oakley, my involvement with the women's peace organization CODEPINK sprang from one of Hannah's auditions the year before. Perhaps you've seen us—women in pink holding signs of peace at congressional hearings, dropping enormous "pink slips" from the sides of buildings, or causing a ruckus at political conventions.

I had been on the CODEPINK mailing list since it was founded in 2002 and had wanted to get involved, but somehow hadn't found the right opening to do so yet. Then, in the summer of 2005, I saw that their L.A. group was going to be staging a play about election reform and they needed local actors, including young ones. I asked Hannah—an emerging activist at the time, as well as a budding thespian—if she'd like to go to the audition.

"It's near Hollywood," I said, knowing that would appeal to my daughter's dreams of acting, "and it's about inspiring change." Hannah's eyes lit up.

"Let's go," she said.

We drove down to a funky little bungalow in Venice, which turned out to be full of women of all ages wearing pink T-shirts— some with CODEPINK logos. Hannah particularly liked one young woman's pink tee, which featured a drawing of a television set, "I lie to you" written across its screen.

The director gave Hannah a script, brimming with sly references to hanging chads and Diebold and paper trails, and asked her to read. After demonstrating her passionate portrayal of the "child of the future," Hannah was offered a part on the spot.

As we sat in the airy front room, a woman with flaming red hair and a pink scarf draped gracefully around her neck burst through the door and introduced herself as Jodie Evans, one of CODEPINK's cofounders. While the play people talked their playtalk, I followed Jodie into the cozy kitchen.

"I admire your work so much," I told her. "If there is anything I can do to help in any way, please let me know." I told her that I was a writer, that I was always looking for ways to use my voice for good.

"Thanks." She smiled and retreated to her office. About half an hour later, just before Hannah and I were about to leave, Jodie burst back into the room, teary and alive with excitement. She had just gotten off the phone with a woman named Cindy Sheehan, she told us. Cindy had just sat down in a ditch in Crawford, Texas, and said she refused to leave until President Bush told her what noble cause her son had died for in Iraq. Shivers ran up and down my arms.

Jodie turned to me. "Can you write a press release about this?" she asked.

I have been writing for CODEPINK—op-eds and chants and whatever else needs to be put into words—ever since. Last year, I was invited to be part of the national staff as their "communication goddess," and I now write the weekly action alerts that go out to two hundred thousand members. Ever since I was a young girl writing letters to ask Jimmy Carter what I could do to help stop pollution (I got a lovely response from the White House—along with a bright orange, Woodsy Owl–stamped trash bag—suggesting I start by picking up litter in my own neighborhood), I have felt called to find the link between my writing and social responsibility. I know the CODEPINK alerts I write anonymously every week will not only reach more people than my fiction ever has, but will also inspire action and encourage change.

I probably would have been comfortable being a writer-activist the rest of my life, sending my words for CODEPINK out into the world from the comfort of my desk chair, if it hadn't been for my experience in the play with Hannah. But standing onstage and realizing I could send the voice I had been so scared of using out to the rafters, out to an audience, changed me.

As I sang "Anything You Can Do, I Can Do Better," I realized that anything *I* could do, I could do better—and more bravely and generously than I had before. Now I relish the chance to stand up and use my voice, my physical presence, for peace—even when my heart is pounding hard. I recently wrote new words for "There's No Business Like Show Business," turning the song into "There's No Business Like War Business," and am in the process of screwing up my nerve to walk into my congressman's office and sing it at the top of my lungs.

Hannah is thirteen now and doesn't want to be onstage anymore. She doesn't want to put herself out there. She is more concerned than she has ever been about what other people think. Sometimes she chides me for being so "social justice-y." She was just assigned to write a report on some aspect of a natural disaster for school. When I suggested she focus on relief organizations, she rolled her eyes and called me a hippie.

The activist part of her isn't completely dormant, though. After she found out that the squirrels being trapped on her campus were later drowned, she organized actions to protest, even creating some guerrilla theater by putting stuffed toy squirrels in the cages. Hopefully, as she grows through this stage, she will become ready to step into the spotlight again. I look forward to participating in future CODEPINK events with her. Maybe one day we can even go to another tryout together.

These days, I much prefer the word "tryout" to "audition." It takes the feeling of competition away and focuses on exploration, discovery, trying something out—our imaginations, our voices, our power. That's what we do as mothers, as activists, as women, as creative people—we try things out, push our own limits, expand our own boundaries, and watch the effects begin to ripple out into the world. It's astounding what we can accomplish when we simply allow ourselves to step up and try. My hope as a mother is that I can give Hannah the exact same gift she's given me through all of this: the powerful reminder that each one of us is capable of so much more than we ever let ourselves believe.

Good Riddance, Attention Whore

by Cindy Sheehan

I HAVE ENDURED a lot of smear and hatred since Casey was killed, and especially since I became the so-called face of the American anti-war movement. Especially since I renounced any remaining tie I have with the Democratic Party, I have been further trashed on such "liberal" blogs as "Democratic Underground." Being called an "attention whore" and being told "good riddance" are two of the milder rebukes.

I have come to some heartbreaking conclusions this Memorial Day morning. These are not spur-of-the-moment reflections, but things I have been meditating on for about a year now.

The first conclusion is that I was the darling of the so-called left as long as I limited my protests to George Bush and the Republican Party. Of course, I was slandered and libeled by the right as a "tool" of the Democratic Party. This label was to marginalize me and my message. How could a woman have an original thought, or be working outside of our "two-party" system?

However, when I started to hold the Democratic Party to the same standards to which I held the Republican Party, support for my cause started to erode, and the "left" started labeling me with the same slurs that the right used. I guess no one paid attention to me when I said that the issue of peace and people dying for no reason is not a matter of "right or left," but of "right and wrong."

I am deemed a radical because I believe that partisan politics should be left by the wayside when hundreds of thousands of people are dying for a war based on lies that is supported by Democrats and

Republicans alike. It amazes me that people who are sharp on the issues—and who can zero in like a laser beam on lies, misrepresentations, and political expediency when it comes to one party—refuse to recognize those things in their own party. Blind party loyalty is dangerous, whatever side it occurs on. People of the world look on us Americans as jokes because we allow our political leaders so much murderous latitude, and if we don't find alternatives to this corrupt "two-party" system, our representative republic will die and be replaced with what we are rapidly descending into with nary a check or balance: a fascist corporate wasteland. I am demonized because I don't see party affiliation or nationality when I look at a person; I see that person's heart. If people who call themselves Democrats look, dress, act, talk, and vote like Republicans, then why do they deserve my support?

I have also reached the conclusion that if I am doing what I am doing because I am an "attention whore," then I really need to be committed. I have invested everything I have into trying to bring peace with justice to a country that wants neither. I have spent every available cent I got from the money a "grateful" country gave me when they killed my son, and I have spent every penny I received in speaking or book fees since then. I have sacrificed a twenty-nine-year marriage and have traveled for extended periods of time away from Casey's brother and sisters. My health has suffered, and my hospital bills from last summer (when I almost died) are in collection, because I have used all my energy trying to stop this country from slaughtering innocent human beings. I have been called every despicable name that small minds can think of, and have had my life threatened many times.

The most devastating conclusion that I reached this morning, however, was that Casey did indeed die for nothing. His precious lifeblood drained out in a country far away from his family who loves him. He was killed by his own country, which is beholden to and run by a war machine that even controls what we think. I have tried ever since he died to make his sacrifice meaningful. Casey died for a country that cares more about who will be the next American Idol than about how many people will be killed in the next few months while Democrats and Republicans play politics with human lives. It is so painful to me to know that I bought into this system for so many years, and that Casey paid the price for that allegiance. I failed my boy, and that hurts the most.

I have also tried to work within a peace movement that often puts personal egos above peace and human life. This group won't work with that group; *he* won't attend an event if *she* is going to be there; "and why does Cindy Sheehan get all the attention, anyway?" It is hard to work for peace when the very movement that is named after it has so many divisions.

Our brave young men and women in Iraq have been abandoned there indefinitely by their cowardly leaders, who move them around like pawns on a chessboard of destruction. And the people of Iraq have been doomed to death, and fates worse than death, by politicians worried more about elections than about people. However, in five, ten, or fifteen years, our troops will come limping home in another abject defeat, and ten or twenty years from then, our children's children will be seeing their loved ones die for no reason, because their grandparents also bought into this corrupt system. George Bush will never be impeached, because if the Democrats dig too deeply, they may unearth a few skeletons in their own graves, and the system will perpetuate itself.

I am going to take whatever I have left and go home. I am going to go home and be a mother to my surviving children and try to regain some of what I have lost. I will try to maintain and nurture some very positive relationships that I have found in the journey that I was forced into when Casey died. I will try to repair some of the ones that have fallen apart since I began this single-minded crusade to try to change a paradigm that is now, I am afraid, carved in immovable, unbendable, and rigidly mendacious marble.

Camp Casey has served its purpose. It's for sale. Anyone want to buy five beautiful acres in Crawford, Texas? I will consider any reasonable offer. I hear George Bush will be moving out soon, too . . . which makes the property even more valuable.

This is my resignation letter as the "face" of the American anti-war movement. This is not my "Checkers" moment—because I will never give up trying to help people in the world who are harmed by the empire of the good old US of A—but I am finished working in, or outside of, this system. This system forcefully resists being helped and eats up the people who try to help it. I am getting out before it totally consumes me or any more people that I love.

Goodbye, America . . . you are not the country that I love, and I have finally realized, no matter how much I sacrifice, I can't make you be that country unless you want it.

It's up to you now.

Adoption in III Acts

by Kathy Briccetti

A LITTLE BEFORE NINE O'CLOCK, Pam, Benjamin, and I passed through metal detectors in the lobby of the Alameda County Superior Court. Pam's anxiety was palpable; the tilled lines of her forehead and her wind-scattered curls told me everything. Balancing our seven-month-old on a hip, she stepped into the elevator and I followed, a plum-colored backpack—filled with mini–rice crackers, extra diapers, a camera, and an envelope of legal papers—slung over my shoulder. My slacks pinched at the waist with the extra pregnancy weight; standing at the back of the elevator as we ascended, I reached underneath my blazer and surreptitiously released the top clasp.

The courthouse—a granite wedding cake with terra-cotta trim—overlooked Lake Merritt. Despite a chalky December sky, the lake was a bucolic tease in the center of Oakland. With winter-greened hills heavy with the homes of the affluent to the east, and an incongruously placed Greek proscenium arch reflected in the water, joggers circling the lake could briefly forget where they were.

We had come to court for a rare event in 1993: a woman adopting a baby boy in order to up his number of legal mothers to two. A second-parent adoption. We were still a decade ahead of the gay-marriage extravaganza that would take place across the bay in San Francisco, when gay parents would charge out of closets—men in tuxedos cradling infants, women in matching wedding gowns with toddlers on their hips, and scores of working parents pulling kids out of school to rush to city hall. Although these marriages eventually would be nullified by the courts, the attention paid them would nudge the country another baby step closer to acceptance of our kind of family.

But that day, we were forging new ground. As the elevator made its climb, I worried something would go wrong, that we would be rebuked, sent away without our adoption decree. The day after I'd given birth to Benjamin, a hospital administrator in a skirt the color and sheen of eggplant had watched me fill in the draft of his birth certificate. Peering over her glasses, she saw me scratch out the word "father" and write in "mother," and then add Pam's name. But the administrator wasn't with me six weeks later when I tore open the envelope from the state of California, pulled out my son's birth certificate, and read the sole word typed in the space under "father": "withheld." That one word made me feel like a teenage mother of an illegitimate child.

Ever since Pam and I had visited the sperm bank to choose a donor, I'd struggled with the idea that my family's blueprint—three generations of adoptions and absent fathers—had somehow caused me to create a child who would not grow up with a father. My son's relationship with his biological father, if he ever met him, would mirror my relationship with my own father. Because the sperm donor had agreed to release his identity when his offspring turned eighteen, if Ben wanted to find the man whose genes he shared, he could. But by that time, Ben would almost be a man himself, and the donor would be not a father, but a stranger.

In 1961, a few months before my fourth birthday, my mother tossed suitcases and a cardboard box of toys into the trunk of her Chevy Corvair and slammed it shut. With care, she placed her violin case on the floor of the back seat and then called to my brother and me. The magnolia in the front yard of our Kentucky home still clenched its flame-shaped buds, new leaves glowing like green embers, and in its shade, my father bent his reed frame to embrace me. When his smooth cheek brushed mine, I filled up on his Daddy smell—spicy mouthwash and the musty velvet-and-rosin scent he carried from his cello case. He patted my back, lingering a second before unfolding and standing again. I grabbed his legs, and with my cheek felt his knees jutting against the soft fabric of his slacks.

"Come on, honey," he said, peeling back my fingers from around his shins. "Be a good girl and get in the car." He spoke as if my little brother, my mother, and I were heading to the park for the day, but something in his voice was off. I climbed into the front while Michael, not quite two years old, settled onto the back seat, the car's lap belts dangling like abandoned playground swings. My mother backed the car down our driveway, and I swiveled to catch a last glimpse of my father through the rear window, a cloudy oval framing the moment. His hands in his pockets, he stood fixed at the end of the drive, swaying slightly. His face melded into the shadows cast by the magnolia, and as the car headed down Oakdale Street toward the expressway, my father slowly shrank, then disappeared.

My mother remarried in Florida when I was eight, and a year later my brother and I were adopted by our stepfather. The morning of my adoption, I buckled the skinny straps of my new patent leather shoes while Michael sprinted back and forth past my bedroom door in the suit he had worn to Mom's wedding. The pant legs were too short, and the sleeves of his dress shirt exposed his skinny wrists. His hair was white-blond like mine, and the cowlick above his forehead, left longer than the rest of his crew cut, had rebelled against our new father's water-and-comb treatment.

"It's Spaghetti Day," Michael sang as he sped by again. He still had difficulty pronouncing our new name, Briccetti. "The two c's sound like 'ch,'" Mom had taught us. Earlier, I had sat at the kitchen table with a piece of lined notebook paper and practiced spelling the long name over and over, in case the judge quizzed me. I would no longer be Kathy Manfred.

"What will we have to do?" I asked Mom as she stood behind me and buttoned my dress—my favorite, the one with lace around the collar. The scent of her body powder merged with a perfume I didn't recognize.

"Probably nothing. We're just going to court so the judge can sign the adoption papers. You get a new father today." Her tone was the one she used when trying to convince me that I would enjoy eating the liver draped with onions on my dinner plate.

I wanted to know if we'd be sworn in on a Bible, if we'd see any holstered guns on deputies, if we'd join robbers or murderers standing before the judge.

"He might ask you a couple of questions."

What questions? I wanted to ask, but Mr. Briccetti tooted the horn and Mom shooed us out the door.

Driving to the Florida courthouse that day, I thought about the man who would become my adoptive father, a man so unlike my lanky father with his hushed voice and tentative kisses. I was just getting to know this new man with a Roman nose and shiny, coffee-bean hair past his ears, the man who grabbed us in bear hugs, pinched our cheeks, and added terms of endearment to his proclamations: "Look at this, sweetie" or "Pass the bread, honey-bunny." He drove us to the beach in his Austin Healy, the "zoom-zoom car," my brother called it, us kids crammed into the space behind the seats made for two grocery sacks, not for two children. We'd clutch the seats in front of us, my corn-silk hair whipping into my eyes and mouth, my mother's silk scarf, emblazoned with a map of the world, flapping next to my bowed head. My new father was a musky intermingling of cigarettes, Certs, and Old Spice, and despite his foreignness, when he let me sit on his lap and steer his Austin Healy, I felt oddly sheltered in his embrace.

Inside the Florida court building, the chilly air raised bumps on my bare arms and legs. A bailiff—his holstered gun prominent on his hip—directed us to the judge's chambers, a large, luminous room with modern office furniture and floor-to-ceiling windows with a view of silky heat mirages on parking lot asphalt. The four of us settled into swivel seats at one end of a vast conference table, and I spun my chair around twice before Mom reached over and placed a hand on my knee. The judge entered—he seemed a giant of a man to me then—with neatly parted gray hair, a starchy suit, and a skinny tie. He shook hands first with Mom and Mr. Briccetti, then with Michael and me. He sat, rolled his chair into position at the head of the table, and looked us over.

"So, why do you want to be adopted?" he asked, smiling and glancing from Michael to me. I peeked at Mom, who leaned forward and then back, as if she wanted to coach me but knew it was too late. Most of her cherry-colored lipstick had rubbed off, but her Jackie Kennedy haircut was perfect. I didn't answer. The judge raised his eyebrows at me, expectant, his smile fading.

Thinking about this now, I'm appalled that a judge would put this question to a child, would force her to answer a question when he didn't understand its ramifications: the loyalties she would be forced to betray. That day I wasn't sure I wanted to be adopted, because I didn't know what it would do to summer visits with my father. I was beginning to forget the spicy mouthwash and the rosin scent from his cello case. Lacking photos, I was also beginning to forget his face. I wondered if this adoption meant I was supposed to pretend that my father, Cyrus Manfred, no longer existed.

Although I balked at the weight of the judge's question in the Florida courthouse, the brief taste of power also made me giddy with possibility. I could have said, "No one asked me how I felt about this. Now that I think about it, I *don't* want to be adopted." But I knew

I needed to give the right answer. I couldn't risk making the adults angry, and the pressure pushed at my chest.

"Because we love him?"

The adults sighed in unison like a spent church choir, their faces settling into satisfied smiles. The judge arranged the adoption papers on the table and handed his shiny gold and black pen to my mother, then to Mr. Briccetti. "You can call him Dad now," my mother said, smiling.

Minutes later, the four of us skipped down the court steps holding hands like a family in a television commercial. I didn't understand why we were supposed to be happy.

Pam, Ben, and I left the elevator and made our way down the hall to the family court. Neither the state of California nor the county's Department of Social Services had approved Pam's adoption of Benjamin. Our lawyer had warned us that in our county only two judges had ever overruled the Social Services policy and granted adoptions by same-sex couples. In neighboring counties, none had. Some states were testing the process, but in most, it was still against the law.

It was Pam who had thawed the vial of frozen semen under her arm, and in our bed had released the awakened sperm into me. Even though nine months later, holding our baby under his slippery arms, she pulled him out of me and cut through his umbilical cord, and even though she cooked and pureed and froze organic vegetables in ice cube trays and pushed him in his doorway swing so I could eat dinner first, the state had deemed our family unsanctioned, morally lacking, illegitimate. Children need both a mother and a father, we'd heard over and over in the media, or they risked personality disorders and "sexual deviance" of their own. Of course, there were no data yet, no long-term studies of children of gay and lesbian parents like those that would come later and prove the frightened, conservative pundits wrong. Just hype and horror stories.

The Alameda County child-welfare worker who had overseen our home study was a married woman with teenage children. Mary Louise wore skirts and stockings and makeup, and she looked as if she lived "through the tunnel" in one of the suburbs, past the line delineating the liberal Bay Area and into more conservative territory. We worried that she'd be uncomfortable in our home, that she'd write a negative report about us simply because lesbians gave her the creeps. We cleaned house as if we feared it would be repossessed on her whim.

She had visited when I was pregnant in order to interview us, inspect our home, and collect the thick questionnaires that Pam filled out: intrusive queries about drug use and psychiatric history. Mary Louise came again after Ben was born, inspecting his room, waking him from a nap because she had to lay eyes on him. "Had to make sure he wasn't bruised and emaciated," I'd grumbled to Pam.

On her final trip to our house, a month before the court date, she sat in our living room, shuffling through papers on her clipboard. Pam held six-month-old Ben on her lap, from time to time planting razzing kisses on his bare soles. This made him laugh, and I was aware that this made us look good. "So, how'd we do?" Pam asked near the end of the visit, the strain evident in her voice. "Did we pass or fail?"

Mary Louise placed her clipboard in her briefcase, stretching out the moment, as if she was in a made-for-television special. "You guys are great," she said, and it took me a few seconds to take in the compliment. "You've got a beautiful home, and this baby is obviously well cared for." As if on cue, Ben cooed, a poster baby for second-parent adoption. "I have to warn you, though," Mary Louise said. She placed her briefcase at her feet and looked at each of us in turn. "About what my report will say."

We received Mary Louise's report a week before the court date. Although it praised Pam's suitability as a parent and supported our desire to "legalize a relationship that already exists," Mary Louise had been bound by current policy.

"In this worker's opinion, the petitioner's suitability to adopt the minor is not in question. She has lived with him and has been committed to him since his birth. Both women obviously love this child and share the responsibilities for his care and development." And then:

> Despite the fact that the petitioner and the natural mother are not married, they have formed with the minor what is a viable family unit. They now want the adoption granted in order to give the minor the protection and support of two committed parents. They believe, and this worker concurs, that the minor can benefit from the security that this adoption will provide, and that his best interests will be served by the granting of this petition.
>
> However, the Agency and State policy recommends denial of same-sex adoptions because the child does not benefit from a legal marriage. The undersigned worker, while viewing the petitioner as eminently qualified to adopt, will abide by that policy.
>
> RECOMMENDATION: The Social Services Agency of Alameda County recommends that the petition of Pamela Harris-Craig for the adoption of Benjamin Ross Craig be denied.

In the fall of 1930, just before Thanksgiving, in a small town in the boot heel of Missouri, my sixteen-year-old grandmother, Mavis, tried to bring her baby boy home from the Children's Home Society in St. Louis, where she had given birth.

"You may not enter this house with that child." Her father, a farmer and part-time minister, stood on the top step of their porch with his arms crossed. "That bastard child," he whispered. Mavis's mother, and a brother, had died in the influenza epidemic when she was four, and now her stepmother, partly hidden in the shadow cast by the porch roof, did not intervene in this homecoming standoff.

Mavis turned and headed back down the dirt driveway. One of her sisters hopped off the porch and caught up with her. On that day in late fall, the two girls took turns carrying the baby a dozen miles out in the country, past pungent dairy and cattle farms, alongside empty soybean and watermelon fields, to an even smaller town. It wasn't even a town really, but a cluster of four houses holding down an intersection of two unpaved roads—damp dirt tilled into naked rows creeping out behind each of the houses. The girls knocked on the door of the home on the northwest corner, that of the baby's father, a married man with his second child on the way. When his wife answered the door, Mavis placed her baby in the woman's arms, and then she and her sister turned around and walked back home, both of them crying for the first few miles.

Six months later, on a spring day just before her son turned a year, Mavis was summoned to that house to collect him. One of the other children was ill, and the family was too poor to keep her baby any longer. The day before my father's first birthday, Mavis handed him to a social worker at the Children's Home Society. He was adopted the next day.

Mavis wrote to the social worker several months later. I keep a copy of her letter in the envelope with the three adoption records—my father's, mine, and Benjamin's—that I have saved.

> I don't know why I did it. They were telling me to hurry up and get it over with, and I was crying so; I didn't hardly know what I was doing. That was the hardest day of my life having to give him up. If I hadn't been such a fool to sign papers. His birth father arranged it; I certainly hope he feels all right over it. I'll remember until the very day I die about my dad forcing me to give my baby up. If I could only get him back, I'd do anything.

When I searched for her a few years after Ben's adoption, her sister told me that my grandmother Mavis, twice divorced, had died at forty-nine, her liver destroyed by alcohol. She had no other children and did not see her son again, nor did she ever meet any of her descendants.

My father's adoption record begins: "IN THE MATTER OF JIMMIE EARL SAUNDERS. The court finds that Mavis Saunders is a single and unmarried woman and that she has given her written consent for transferring custody of her said child to the Children's Home Society."

When my father was three, his adoptive mother, a woman who would live 103 years, stood before a judge in the Circuit Court of St. Louis with her lawyer at her side. Her husband did not attend this hearing to finalize the adoption of their son—their only child—possibly because he was working or looking for a job. Or maybe it was another reason, because a year later, when my father was four years old, his adoptive father packed a suitcase, walked out the door, and did not return.

When I was sixteen, my stepfather, the man who'd given me the name Briccetti, took a job in another city, eventually rented a house there, and returned home a couple of weekends a month. After each of his visits, a few more belongings—the denim jacket he always hung on the coat tree in the hall, the tin of spicy mints in the pantry, the clay ashtray I made for him in fourth grade—disappeared. I wasn't there the day the movers came for his piano. And I wasn't home the morning he backed a U-Haul truck into the driveway, loaded it with the rest of the furniture from his study, and drove away. He had left so gradually, I don't think we ever said goodbye. I just remember walking into his empty study, facing its wall of windows, and staring at sunlight striking newly bared carpet, three potted plants left behind on windowsills, and a small blue pencil sharpener lying on its side in a corner.

Entering the Oakland courtroom, Pam, Ben, and I paused at the doorway, succumbing to a reverential hush. The room was plain— boxy, with an unadorned, absurdly high ceiling that siphoned off voices. A row of windows placed high on the wall broke the vastness of the mahogany paneling.

Pam and I had considered using a known donor instead of an anonymous one, but we didn't want to risk the chance that he might change his mind someday, taking us to court for custody. We used a donor who relinquished his ties to our child by giving his semen to a sperm bank instead of directly to us, but I still worried that if we didn't complete this adoption, a judge might—in a legal fluke—take my child from me and give him to the donor and his wife, simply because my partner was a woman. There was precedent for this.

If we didn't get one of the two judges in our county who routinely overruled Social Services, our adoption would be denied and we would be left no recourse. It was statistically unlikely, but the possibility still frightened me. I was holding something back, too, not coming clean with Pam. "We need to ensure your rights," I'd said. "We don't want the donor, or a judge who doesn't know any better, taking Ben away from you." But I hadn't admitted my deeper fear, the possibility of our breaking up someday, and what might happen to Ben if we did. One of the couples in our lesbian moms' playgroup had already separated, and now they shuttled their eighteen-month-old between two houses. A lesbian couple in another state was fighting for custody of their six-year-old, also a product of a trip to the sperm bank. Because the nonbiological mother had not adopted, in the eyes of the court she had no rights, and she'd been denied visitation rights with the child she'd raised since birth.

I didn't admit that part of me wanted to skip this adoption and hold on to legal custody of Ben. I could imagine a time when I might want him to myself, and this frightened me—my potential for behaving badly. But, I wondered, how could I, of all people, deprive my son of a parent? Could he grieve something he never lost? I knew that abandonment was not genetic, but I *was* aware of the power of repetition over generations, and I feared that this unknown force would somehow exert itself over my child.

As we settled into one of the hardwood, theater-style seats in the observers' section, Pam removed Ben's jacket and handed him a rice cracker. I went to fuss with his socks, but Pam beat me to it, pulling them up over his chubby legs. She had dressed him that morning, in blue overalls that had a small teddy bear appliqué on the center of the chest. A large, red heart filled the center of the bear. It was an outfit he'd worn several times before, and I didn't think about its significance until later, when I looked at photos taken that day and wondered whether Pam chose that piece of clothing deliberately or whether it had been an unconscious act to show our love to the world, and she had been sending the judge a subliminal message.

I wanted to reach over and squeeze her hand, but resisted. One night, a couple of years before Ben was born, a drunk we'd passed on our way home from the movies had shouted at us, "Fucking lezzies!" Pam and I had never spoken about it, but we kept our displays of affection inside our home, where, with curtains drawn, we embraced, kissed, caressed each other's faces. Now Pam smoothed Ben's hair at the temples and kissed his cheek. He gummed his rice cracker and babbled with pleasure.

The light from outside the courtroom, eking in from the windows above, shone winter-weak. Other families wandered in through the double doors, equally burdened with baby paraphernalia and legal papers, and found seats around us. Across the aisle, a Caucasian woman and man in their early fifties took turns chasing an Asian toddler in a lacy, rose-colored dress around the seats. In the row in front of us, a woman with skin a shade lighter than the mahogany walls adjusted an ebony-skinned boy's necktie while a fair-skinned blond man, his hair in dreadlocks, tapped his fingers in a restless rhythm on the boy's shoulder.

Ben squawked, joining the other babies in an infant opera. Parents shushed their children, but the noise mounted and the room began to sound more like a daycare center than a courtroom. We were the only lesbian couple waiting with a baby, and Pam hovered over Benjamin, in high-maintenance-mother mode. "More crackers?" she asked. "Do you want Mama to get your bottle?" A meltdown would not have looked good at that moment. It seemed we'd tacitly agreed that she'd carry him into the courtroom that morning, that she'd take care of him during this event. It was like a job interview. We'd show whoever was watching what a good parent she was, and how lucky he was to have her.

I forced myself to sit still, resisted leaping up and pacing. I bounced my knee as if Ben was on it and wiped my palms on my slacks over and over. Maybe the judge had called in sick and the substitute judge would refuse to see us. Or he would usher us in only to scowl, lecture us on the necessity—the right—of a child to have a mother and a father, and then send us away. Because she was expensive, we'd asked our lawyer not to accompany us to court. All the paperwork had been filed, and we were gambling that this would be an uncomplicated formality. I worried maybe that had been a mistake, that she should have been here in case something went wrong.

I pulled the sheath of papers from the backpack and pretended to study the one on top, the order terminating the sperm donor's parental rights—one of the documents necessary for this adoption to proceed. I studied it even though I already knew every word on it and how many ways it said that my child was fatherless.

1. BENJAMIN ROSS CRAIG has no presumed father under California Civil Code section 7004 (a).

2. BENJAMIN ROSS CRAIG having been conceived through artificial insemination by donor, the sperm donation having been made through a licensed physician, has no legal father pursuant to California Civil Code 7005 (b).

3. No man has formally or informally claimed to be the father of this child.

The clerk's voice rang clear in the cavernous room. "Benjamin Ross Craig. Pamela Harris-Craig. Katherine Briccetti-Craig." It was the first time I'd heard our family name spoken by someone other than us. Pam and I had only begun using our hyphenated names a year earlier, a name we'd found on both of our family trees, and hearing it called across the room sounded strange and comforting at the same time. I wanted the world to know that the three of us shared a name. I wanted to stand up and shout that even though there was no father, we were still a family.

As we gathered our belongings, the process began to feel even more like a commitment ceremony than when Pam and I exchanged rings seven years earlier, perched on a boulder overlooking the glistening Pacific Ocean. It would prove more binding than registering with the city of Berkeley, and later with the state of California, as domestic partners. Like in divorce, those contracts could be nullified. Not so with adoption. Ben's adoption decree would tie me to Pam forever; because no matter what happened in our lives, if we stayed together or drifted apart, we would always have this child binding us together.

We followed the clerk, who wore a bold, floral dress, past the judge's vacant bench into the hall leading to his chambers, Pam carrying Ben chest to chest, me trailing with the gear, like the family's

Sherpa. As the birth mother, I had already signed papers allowing her
to adopt my biological child. I would not be giving up my parental
rights, and that was what made this a second-parent adoption. No
one would be able to take our child away from Pam. Not my family,
not the court, not me. That is, *if* this judge overruled the Department
of Social Services and granted our adoption.

In his chambers in the Oakland courtroom, bespectacled Judge
Morimoto, wearing a white, starched shirt with rolled-up sleeves
and an off-center tie, reached across his cluttered desk to shake our
hands. He had a wide, round face that was large for his body. His
careless attention to his tie—it looked as if he'd pulled it to the side in
a fit of discomfort—could have signaled boredom, irritation, or simply a laid-back approach to the job. I searched his face for a clue as
to how this would go. When Pam leaned forward, Ben tilted toward
the judge, who took that opportunity to stroke Ben's marshmallow
cheek with thick fingertips. "Say hi," Pam told Ben, and she waved
his chubby hand at the judge. Ben stared at the man, mouth open, not
blinking. Given the distractions—children to watch in the courtroom
and now this unfamiliar man making eyes at him—he had not fussed
once that morning. And for a minute I too was distracted. I glanced
out the judge's window at the lake, where a crew team shuttled across
with smooth, dashlike strokes. It was dreamlike, what we were doing. Part of me wished it was already over, that we were out rowing
on the lake, too.

"Tuesday mornings I do the adoptions." He peered at us above
thick glasses, and I couldn't read his expression. Next to him, the
clerk arranged papers in some kind of order in front of him; because
she stood so close, it looked for a second as if the judge had a second
pair of hands. "It's the best part of my job," he added, looking up
and smiling. A whisper of calm settled inside my chest.

I glanced at the decree of adoption our lawyer had optimistically prepared. And as Judge Morimoto signed his name to it, I read a few of the upside-down words. IT IS THEREFORE ORDERED, ADJUDGED, AND DECREED that the petition for adoption is granted.

He looked up. "Congratulations," he said, scooping up the papers and straightening them against the desktop before handing them to his clerk. I checked Pam's face and, for the first time that morning, I saw her smile.

"We're legal, little boy," she said, brushing her lips over Ben's hair. I put my arms around the two of them and squeezed, smashing us together. "Group hug," I said, kissing Ben's cheek. He squealed and kicked his legs. Something inside my chest released; I was tossing away ballast, my body was becoming lighter.

Pam and I exchanged a glance. I knew she was relieved, but for me it was complicated. I was relieved too—I felt as if we had fought hard for something that we deserved—but it was also daunting, what we had done, undergoing this family-forming rite.

A minute later, Judge Morimoto took his black robe from a coat rack in the corner, slipped it over his shirtsleeves, and met us in front of his wall of legal volumes. His clerk snatched our camera, and as the four of us positioned ourselves, I pulled in my stomach, furtively refastened the clasp on my slacks, and smoothed my blazer. Ben wriggled in Pam's arms, ready to get down. "It's okay, big boy," she whispered to him. "We're almost done." We flanked the judge, who spoke to Ben in a voice used only with babies. "Say 'Happy Adoption Day' for the camera," he said, cooing like a proud grandfather. Ben babbled, imitating the judge's intonation. From behind the desk, the clerk, bending at the waist, framed us through the lens. And I saw in the photo, after we had it developed a couple of weeks later, that all of us were laughing.

Performing Mother Activism

by Beth Osnes

MY FIRST EXPOSURE to an activist mother was in *Mary Poppins*. If you remember, the children's mother, Winifred—a woman who neglected her children because of her commitment to her activism—was portrayed as privileged, silly, ineffectual. By the end of the film, she renounces her cause, discarding her suffragette sash to take on her rightful duties as wife and mother in the privacy of her home. A subliminal message was sent to me and every other viewer of that film: Being politically active and being a good mother are mutually exclusive.

A few years ago, I wrote and performed my own one-woman show. I did it because I was tired of the complicated multimedia performances I had been engaged in, and with my hectic schedule of being a mother, a teacher, a performer, and an activist, I wanted to *simplify*. No tricks or spectacle, just direct and intimate contact with the audience, telling stories that mattered to me.

The material that naturally emerged during the creative process was all about mothering and activism, since I had been immersed in both of those activities for twelve years. It included the kind of inner negotiations that we mothers go through in daily life, the results of which, collectively, have enormous ramifications on the world. Negotiations such as whether or not to buy that cute skirt at Old Navy, marked down to $3.99 but probably made in a sweatshop in Vietnam. I'd ask myself, *But if I'm buying it well below cost, am I exempt from the karma of supporting their lousy business practices?*

The first piece in my show has me stepping out in front of the audience to explain why I want to perform this piece for them:

I feel like a miner. Like I want to dig down deep into the mounds of diapers, wives' tales, errands, dishes, and silence, all that stuff, to discover that thick vein of mother wisdom deep in the earth. I want to carve off a big chunk and carry it up top, into the light of day, where it can be seen for its extraordinary value. As they say in mining, I want to hit the mother lode.

I go on with scenes like "Ben Hur, Done That," in which I describe the time I took my children to a Chartlon Heston–associated antigun rally. "Are we to be disimpassioned presenters, fairly elucidating each view and position?" I ask.

My God, our children would end up with as much passion as Wonder Bread. So then, do we simply couch everything in "This is what we believe, but not everyone sees it this way," which works well when talking about Hindus . . . but works worse when discussing a pro-gun protestor who is standing four yards away, screaming, "We will not disarm!" Then I can't help but say, "Look, kids, here's a raving lunatic: the last person on Earth I would want to entrust with a weapon."

I go on with scenes that tackle the onslaught of societal expectations and repressive forces that creep into a woman's life once she becomes a mother: "It happens one day. You find a large parcel on your front porch. You open it to find the status quo being delivered to you . . . well, actually, the status quo manual. It's titled, 'The Ideal Mother.' You flip through the pages. Page 16: 'Giving Up Swearing.' Oh, fuck."

I go on with scenes that lambaste the fearmongering that goes on in our government and media: "The status quo wants you to dumb down, mother. It will tell you who to trust and who to fear." I remind mothers that we must think for ourselves: "I say rage, mother. Do not go gently into that good night. Rage, *rage* against the dying of your light."

And just as the text starts getting too didactic, I ask, "Is this preachy? What, you thought mothers weren't *preachy?!*"

The performance ends with a tribute to my own mother's wisdom and a call for mothers to work together to find solutions for this troubled world:

> In conclusion, I would just like to say that I fully believe that if my mom ruled the earth, she would have fixed all the problems in the Middle East by now. She would have touched the hearts of white supremacists. She would make corporate America clean up its mess. All children would be growing up with healthcare, enough to eat, and with love. We have the means. We lack the will. But if my mother were in charge, there would be a new world order.
>
> Some may doubt she could. I've seen my mother move mountains. She raised ten children, all good people. I've seen my mother endure great sadness and come out on the other end with a pure and thankful heart. I have seen mothers, so many mothers, do amazing things.
>
> How did you do that? Talk about it.

It's always struck me how similar activism is to performing. Both force you to present yourself in public and express some predetermined content. As a performer, I would be terrified to be on the stage in public without rehearsing; in fact, it's one of my stock nightmares. It only follows that people new to civic participation would feel much more comfortable and confident after rehearsing as well—after learning how to release tension, which blocks expression; after learning how to use full breath, which gives life to what we express; after learning how to make authentic contact with the audience, whether it's one person or thousands.

That's why, a few months after I first performed my show, I presented a workshop called "Rehearsal for Activism" for Mothers

Acting Up (MAU), a movement I cofounded that mobilizes mothers to advocate for the world's children.

In it, I asked the participants to identify one thing they could and would do within the next month to advance some aspect of social justice. After each person described what they could and would do, we all acted out what each person described so they could encounter potential obstacles to their intentions in a rehearsal setting. One man, who wanted to adorn his bike with a sign on the basket calling for a U.S. Department of Peace, realized, once we acted out the scene, that he might want to keep handouts in his backpack that explain HR 808, a bill before the House of Representatives calling for the establishment of a cabinet-level Department of Peace and Nonviolence. A woman practiced calling her senator to ask him to support funding for the UN's Millennium Development Goals; other participants coached her on how she could speak more effectively and include more specific information about the organization and about what she was asking her senator to do.

At a workshop in Oklahoma City, one woman nodded her head, ultimately recognizing herself as someone who would speak out in public, saying, "I can do it if it's positive."

During a recent MAU visit to the office of my senator (an extremely conservative man), I watched his aide, with whom we were meeting, literally puff up his chest and stand when we questioned our nation's rationale for still being in the Iraq war. He was performing male domination and was—most likely unconsciously—attempting to intimidate us into submission through his bodily stance. He's had a lot of practice being in public; many men have.

As I watched a fellow visitor continue to express her convictions—in spite of his physical stance—with direct eye contact, full breath, and compassion, I knew she had overcome the limiting stereotypical role of mother. This was a new performance of mother—confident, self-scripted, and audacious—performed for a rapt audience. Had etiquette allowed, I would have given her a standing ovation.

Like so many other plays and books and films, *Mary Poppins* offered up the mother as a bit player. Mothers Acting Up is a response to just that misperception, a nudge to mothers everywhere to forgo the secondary role as witnesses and nurturers and to step up into the lead role, knowing that, unlike Winifred's portrayal, it will only make them better mothers.

The process of integrating my theater with my motherhood and my activism has been ridiculously invigorating. It has brought the pieces of my self back together: Now my life experience, my creativity, and my intellectual development—all of it is out there on a platter, being offered to the audience.

I have traveled on this transformational journey with minimal guidance and few road signs, and quite frankly, it took over a decade to claim my full self in this way. Perhaps it wouldn't have taken so long if I'd had more role models. Only now are mothers in public positions being shown in the media: Geena Davis as the U.S. president on the television show *Commander in Chief,* Speaker of the House Nancy Pelosi speaking as a mother in public statements, and Angelina Jolie letting her role as mother be primary in the media.

As we mothers claim our own voices and assert our priorities in the world, our impassioned monologues will be heard in governmental offices, corporate boardrooms, and public podiums. And we will land the starring roles in this world's melodrama, deciding how our resources are allocated, how our conflicts are resolved, how our earth is treated, and how our future is charted. Indeed, a star is born.

Mother, take the stage.

Pregnant in New York

by Anna Quindlen

I HAVE TWO ENDURING MEMORIES of the hours just before I gave birth to my first child. One is of finding a legal parking space on 78th Street between Lexington and Park, which made my husband and me believe that we were going inside the hospital to have a child who would always lead a charmed life. The other is of walking down Lexington Avenue, stopping every couple of steps to find myself a visual focal point—a stop sign, a red light, a pair of $200 shoes in a store window—and doing what the Lamaze books call first-stage breathing. It was 3:00 AM and coming toward me through a magenta haze of what the Lamaze books call discomfort were a couple in evening clothes whose eyes were popping out of their perfect faces. "Wow," said the man when I was at least two steps past them. "She looks like she's ready to burst."

I love New York, but it's a tough place to be pregnant. It's a great place for half sour pickles, chopped liver, millionaires, actors, dancers, akita dogs, nice leather goods, fur coats, and baseball, but it is a difficult place to have any kind of disability, and as anyone who has filled out the forms for a maternity leave lately will tell you, pregnancy is considered a disability. There's no privacy in New York; everyone is right up against everyone else and they all feel compelled to say what they think. When you look like a hot-air balloon with insufficient ballast, that's not good.

New York has no pity: It's every man for himself, and since you are yourself-and-a-half, you fall behind. There's a rumor afoot that if you are pregnant you can get a seat on the A train at rush hour, but it's totally false. There are, in fact, parts of the world in which pregnancy can get you a seat on public transportation, but none of them are within the boundaries of the city—with the possible exception of some unreconstructed parts of Staten Island.

What you get instead are rude comments, unwarranted intrusions and deli countermen. It is a little-known fact that New York deli countermen can predict the sex of an unborn child. (This is providing that you order, of course. For a counterman to provide this service requires a minimum order of seventy-five cents.) This is how it works: You walk into a deli and say, "Large fruit salad, turkey on rye with Russian, a large Perrier and a tea with lemon." The deli counterman says, "Who you buying for, the Rangers?" and all the other deli countermen laugh.

This is where many pregnant women make their mistake. If it is wintertime and you are wearing a loose coat, the preferred answer to this question is, "I'm buying for all the women in my office." If it is summer and you are visibly pregnant, you are sunk. The deli counterman will lean over the counter and say, studying your contours, "It's a boy." He will then tell a tedious story about sex determination, his Aunt Olga, and a clove of garlic, while behind you people waiting on line shift and sigh and begin to make Zero Population Growth and fat people comments. (I once dealt with an East Side counterman who argued with me about the tea because he said it was bad for the baby, but he was an actor waiting for his big break, not a professional.) Deli countermen do not believe in amniocentesis. Friends who have had amniocentesis tell me that once or twice they tried to argue: "I already know it's a girl." "You are wrong." They gave up: "Don't forget the napkins."

There are also cabdrivers. One promptly pulled over in the middle of Central Park when I told him I had that queasy feeling. When I turned to get back into the cab, it was gone. The driver had taken the $1.80 on the meter as a loss. Luckily, I never had this problem again, because as I grew larger, nine out of ten cabdrivers refused to pick me up. They had read the tabloids. They knew about all those babies christened Checker (actually, I suppose now most of them are Plymouths) because they're born in the back seat in the Midtown Tunnel. The only way I could get a cabdriver to pick me up after the sixth month was to hide my stomach by having a friend walk in front of me. The exception was a really tiresome young cabdriver whose wife's due date was a week after mine and who wanted to practice panting with me for that evening's childbirth class. Most of the time I wound up taking public transportation.

And so it came down to the subways: men looking at their feet, reading their newspapers, working hard to keep from noticing me. One day on the IRT I was sitting down—it was a spot left unoccupied because the rainwater had spilled in the window from an elevated station—when I noticed a woman standing who was or should have been on her way to the hospital.

"When are you due?" I asked her. "Thursday," she gasped. "I'm September," I said. "Take my seat." She slumped down and said, with feeling, "You are the first person to give me a seat on the subway since I've been pregnant." Being New Yorkers, with no sense of personal privacy, we began to exchange subway, taxi, and deli countererman stories. When a man sitting nearby got up to leave, he snarled, "You wanted women's lib, now you got it."

Well, I'm here to say that I did get women's lib, and it is my only fond memory of being pregnant in New York. (Actually, I did find pregnancy useful on opening day at Yankee Stadium, when great swarms of people parted at the sight of me as though I were Charlton Heston in *The Ten Commandments*. But it had a pariah quality that was not totally soothing.)

One evening rush hour during my eighth month I was waiting for a train at Columbus Circle. The loudspeaker was crackling unintelligibly and ominously and there were as many people on the platform as currently live in Santa Barbara, Calif. Suddenly I had the dreadful feeling that I was being surrounded. "To get mugged at a time like this," I thought ruefully. "And this being New York, they'll probably try to take the baby, too." But as I looked around I saw that the people surrounding me were four women, some armed with shoulder bags. "You need protection," one said, and being New Yorkers, they ignored the fact that they did not know one another and joined forces to form a kind of phalanx around me, not unlike those that offensive linemen build around a quarterback.

When the train arrived and the doors opened, they moved forward, with purpose, and I was swept inside, not the least bit bruised. "Looks like a boy," said one with a grin, and as the train began to move, we all grabbed the silver overhead handles and turned away from one another.

The Born

by Anne Lamott

EVERYTHING WAS GOING swimmingly on the panel. The subject was politics and faith, and I was onstage with two clergymen with progressive spiritual leanings, and a moderator who was liberal and Catholic. We were having a discussion before an audience of 1,300 people in Washington, D.C., about many of the social justice topics on which we agree; we were discussing the immorality of the federal budget, the wrongness of the president's war in Iraq. . . . Then an older man came to the mic and raised the issue of abortion, and people just lost their minds.

Or at any rate, I did.

Maybe it was the way in which the man couched his question, which was about how we should reconcile our progressive stance on peace and justice with the "murder of a million babies every year in America."

The man who asked the question was soft-spoken, neatly and casually dressed. Richard, the Franciscan priest, answered first, saying that this was indeed a painful issue, but that it was not the only pro-life matter with which progressives—including Catholics—should concern themselves during elections. There were also the pro-life matters of capital punishment and the war in Iraq, poverty, and HIV. Then Jim, the Evangelical minister, spoke about the need to reduce the number of unwanted pregnancies, and the need to defuse abortion as a political issue by welcoming pro-choice and pro-life supporters to the discussion with equal respect for their positions. He spoke cautiously about how "morally ambiguous" the question was.

I sat there frozen. The moderator turned to me and asked if I would like to respond.

I did. I wanted to respond by pushing over the table.

Instead, I shook my head. I love and respect the Franciscan and the Evangelical, and I agree with them 90-plus percent of the time. So I did not say anything at first.

When I was asked another question, though, I paused. There was a loud buzzing in my head, the voice of reason saying, "You have the right to remain silent," and the voice of my conscience, insistent. I wanted to express, calmly and eloquently, that people who are pro-choice understand that there are two lives involved in an abortion—one born (the pregnant woman) and one not (the fetus)—and that the born person must be allowed to decide what is right: whether or not to bring a pregnancy to term and launch another life into circulation.

I also wanted to wave a gun around, to show what a real murder looks like. This tipped me off that I should hold my tongue until further notice. And I tried.

But then I announced that I needed to speak out on behalf of the many women present, including myself, who had had abortions, and the women whose daughters might need one in the not-too-distant future. On behalf of people who must know that teenage girls will have abortions, whether in clinics or dirty back rooms. Women whose lives had been righted and redeemed by *Roe v. Wade*.

My answer was met with some applause, but mostly a shocked silence. *Pall* is a good word. It did not feel good to be the cause of that pall. I knew what I was *supposed* to have said as a progressive Christian: that it's all very complicated and painful, and that Jim was right in saying that the abortion rate in the country was way too high for a caring and compassionate society.

But I did the only thing I could think to do: plunge on and tell my truth. I said that this was the most intimate decision a woman could make, and she made it alone, in her deepest heart, though sometimes with the man by whom she was pregnant, with her dearest friends, or with her doctor—but without the personal opinion of, say, Tom DeLay or Karl Rove. I said that I could not *believe* that men committed to equality and civil rights were still challenging the basic rights of women. I thought about the photo op at which President Bush, having signed legislation limiting abortion rights, was surrounded by nine self-righteous white married males, who had probably forced God knows how many girlfriends into doing God knows what. I thought of Bush's public appearance with children born from frozen embryos, whom some people call "snowflake babies," and of the embryos themselves, which he called the youngest and most vulnerable Americans.

And somehow, as I was speaking, I got louder and maybe more emphatic than I actually feel, and said that it was not a morally ambiguous issue for me *at all*. I said that fetuses were not babies yet; that there was actually a difference between pro-choice people, like me, and Klaus Barbie.

Then I said that a woman's right to choose was nobody else's goddamn business.

This got their attention.

A cloud of misery fell over the room, and the stage. At last Jim said something unifying enough for us to proceed: that liberals must not treat with contempt and exclusion people who hold opposing opinions on abortion, partly because it was tough material, and partly because we would never win another election.

Not until the reception afterward did I realize part of my problem—no one had told me that the crowd was made up largely of Catholics. I had flown in at dawn on a red-eye, and in my exhaustion and hibernation I had somehow missed this one tiny bit of information. I was mortified; I had to eat several fistfuls of M&Ms just to calm down.

Then I asked myself: Would I, should I, have given a calmer answer? Wouldn't it have been more effective, and harder to dismiss me, if I had sounded more reasonable, less spewy?

I might have presented my position less stridently, less divisively. But the questioner's use of the words "murder" and "babies" had put me on the defensive. Plus, I was—I am—so confused about why we still have to argue with patriarchal sentimentality about miniscule zygotes, when real, live, already born women—many of them desperately poor—get such short shrift from the government now in power.

Most women like me would much rather use our time and energy to make the world safe and just and fair for the children we do have and do love, not to mention the children of New Orleans and Darfur. I am tired and menopausal and would like for the most part to be left alone: I have had my abortions, and I have had a child.

But as a Christian and a feminist, the most important message I can carry and fight for is the sacredness of each human life, and reproductive rights for all women are a crucial part of that. It is a moral necessity that we not be forced to bring children into the world for whom we cannot be responsible and adoring and present. We must not inflict life on children who will be resented; we must not inflict unwanted children on society.

During the reception, an old woman came up to me and said, "If you hadn't spoken out, I would have spit," and then raised her fist in the power salute. We huddled for a while and ate M&Ms to give us strength. It was a communion for those of us who continue to believe that civil rights and equality, and even common sense, may somehow be sovereign one day.

Signora

by Gigi Rosenberg

I WATCHED THEM at the Piazza Gramsci bus stop as I waited for the number 1 in Siena. Him so close: not touching, but whispering quietly and insistently into her face. I wanted to look away, to leave them to their lovers' privacy, but I couldn't take my eyes off them.

How expressive Italians are in public, compared with us, puritanical Americans, I thought, stealing peeks at them. Then the woman turned her back on the man and he curved around to find her face again, trailing her with his incessant murmurs. Were they lovers? I couldn't tell.

I was on my way to meet Rita, my new Italian friend and "language partner." We met once a week to practice speaking—she her English and I, my beginning Italian. Amidst the double-decker tour buses and Fiats speeding by, the number 1 minibus arrived. I climbed on and so did the woman, sitting right behind me. The man stayed on the sidewalk, his stare drilling a hole in the woman's head while she looked out the opposite window. She was in her twenties, with long brown hair framing a pale face, her body lithe but listless.

Because the bus was ahead of schedule, it idled at the bus stop, doors open. I picked up my book to read. Within a minute, the man climbed on the bus too, muttering words I couldn't decipher. As he closed in on the woman behind me, I saw his dark, bloodshot eyes and inhaled his smell of sweat, old wine, and sleep.

I moved toward the front of the bus and found a seat facing them. Was she in trouble? The handful of others on the bus, mostly single women, didn't seem to notice them. Would she call for help if she needed it?

She turned to him and spoke for the first time, motioning with her hands both a question *(Why are you talking to me?)* and a request *(Leave me alone)*.

I stared at my book. *Let somebody else do something. This isn't my country.*

When I looked up again, the man grabbed his crotch and stuffed his whole package—balls and all—into his hand. Masturbating? An itch? A readjustment?

Come on, people, I thought. *Do something. Why isn't this woman calling for help?* I imagined yelling the one word that my Italian teacher in Oregon had taught me to use if I ever got hassled in Italy: *"Via!"* Or was it *"Vai"? Shit. This isn't my language.*

After four months of living in Siena, I still practiced Italian phrases in my head before I said them. As a foreigner, I was often on high alert in public, scanning body language and facial expressions when the words made no sense.

But while I wasn't a native, I wasn't a tourist anymore, either. After 120 nights of sleeping under windows that opened onto the Piazza del Campo, I felt that Siena was my city, too. I might not have noticed this couple on a bus in Portland. But now I possessed an unusual combination: the alertness of a stranger and the pride of a citizen.

And something else: No matter my nationality, I was now also a mother and, since becoming one nine years earlier, I had discovered the she-bear side of myself. At home, in the States, I had broken up playground fights when no other adults were present to intervene. I had stopped to help lost children in public places until their parents were found. But I'd never before lived on foreign soil as a mother. I didn't know the customs, the nuances. I was at a loss for words. But

I did know this: If this were my daughter, I would want someone to do something, even in a broken language.

My heart beat faster. *Get away from her,* I wanted to shout. *Stay away from this* signorina. That could be my daughter someday. But I didn't want to make a fool of myself. I didn't want anyone to laugh at my Italian. *Maybe those two know each other.* But it was too late to stop myself. *Basta.* Enough was enough.

Because since I had been living in Italy, something else had changed: I had noticed that shopkeepers and my daughter's teachers addressed me as *"Signora."* At first I didn't know they were talking to me. I looked around, expecting to see an aged, buxom beauty dressed to the nines—a real *Signora.* But there was nobody standing next to me. There was just me in my Gap jeans, Birkenstocks, and Patagonia raincoat. I was clearly no Italian. I was no *Signora* either, in my own eyes, but in Italy you become a *Signora* whether you want to or not.

No matter how much I imagined myself an eternal *signorina,* I didn't fool Italians. Was it the American in me that still acted perky and coy, even though I was way past that? Or the middle-aged woman who hadn't looked in the mirror in too long? In Italy I was old—old enough to be a *Signora.*

But *Signora* isn't "ma'am," which I hate—like the bleating of a lamb: weak and of no consequence. *Signora* is grown-up and full-bodied. *Signora* is the staccato stamp of a high-heeled boot. *Signora* is a plunging neckline, revealing the power and beauty of her female body. She is also the gray-skirted grandmother in a long, black sweater, with stockinged legs and flat, lace-up shoes. *Signora* lets her breasts lead the way, whether they are exposed or hidden. She is not perky, coy, or cute. She commands respect. She knows when it is time to stand up.

I stood up.

I remembered that we were on a bus and that buses have drivers.
I found ours at the front behind a half partition—a beautiful, boyish
man with black hair trimmed close. Keeping one eye on the man and
the *signorina*, I leaned into the driver's fresh face and green eyes and
opened my mouth. It was the first time in Italy I didn't rehearse.

"Un uomo disturba una donna qui," I said, which I hoped
meant: "A man disturbs a woman here." I pointed to the back of
the bus. The driver looked at me with the confused look that native
speakers have when their language emerges from a stranger's throat.
He breathed in to speak. But before he could answer, the man backed
up from my *signorina*, twirled to face the door, and wobbled off the
bus with the sea legs of a drunk.

The man never looked at me. But he saw me. *Signoras* cannot
be dismissed.

"Ahh, *tutto bene*," I said to the driver. "All is good."

As I walked back to my seat, down the short aisle, I glanced at
the *signorina*, who locked eyes with me.

"Grazie," she said.

"Niente," I answered, like I'd heard other *Signoras* say. "That
was nothing."

As we pulled away from the stop, down Via Federico, I saw the
man lurch toward a group of robust *signorinas*, his lips moving non-
stop. They listened for an instant and then all turned their backs on
him. They looked tougher than my *signorina*, who had gone back to
staring out the window.

I wanted to ask her: *Did you know him? Why didn't you get
help?* But I tried not to gape. My body cooled down. I read my book.
We descended off one of the seven hills that make up Siena's walled
city, past San Domenico Church, which houses the actual preserved
head and right thumb of Saint Catherine—Italy's patron saint. We

flew past Fortezza di Santa Barbara, then down Strada di Pescaia, past gas stations and stone buildings, a mishmash of the tacky and the medieval.

On Strada dei Cappuccini, two stops before my stop, the *signorina* pushed the button to signal the driver. The bus slowed. She stepped down one step, then two, then turned to face me. Looking me right in the eye, she said, *"Arrivederci."*

"Arrivederci," I echoed, her goodbye reminding me how Italians, unlike Americans, don't arrive or depart without formality: a kiss for friends, a *buon giorno* or *arrivederci* for acquaintances.

The bus doors squeezed shut behind her.

Arrivederci, I thought. Buried in that word is the verb *vedere,* which means "to see," and *ci,* which means "each other." The literal translation of the word is "until we see each other again." Within each Italian goodbye is the promise of the next meeting, the promise that the *Signora* and the *signorina* will meet again.

Later, at Rita's kitchen table, over coffee and sweet bread, I tell her what happened.

"Brava!" she calls me for doing what I did.

"Non era niente," I say. "It was nothing."

For a *Signora,* that *was* nothing.

Raising Small Boys in a Time of War

by Shari MacDonald Strong

DURING THE SUMMER before the 2004 election, I taught my children to call out "Peace!" when I asked, "What do we want?" and "Now!" when I prompted, "When do we want it?" I bought them tiny "JOHN KERRY FOR PRESIDENT" T-shirts. They learned that the question "Who do we want for president?" was their cue to shout out, "John Kerry!" This was also the summer that I taught them this version of call-and-response:

> Me: "Who loves you?"
> Boys: "Mama!"

For weeks, however, my year-and-a-half-old boys mixed up the two:

> Me: "Who loves you?"
> Boys: "John Kerry!"

I always nodded when they said this. "That's right," I told my budding Democrats. "He does. And his policies show it, too."

Other than voting, this was my greatest contribution to the election year, but I didn't worry about my paltry efforts at the time. I live in a state as blue as the Atlantic, where liberal empathy reigns over conservative rigidity, and Democrats generally serve as the voice of the people. I did my civic duty: (a) reminding neighbors, friends, and acquaintances to vote, and (b) urging them to vote Kerry/Edwards. But I'd barely get more than a few words out before the person would say something to the effect of, "Are you *kidding?* I mean, *who's not going to vote?"* When I asked whom they would vote for, people laughed aloud or snickered ironically. As in: "Do you really have to ask?" As in: "Like *anyone* who's been paying the *least bit* of attention would vote for Bush now?" As in: "Oh my god, could you *imagine* what would happen to this country if that moron actually got elected again?"

At the time, we couldn't picture it, didn't dream that the blessed certainty we all felt was, in fact, catastrophic overconfidence. When the Swift Boat Veterans for Telling Bald-Faced Lies started their multimillion-dollar smear campaign against Kerry, I shook my head and thought, *How sad. Do they really think that the country is going to fall for* that?

"What if Bush actually wins?" we moms asked one another in line at the grocery store, at our kids' summer camps, at the office, when we met on the street.

"It won't happen," we would assure one another, shaking our heads. "It *can't*. It would be the worst thing that ever happened to our country, and *people know it*. There's no way they'll let it happen. It won't even be close."

The night of the election, I sat with my knees almost touching the television set, which I'd pulled up near to the couch. When things started looking touch-and-go for the Democrats, at first I enjoyed the moment, imagining it was like the tension of Andre Agassi going one set down before pulling out match point to win a Grand Slam. The stress triggered by those random upsets in swing states, I thought, would make the inevitable Democratic win even sweeter. I figured that the news programs were purposely playing the whole thing up, making the situation look better for the Republicans than it was, just to add to the drama. My husband went to bed at eleven thirty that night, utterly despondent, but I hung on until the early morning hours, convinced it all had to be a crafty news angle, or a mistake, or a joke.

The next morning, I sat on the couch, trying to wrestle my preschool daughter's shoe onto her foot. I couldn't get it on; nothing was working out the way it was supposed to. Dropping one Buster Brown onto the oak hardwood, I pressed my hands to my face and tried to catch my breath.

"What's wrong, Mama?" We had adopted Eugenia from Russia one year earlier. Her voice still sounded a little exotic. She laid one little hand on my arm.

"John Kerry . . . didn't win," I told her, my voice breaking.

Genia considered this. "Well," she said at last, "maybe he'll win today. If he doesn't, call Papa, or call Miss Pamela." She patted my sleeve. "And I'll come home."

I took her in my arms and held her close, crying into the softness of her hair. Eventually, I pulled myself together enough to drive her to school, then spent the rest of the morning pacing the house, clutching my babies—my boys—to my chest, pressing my lips, my fears, against the soft pale skin of their cheeks and necks.

What are we going to do?

I wasn't in despair only about George Bush. A week earlier I had found out that a heart condition I'd been born with had worsened. The doctors had scheduled open-heart surgery for just ten days after the election. In a little more than a week, my body would undergo the most traumatic physical event of my life.

But in some ways the emotional trauma from the election turned out to be worse.

I spent most of November and December convalescing, my broken breastbone slowly knitting itself back together over my bruised heart. One by one, my children tiptoed to my bedside to smile shyly at me, to kiss my fingers, to hold my hand, and—as I grew stronger—to gently snuggle up beside me in my bed. Painfully, I coughed to get my lungs working properly again, as the doctors instructed. I sat up, slowly, gingerly. I got out of bed, I walked. I warmed a cup of broth in the microwave. One day, I was able to lean over and change a diaper again, and this was the best day of all.

Day by day, my health got better.

Day by day, the state of my country got worse.

Years later, my November 2004 surgery is nothing but a thin white scar and a pale memory.

But I think about the consequences of that election every day.

The Butterfly Effect theorizes that the tiniest action—say, of a butterfly flapping its wings—can be felt on the opposite side of the world. I can't imagine where all the effects of the 2004 election are felt, but I'm primarily concerned about its impact on the little people in my home, especially those who will one day be of recruiting age. In an August 2007 interview on National Public Radio's *All Things Considered*, Army Lieutenant General Douglas Lute—George W. Bush's "war czar"—said of a potential military draft: "I think it makes sense to certainly consider it. And I can tell you, this has always been an option on the table."

Of course it has. What *isn't* an option on the table for George W. Bush? Illegal wiretaps? Torture of detainees? The ironically named "Patriot Act"? Sending our country's sons and daughters off to kill and be killed—for what, exactly? To make our country "safer"? Are there truly still U.S. citizens who believe that The Decider's policies have made us anything but more isolated, more mocked, more despised?

After the election, I read that "security moms"—mothers like me, moms who love their children as desperately, as completely, as I love mine (is that possible?)—played a key role in getting Bush re-elected. I have trouble believing it: How can any woman acting out of her deepest mothering instincts support this man, this war? I look around and I feel confused, demoralized. Where are our massive protests? Where are the mobs of mothers? Where is our righteous indignation?

Even I, at my pacifist core, know that a country must be protected in some way. But this? The Bush administration told us we needed to go to war against Iraq because of 9/11—but there wasn't a single Iraqi involved in the attack that day. Why aren't we mothers saying anything? Why, year after year, are we—as dictated by a former baseball team owner and war contractor Halliburton's former CEO—overriding our maternal instincts, continuing to sit by and watch our children, and the Iraqi mothers' children, die? Where is that part of ourselves that would—acting solely on instinct, without question or hesitation or a moment's regret—throw ourselves in front of the bus to save our daughters and sons?

When I think about the U.S. presence in the Middle East, I think about the future. I think about the possibility of a draft. I think about my sons: about Will, my loving, dark-haired charmer, who at five years old still has the velvety skin of a baby, who told me this morning, "Mama, I *googleflex dog dare you*—to buy me a pet cheetah!" Will, who slips into our bed each night to sleep in the circle of my arms; who is miraculously still a little in love with me, and whose most often repeated phrase is: "I want to be with Mama"; whose blue eyes could melt more ice caps than global warming.

I think of Macky, the first of our babies I held, born a half hour after his brother because he turned around in the womb, uncertain that the wider world was a place he wanted to go. Macky, who calls *The Incredibles* "The Increstables" and his sister's orthodontist "the orthodentist," who was born with an extra eye tooth, and who advised me, Buddha-like, one morning last winter after I complained about a

snow day wrecking my schedule: "Nobody knows this day. Not even
this family. Nobody in the whole wide world knows this day."

I think of my daughter, too. Strong and smart: the sort of as-
set any organization, including the armed forces, would want. Since
she's being raised as a Quaker, it's unlikely that she'll ever enter the
military. But my boys, equally strong and smart, may not have the
same options. I wonder what the effects of the United States' actions
in the Middle East today will be in ten, twelve, thirteen years.

"I love you, baby," I say to my sons, and they scowl.

"I'm not a baby, Mama. I'm a *big boy.*" Oh, I know, my sweetie.
I know. And I am proud. But if I could keep you this size forever,
would I? Would I sacrifice your teenage years, teaching you to drive,
watching you fall in love for the first time? Would I give up seeing
you graduate college? Surrender dancing with you at your wedding?
Forfeit grandkids? Would I keep you small, hold you close forever,
if it meant that you would never be big enough to sign a legal document, that you could be neither conscripted nor summoned by Uncle
Sam, that you would never hoist and shoot a gun?

I watch my sons—playing Baby Kitties, playing Spiderman, in the
back yard—and I think, *Over my dead body. I will never let them
get my boys.*

Will shoots me with an invisible gun. "*Pew, pew!*" he shouts,
pointing a finger in my direction.

"Honey, we don't play shooting games, remember?"

"But," Will says, "I'm shooting *love.*"

The war plotters will have to go through me first, I think. *I will
never let them get within one hundred feet of my children.*

But how many mothers throughout history have mistakenly
thought this very thing—that they could protect their children

through the power of mother love alone? How many mothers tried—
and failed—to keep their sons from being shipped off to Vietnam,
clutching their boys' arms, begging them to flee to Canada? How
many Iraqi mothers have prayed similar words before a bomb or
mortar shell or contaminated water caused the breath to be extin-
guished from lips that once nursed at their breasts?

Is it arrogance? Privilege? Naiveté? What makes me think that
I can somehow save my boys if the worst happens, when so many
other mothers could not?

And if there is nothing I can do when the time comes, is there
something—anything—I can do now?

Three years after the 2004 election, our family is vacationing on an
island just south of the Canadian border. The children and Craig
are back at the beach, wading through tide pools and stomping on
the sand, making the "gooey duck" clams squirt. I'm at an Internet
café, reading through submissions for the magazine where I work,
but George W. Bush's face bears down on me from the widescreen
monitor mounted high on the wall.

"They are dangerous people," he says with smug certainty,
"and they need to be confronted." I'm not sure who "they" are,
which "dangerous people" he's talking about now. Iraqis, Afghanis,
Iranians? Does it matter?

"Idiot," I mutter. I try to imagine doling out this "advice" to one
of my children. "Honey, you know that dangerous boy in your class?
I want you to go in there and *confront* him!"

I still can't believe this is my country's president.

I look out the window, trying to catch a glimpse of the Canadian
Rockies, just north of here. I picture an imaginary line, drawing the
waters between the U.S. San Juan Islands and the Canadian San Juans
in two. *So close,* I think. *Just a simple ferry ride.*

"All these liberals who hate the country so much . . . " My dad spits out the words, each one a bitter seed. "They should just leave, go live somewhere else. They're as bad as the Frogs." He resents the French for openly despising U.S. tourists; he's still angry at them for not showing enough gratitude after World War II. Something about de Gaulle.

"Maybe they'd like to," I say. "Maybe they'd rather live someplace else than have their sons killed for a war about oil." I don't tell him that I'm tempted to move to another country myself, but he looks at me like he suspects it. My dad loathes my politics with the fire of a thousand hot, burning suns. But if I could prove to him that those same politics would save his grandsons' lives someday, I doubt that he'd quibble.

Because I don't want the political questions about motherhood and government to be rhetorical, I sign up for a Women and Politics class at a local university—hoping to find some answers, a road map, some hope. One day, a classmate announces that her biggest worry about the war is that someday women will be drafted.

"I think women should be subject to the draft to the same degree that men are," I say. I think about my daughter. Would I be willing to let my sons die so that I could save her? The question is absurd. "Which is to say, none of them should be."

I remember the ending of Andre Dubus's "A Father's Story," about a devout Catholic father who comes to the aid of his daughter under tragic circumstances. The man prays—contrasting his own defense and protection of his daughter with a male god's sacrifice of his son. "I could bear the pain of watching and knowing my sons' pain," the man says, "could bear it with pride as they took the whip and nails. But You never had a daughter and, if You had, You could not have borne her Passion."

The woman in my class reconsiders. "I don't know. Maybe if women were drafted, that would be the end of it. People would rise up and stop the war."

It occurs to me that, while people are aware that courageous and brilliant women serve in the military, we still think of the armed forces as largely male; I realize that the majority of U.S. casualties in Iraq and Afghanistan still are men. I wonder, *What is it that makes us willing collectively to bear our sons' Passion in a way that we would not our daughters'?* And I wonder if the woman from my class is right.

On the morning after the 2004 election, the first thing I did was cry. The second thing I did was Google "Canada" and "immigration." I wasn't the only one. Reuters reported that on that Wednesday, the Canadian immigration website, which usually gets 20,000 visits per day, received more than 115,000 hits.

But, painful as it feels at times, the United States *is* my home. It's here that I voted for the first time (for a Republican, god help me), here that I became a feminist. Here that my babies were born, here that I hope to die (preferably many decades from now), here that I watch *The Daily Show* and *The Colbert Report*. Here that I became a mother.

In other words, this is the place where—at least for now, in more ways than not—I'm still free to be myself, still free to stand up and fight, still free to use my voice: to teach my children to resolve conflict peacefully, to call my representatives, to march, to protest, to run for office if I want. To fundraise, to (wo)man the phone banks, to vote, to join or start a movement. To say whatever I want. To call my president a moron. (And I do.)

Our culture doesn't tell me—as a woman, as a mother—that I can change the world. But no one's stopping me, either—not really.

Yes, we live in a patriarchal society, in a culture where far too many people care more about what's on their television set than about who wins the White House or who's dying on the other side of the world. But people can change. Somebody just has to lead them. I'm hoping that—starting now—it will be the mothers. We are the ones who guide the children we love in their journey to become the very best human beings they can be—the wisest, the most compassionate; the most generous, discerning, and circumspect.

There's no reason on earth we can't do it for our country, too.

Thankfully, there's another election coming. And another one after that. Of course, no one knows what the outcome will be. My boy is right: *Nobody in the whole wide world knows this day.*

But I do know that I'll be in it up to my elbows, that I'll be fighting harder than ever before. I know that I'm ready to stand in the street, to wave my arms in the air, to do everything I can to stop that runaway bus. Because that's what mothers do.

And, for that matter, fathers—and people without kids. I saw that this last summer, when I dragged a fold-up wooden chair out to the parking strip so I could watch our children playing in the front yard while my husband worked inside the house, some fifty feet away. I was sitting in the sun, reading a book and watching the kids crashing across the green grass, when an old Lincoln pulled up in front of the house and the driver shouted something at our family.

I turned and saw that he was waving an arm at the sign we had posted on the corner, among the weeds: WAR IS NOT THE ANSWER. A woman sat beside him.

"Is right!" the man shouted at my daughter. "No war! Not the answer." I couldn't place his accent.

My daughter smiled and waved back at him and then took up the cry. "War is not the answer!" she called. "War is not the answer!" And she rode down the sidewalk on her old red Schwinn Stingray, ringing the bell like a modern-day, reverse-order Paul Revere: calling U.S. citizens not to fight, but to disarm.

I watched her go, then looked back at the couple in the car, and we smiled at one another. As the man cranked the wheel and turned his car back into the street, Will dug in the mud and Macky rolled away on his orange-handled scooter, and I took a picture in my mind to preserve this perfect summer day when we were all together, and everyone was alive and whole and safe.

The Mother is Standing

by Denise Roy

The practice of the presence of the Mother
Demands and gives everything.
    —Andrew Harvey, *Son of Man*

I WAS A GOODY TWO-SHOES for much of my life. I rarely broke a rule, even a grammatical one. Although I've grown more comfortable with breaking rules as I've aged, the fact that I was about to be arrested was still a stretch for me.

It was a beautiful Good Friday morning. Paul and I carpooled with other members of our church community to a sunrise service held at the gates of Lawrence Livermore National Laboratory. We had come to join with hundreds of other people—women and men, nuns and priests, children, the healthy and the sick—to pray in quiet witness for peace as we walked the Stations of the Cross at the nuclear weapons facility.

We parked and walked toward the crowd gathering at the corner. Truck drivers passing by honked their support. I waved across the street to men in black SUVs who sat sipping coffee and keeping an eye on things. Several unmarked helicopters buzzed overhead.

"I've got to go to the bathroom," I told Paul. I slogged through the mud to the blue porta-potty that had been set up for our group's use. That was the first of five trips I would take to the bathroom.

Originally, I hadn't planned to participate in the civil disobedience. But earlier in the week, I woke up and heard myself say, "It's time for you to cross the line."

Those of us who were going to kneel in the road to the entrance
of the lab wore cloth stoles around our necks. Other people wrote
their names on our stoles, symbolizing that we were taking them all
along with us. Paul wrote his name and our children's names on my
stole, and the people from our church wrote theirs as well.

Our group moved together to the first station and began to sing a
familiar song. It was "Stabat Mater," which is Latin for "The Mother
Was Standing." At each station we sang it:

> At the cross her station keeping,
> Stood the mournful Mother weeping,
> Close to Jesus to the last.

When I was a little girl, I attended Catholic elementary school,
and each Friday during Lent, we processed over to the church to
make the Stations of the Cross. At each station, we sang this song
with its haunting melody; even then, it made me cry. A mother is
staying with her son—her only child—as he is dying. Her heart is
broken; she is unable to prevent his death, but she stays. She remains
faithful in her great love for him.

She stayed. That's the thing. She stayed. The men ran away, fearing arrest, but the women stayed, and the mother stayed. She stood
with her son in silent and grieving witness. When she was pregnant
with him, she was the mother who sang the Magnificat—that song of
praise to the Holy One who sides with the poor and with those who
suffer injustice. She had raised her son singing that prayer.

I didn't know it when I was a little girl, but this mother was
becoming part of me; she was inviting me into her vision. She modeled how a mother stands, stays, bears witness, prays, and will not
be moved.

That morning at the lab, as we walked the fourteen stations, we
prayed and sang, over and over, "Stabat Mater." Finally, we arrived
at the gate. There were so many men wearing suits; some worked

at the lab, others at Homeland Security. There were even more riot police, dressed in full gear—helmets, reflective visors, bully sticks, Mace. My stomach did a somersault. I said a quick prayer.

A line of fifteen riot police marched across the road by the gate, their boots pounding in unison. Ten members of our group filed quietly in front of them and then knelt in the road. From the sidelines, I looked at the police officers and was surprised to see how young they were. Most were not much older than my sons. They did not speak or look at anyone, although Paul, ever the comedian, got one to crack a smile at a joke.

Some members of our group weren't able to kneel because their knees were too arthritic. Several women had MS; they hobbled to their place on the road using their canes. One by one, each person was read the official demand to leave or be arrested. One by one they refused. They were helped to their feet by an officer and escorted through the gates to be handcuffed and processed.

We began to sing a Taizé song, "Ubi Caritas": "Where charity and love prevail, there is God." Over and over, we sang, and the music helped me to drop into my heart. I realized I wasn't afraid anymore. Crossing the line may not change what happens at the lab, but it had changed me. I knew that this was exactly where I needed to be: praying on this Good Friday with this little hobbled group of people, witnessing the fact that we see, that we care, that we protest the normal way of doing things, that we believe in resurrection. I looked at the faces of the police and the lab officials and realized that it was likely that they, too, all wanted peace. I prayed for all of us.

As the first line emptied, I joined the second group and knelt in the road. After a few moments, an officer came to arrest me. A reporter from a local news station was there, and she put a microphone up to me as I was being led away. "Why are you doing this?" she asked. "For my children," I heard myself say.

The police took us to the side of the road, asked us to remove everything except our basic clothing, and then handcuffed us. Large white vans were waiting to take us to holding pens on the other side of the facility. As I got into one, I saw a friend of mine already in the back seat. He introduced me to others in the van, and we discovered that many of our paths had crossed before. We were taken to the outdoor pens, and ten or so people were locked up in each. The guards kindly brought folding chairs for the women with MS to sit on while they waited for processing.

Eventually, I was escorted into a large warehouse to be fingerprinted and photographed. There were tables set up, like at a college registration, and women sitting at different stations to take down our information. They issued me a citation and said that I would hear within several weeks whether the district attorney would prosecute. Then they took me to another, larger holding pen, where I met one of my professors from my seminary training twenty-five years ago. After a while, we were taken to another van, driven outside the gates, and released. I met Paul and our friends, and we left to go to our church's Good Friday service.

Our protest on that Good Friday morning did not change the world, at least as far as we can see. Nevertheless, it changed me, and it changed our community. A reporter once asked A. J. Muste—a social activist who, during the Vietnam War, stood outside the White House night after night—"Mr. Muste, do you really think you are going to change the policies of this country by standing out here alone at night with a candle?"

"Oh," Muste replied, "I don't do this to change the country. I do this so the country won't change me."

When I am willing to cross the line of how much I think I can love, I am changed. When I am more in touch with what I love than with what I fear, I take a stand. My prayer is that more and more of us, on behalf of all children, will use the energy of a mother to touch the seeds of courage and love within us for the sake of the world.

The Mother is standing. And the Mother is a multitude when we stand together.

Peace March Sans Children

by Valerie Weaver-Zercher

IT IS SIX THIRTY on a Saturday morning in January. I am walking sleepily around the house, piling on layers of socks and shirts and packing water and sandwiches. Lacing up my hiking boots, I catch a glimpse of my bulky parka and mama-cut jeans. I reach for lip balm in my coat pocket and instead pull out two pacifiers and a lollipop stick. I am heading to an antiwar march, and I look like I am headed to playgroup.

I haven't been to a real protest in years. Since I had children, vigils and marches have gone the way of candlelit dinners and New Year's Eve parties. Before having kids, and even during the first few years of parenthood, I considered myself something of an activist. I ran the peace and justice club in college, protested the first Iraq war, went to anti–death penalty rallies, helped to plan a peace vigil after 9/11, and organized a church group to advocate for Palestinian villagers whose homes were threatened with demolition. Even after the babies started coming, I still thought I could do the usual activist shtick. I fancied myself one of those calm, collected mama types who do occasionally appear at rallies, with children strapped into various combinations of stroller, sling, and backpack.

After a couple attempts at activist multitasking, however—standing on a street corner downtown, holding an antiwar sign while the baby howled in the sling and the toddler tried to fling himself in front of passing cars—I gave up. Recently, I felt good if I had enough energy to go to one of those activist websites, where all you have to do is type in your name and address and click "send."

Motherhood had catapulted me from a world of ripped-jean, defiant idealism into sleep-deprived, thirtysomething cynicism. While I don't fully buy the idea that standing on a street corner with a sign can change anything, before kids, I could afford to sustain the temporary illusion that it might. After kids, the luxury of dreaming had abandoned me, and I had eventually stopped praying for much more than the baby to stop crying, the toddler to start sleeping, and the preschooler to stop talking. Three children in five years had simply knocked my activist self—along with my erotic self, professional self, and all the other selves I could think of—into a coma. I comforted myself with something I'd heard one time about the comatose—that when they awaken, they rarely remember the pain.

Although my youngest son was now two years old, I was still awakening, bleary-eyed, from the stupor of early parenthood. Looking around at my strange new surroundings—three sons, a mortgage, and a country at war again—I realized that the adult complacency that I'd been griping about for years often has less to do with *not* caring about important issues and more to do with caring *a lot*—for the young.

Caring for the world or caring for the kids: It seemed counterintuitive, even wrong, that the two would be incompatible. Yet I couldn't deny that, in my own life at least, the two were as quarrelsome as brothers vying for the attention of their mother.

A mother who was just waking up.

The day before the march, a newspaper reporter, having found my contact information on a peace calendar I used to edit, calls to ask if I am going to the protest in D.C. At precisely the same moment that I pick up the ringing phone, the toddler yanks the hair of the four-year-old, who promptly falls off his kitchen stool.

"Hello, this is Valerie speaking," I say into the receiver as little boys begin to pummel each other at my ankles. I cannot hear anything above the screaming and crying except "reporter" and "march tomorrow" and "questions." After twisting free from the wrestling championship taking place on my linoleum, I move into the living room, a finger pressed against my free ear. The wrestlers change venues and follow me, still screeching and writhing. I hear the caller suggest, drily, that I call him back when things are a little calmer. That sounds good, I say, until I realize that I will not be able to hear his name or phone number, and that the pens and paper down the hall might as well be in Nepal. I suggest that he call back in half an hour, click off the phone, and stomp around the living room, yelling at my little wrestlers who are now, quite prudently, racing into corners to hide. So much for the peaceable kingdom.

Later, when the youngest is sleeping and the older two are watching a video, the reporter calls back. He asks me to talk about the reasons I am going to the march. I come up with something pretty decent, about how I believe that the war has only made the world more dangerous, how I worry about its eventual impact on my sons' futures, and how invading a sovereign country based on false information probably hasn't won us many friends.

I do not tell him my ulterior motives for going to the march, the ones that I have not quite admitted to myself yet. I do not tell him that I am going to this march to remind myself that I am more than a suburban housewife and mother. I don't mention that I am going because I want to remember what it feels like to care about more than how to keep lettuce fresh, how to clean curtains, or how to calibrate the length of time-outs to a child's age.

That afternoon a photographer comes to take my picture to go along with the article in the next day's paper. He cases out our first floor and the basement, looking for good light. Do I have any signs that I plan to carry that I could hold for the photograph, he asks. No, I say. Some peace paraphernalia that could serve as a backdrop, perhaps? Not really, I tell him. I do have a little WOMEN AGAINST WAR lapel button, I offer hopefully. Yeah, I guess you can go ahead and put that on, he says flatly. He seems disappointed.

I think he was looking for someone a little more picturesque. A hippie with dreadlocks, maybe, or at least a *keffiyeh* or a tie-dyed shirt. Instead he got me: a suburban mother of three, in jeans and a nondescript sweater, looking forward to getting out of the house for a day.

The article appeared in the paper the next day. The photo didn't.

On the subway into the city, a toddler sits in his stroller next to his mom while his father films him with his video camera and narrates. "This is Paulie going to his first peace march. Wave, Paulie! Paulie is convinced that this war is being waged on false information. He thinks that our military action in Iraq is the latest in a string of colonialist actions by our government in a postcolonial world. Right, Paulie?" The rest of us on the train smile and laugh—most of us are headed to the peace march, too. Someone gives a thumbs-up to wide-eyed, drooling Paulie and his savvy political opinions.

"Wouldn't that be great to take your kids to a peace march!" one of the college students who has traveled with me intones enthusiastically as she turns back from watching Paulie. *Yeah, right,* I think. I had considered bringing one of my own children along to the march, probably the middle one, who throws the fewest tantrums these days. For several days I had lovely daydreams of holding a son's hand as we strolled along the length of the Mall, listening to speakers and musicians hold forth against the war. I imagined my son growing up with the memory of this march slowly blooming in his mind, and visualized his long and illustrious career as an international mediator, or at least his avocation as a peace activist against whatever wars our country is waging in 2030.

Then I visualized the long line of porta-potties that would be my recently potty-trained son's only place to pee. I remembered the state farm show that we attended with all three kids a couple weeks earlier, with its surging crowds that threatened to engulf my sons and carry them away in an undertow of pants and purses and cowboy boots, and I knew—even hoped—that this crowd would be bigger. I imagined all the snacks and water and books and mittens and hats I would have to bring along. And I decided to go alone.

On the subway I silently wish Paulie's parents the best, thanking God that it's them and not me. I ask God to someday bless that lovely college student with three young sons so that she can have the pleasure of taking them with her—in a car and then a tour bus and then a subway and then a half-mile walk—to a peace march.

When we get to the Mall, I see a crowd that would probably disappoint the newspaper photographer as much as I did. There are a few activist caricatures here, men with grizzled beards and earrings and women with peasant skirts and hennaed hair. There are some college students looking for a party, the women in sleeveless shirts and jeans holding their fingers in peace signs while riding on the shoulders of young men with long manes. Mostly, though, there are a bunch of nondescript folks. Pimply-faced teenagers. Stooping elderly folks searching out benches. Well-dressed women in gray woolen pants and fuchsia hats. Middle-aged people wearing parkas and hiking boots. Humdrum Americans just like me.

The crowd is thin at first, and the small cluster of us who came together talk about walking around a bit, seeing who else we might know. Before too long, however, walking around has become virtually impossible. We are hemmed in on all sides by people. Even turning around soon requires scraping someone else's hips or bumping your head into some tall person's armpit. We chant and sing and shout and listen to people like Jesse Jackson and Maxine Waters and Jane Fonda. I do not hear much of what they say, because I'm getting a headache.

After a while, we begin to march, except that there are so many people that we are not going anywhere. Everyone takes a couple of steps toward the left, as if we're dancers carefully, slowly practicing our moves. We move forward a little, then stop, then creep, then stop again. After fifteen minutes of this, I begin to think that we look a lot less like a graceful dance company in rehearsal and a lot more like a flock of stodgy, befuddled sheep.

We finally start moving in earnest, and I concentrate on staying with the people I know. We meet up with some more friends, and now we're a crew of about twenty trying to stay together in a crowd of one hundred thousand. This is no easy task, now that we're moving faster. We crane our necks and call to each other and motion other people past, and at one point we accidentally get off the march route and find ourselves standing in line for hot dogs. About halfway through the march, we start singing hymns, and that seems to keep us together better than anything else. Other people around us watch awhile and then start to join in. Someone hands my friend Jonathan a bullhorn. "Okay, people, now we're going to do 'We are marching 'cause we hate this war.' Join us!" he calls, loving every moment of his march-within-a-march fame.

By the time we get back to the Mall, it is late afternoon. We smile at the police officers, who wave us off the route, and we head for the subway. The trains are packed, and we finally squeeze onto one at the time when we're already supposed to be back on our bus, ten stops away. The bus waits for us and a few other stragglers, then crawls out of the parking lot toward home.

I lean my head against the bus window and close my eyes. My headache is worse, but I am strangely unbothered by it. In my chest I am feeling that old, familiar activist exhilaration that always follows the chants and steps and songs. I am feeling more hopeful than I have in a long time that maybe the will of the people can actually stop a war.

I am also feeling a yearning that I didn't feel as a college student activist, a yearning that can only be a fraction of what the thousands of mothers of dead American soldiers and thousands of mothers of dead Iraqis must feel. In my chest I am missing my sons, even though I have been away for only a day. I am missing them in that place where rib meets rib. And I am imagining the unspeakable horror of missing them there, every day, for the rest of my life.

Someday I'll take my kids to a peace march. I'll teach them about democracy, about their family's religious tradition that calls us to be peacemakers, and about what it means to demand that their government account for illegal and immoral actions. For now, though, I'm content to let them stay home with their books and their bikes and their daddy.

I have also stopped expecting that caring needs to be a whole and perfect project, like an unsliced loaf of homemade bread. I am coming to accept that, at least for me, caring about the world is much more fragmented, much more like a store-bought loaf that splays open as soon as you open the bag. Here's a slice of caring about antipoverty legislation, here's one of caring for my three-year-old with the flu, here's a slice of caring for victims of our country's warring— and, whoops, here's even a slice of caring about my curtains. I have stopped imagining that caring is pure and unselfish; many people, including me, fashion their identities out of caring, whether for kids or for the world. Still: Bread is bread, and caring is caring. Whole or broken. Homemade or purchased. Consumed or given away.

I'm also learning that social movements will go on, even if nursing mothers or parents of toddlers have to drop out for a while. We will be back, someday, maybe when the youngest turns two or whenever we can again afford to dream like activists, rather than work like dogs. We may be more distracted than before, less available for four-hour brainstorming sessions on how to stick it to the Man. But when we return, we will give a break to someone else who needs it—like those erstwhile college students who may be finding that carting babies to marches is harder than they anticipated.

And when we do rejoin the movement, it is possible that we will agitate and march and advocate from a deeper place within ourselves than we had known existed. It is possible that we will act from that cavity our children have hollowed out of us, that place where breath begins.

ACKNOWLEDGMENTS

OH, HOW I THANK the masses of mothers and others who have walked with, supported, carried, and loved me on this journey. To all the Literary Mamas, especially Amy Hudock, who gave me a chance; Jennifer Margulis, who taught me vast amounts about editing. Kate Haas, for being wise first eyes; Caroline Grant, for sharing the burden and adventure; Marjorie Osterhout and Stephanie Hunt for wisely and skillfully guiding me; Sonya Huber and Susan Ito (and Kate, again) for your patience; and particularly, *especially,* the generous and brilliant Andi Buchanan, for opening those crucial first doors.

To my marvelous agent, Linda Loewenthal, for getting excited about the project and selling it, and to my team at Seal Press—Brooke Warner, Krista Lyons-Gould, Laura Mazer, Wendy Taylor, Andie East, and Dylan Wooters—who "got" and loved the concept from the start. To those women who from the beginning gave me encouraging nods or told me, *Yes, yes, yes, you have to do this!,* including Miriam Peskowitz, Kate Moses, Ann Crittenden, Ariel Gore, Jennifer Baumgardner and Amy Richards, Susan Straight, and Debra Ollivier. To Kim Heggen, for believing in me for the last thirty-five years, and to Liz Heaney, for being the first one who told me I could do it. Thank you, Linera Lucas, for inviting me to your lovely book club, and for connecting me with Mary and Gigi. For making my life easier, not more difficult, during deadline crunch time: Melanie Booth, Meg Roland, and Jackie Fowler. For minimizing my bumbling, thank you, Joel and Heidi Roberts. For a room of my own, thank you, Nella and James Coe, and Erik Smith. For starting it all, Brenda Edin.

Because I'd be nowhere without my dearly loved friends, I must mention especially Sarah Krick, An and Melissa Vu, Lindy Warren Lowry, Kate Melo Wadnizak, Michelle O'Neil, Rachelle Mee-Chapman, Stephanie Drury, Margaret "Thereby Hangs a Tale" Foley, Michelle Freedman, Melanie Weidner, Jayne Calkins, Erica Huber, Dover Norris-York, Claire Nail, and all my West Hills Friends. Because I'd be nowhere without my sanity and soul, I thank those who have helped me connect with myself and with God/Spirit: Steve Spotts, Stan Thornberg, Mirae Grant, Dena DeCastro, Mike Huber, Laurie Schaad, Karen Maezen Miller, and Khadim Chishti.

Because this book would be nothing but blank pages without them—and because they've energized me to a degree I wouldn't have dreamt possible—thank you to the brilliant, much-loved contributors of this book, who have been a powerful inspiration to me and have also become valued friends: Your encouragement, enthusiasm, hard work, extraordinary talent, and love notes have made my life infinitely richer.

To Erin Leichty, Amy Mathews, and Laurie Gill, for loving my children (and me) and for providing much-needed time during which to write; and to Pamela Cripe, Stephanie Fisher-Hunt, and Denee Longen for helping us to raise good citizens.

To my sweet and wonderful mom and dad, Mac and Jean, and the rest of my conservative family and friends (some of whom are listed on this page, and some of whom may hyperventilate at what they read in this book), who continue to love me despite the shock of my turning out to be such a hard-leaning lefty, and to my progressive friends and relatives, who share the journey with me—equal thanks.

And of course—*of course!*—thank you to the brilliant girlfriends who started me on the journey: Bridget Culpepper, Susan Hall, and Dr. Jennifer Bird. To Jolene Lyon, without whose sacrifice and goodness I would have none of my children. To my sweet, funny, gentle, openhearted children—Eugenia, Will, and Mac—for the snuggles, for the love, and for giving me every reason in the world to do this important work. Finally, to my sweetheart, Craig Strong, who is as brilliant as he is handsome, as sweet as he is funny, the champion of pillow origami, and my best friend in the world.

ABOUT THE CONTRIBUTORS

MARY AKERS'S work has appeared or is forthcoming in *Primavera, Xavier Review, Brevity, Literary Mama, Wisconsin Review,* and other journals. She has received 2004, 2005, and 2006 Bread Loaf work-study scholarships and is a graduate of the Queens University of Charlotte MFA program in creative writing.

CAROLYN ALESSIO is the recipient of an NEA Literature Fellowship for 2008. Her work appears regularly in the *Chicago Tribune* and *The Chronicle of Higher Education,* and has appeared in the Pushcart Prize anthology. Her essay "Citizens of Thebes" was one of "100 Notable Essays" for *The Best American Essays* of 2006.

BENAZIR BHUTTO was the two-time Prime Minister of Pakistan (1988–1990 and 1993–1996), the author of *Daughter of the East: An Autobiography* and *Foreign Policy in Perspective,* chairwoman of the Pakistan People's Party, daughter of former prime minister of Pakistan Zulfikar Ali Bhutto, and the mother of three children. She was assassinated on December 27, 2007, two months after her return to Pakistan following years of exile, at the conclusion of a political rally held in Rawalpindi, Pakistan.

GAYLE BRANDEIS is the author of *Fruitflesh: Seeds of Inspiration for Women Who Write, Dictionary Poems, The Book of Dead Birds,* which won Barbara Kingsolver's Bellwether Prize for Fiction in Support of a Literature of Social Change, and her latest novel, *Self*

Storage. Other cool Barbara-related words include a grant from the Barbara Deming Memorial Fund for Women and a Barbara Mandigo Kelly Peace Poetry Award. Gayle was named a Writer Who Makes a Difference by *The Writer* magazine. She is on the national staff of CODEPINK: Women for Peace and is a founding member of the Women Creating Peace Collective. Mom to two teenagers, Arin and Hannah, Gayle lives, teaches, writes, and works for social justice in Southern California.

KATHY BRICCETTI'S work has appeared or is forthcoming in *Dos Passos Review, Under the Sun, So to Speak, upstreet, Bark, The Writer,* the *Chicago Tribune,* and the *San Francisco Chronicle Magazine.* Her essays have been broadcast on public radio and re-printed in several anthologies. She won Honorable Mention in flash-quake's Micro-Flash Fiction contest and was a finalist in the 2007 Writers at Work competition. One of her essays was nominated for a Pushcart Prize in 2007, and she was awarded a residency at Vermont Studio Center in 2008. She has an MFA from Stonecoast and is at work on a memoir, from which "Adoption in III Acts" is excerpted. For more information, see her website at www.kathybriccetti.com.

SUSIE BRIGHT is the host of the podcast *In Bed with Susie Bright,* series editor of *The Best American Erotica,* editor of *Three Kinds of Asking for It* and *Three the Hard Way,* and the author of *Mommy's Little Girl: On Sex, Motherhood, Porn, and Cherry Pie; Full Exposure: Opening Up to Your Sexual Creativity and Erotic Expression; The Sexual State of the Union;* and *How to Write a Dirty Story: Reading, Writing, and Publishing Erotica.*

JENNIFER BRISENDINE is a freelance writer and public school teacher in Pennsylvania. Currently, she freelances for a small educational publisher and teaches eleventh-grade English part-time. Her feature articles have appeared in the fiction database NoveList, and her creative nonfiction has appeared in *Literary Mama*. She is married and has one son.

SARAH WERTHAN BUTTENWIESER went to Hampshire College and the MFA Program for Writers at Warren Wilson College. Her work has appeared in anthologies, as well as the *Southwest Review*, *Literary Mama, Brain, Child, Bitch* magazine, *Mamazine, hip mama*, and the Mothers Movement Online, among others.

J. ANDERSON COATS is a writer living north of Seattle. Her essays have appeared in *off our backs, MotherVerse,* and *Mamaphonic: Balancing Motherhood and Other Creative Acts* (Soft Skull, 2004). She has a cool surgery scar unrelated to childbirth, and she's been given the curse of Cromwell on a back road in Connemara.

ANN DOUGLAS is the author of *The Mother of All Pregnancy Books* and numerous other books about pregnancy and motherhood. She and her daughter Julie cowrote the award-winning preteen body-image book *Body Talk: Straight Facts About Fitness, Nutrition, and Feeling Great About Yourself.* A card-carrying optimist (when she's not suffering from an acute case of political heartbreak), Ann continues to work behind the scenes on her local candidate's political campaign in Peterborough, Ontario, and to blog about making change at www.onewomanoneblog.com.

MONA GABLE is a writer whose articles and essays have appeared in the *Los Angeles Times* Sunday magazine, *Ladies' Home Journal, Family Circle, Health, Los Angeles* magazine, and *Salon,* among numerous other publications. Her essays have been anthologized in two best-selling collections, *Mothers Who Think: Tales of Real-Life Parenthood* and *A Cup of Comfort for Mothers and Daughters*. She also blogs on politics for The Huffington Post. She is currently writing a memoir about her mother's lobotomy.

NINA GABY is a writer, visual artist, and advanced-practice psychiatric nurse living in central Vermont with her husband, teenage daughter, two cats, one dog, and a few fish. She has previously been published in the Seal Press anthology *I Wanna Be Sedated*, as well as in other collections, both print and online. She has currently taken on the international Write a Novel in a Month challenge and is completing a very messy first draft of a novel she has kept notes on for years, putting her postmenopausal insomnia to good use.

VIOLETA GARCIA-MENDOZA is a Spanish American poet, writer, and teacher. Her poetry has appeared in *Mamazine*, *Tattoo Highway*, the *Pittsburgh Post-Gazette*, *Cicada*, and *Soleado*, and her prose has appeared in *Literary Mama*, where she is coeditor of the Literary Reflections department. Violeta posts Bluestocking columns and Bookshelf recommendations on her website, Turn People Purple (www.turnpeoplepurple.com), and writes about food, family, and the writing life in her blog, "Feed Your Loves" (http://feedyourloves .wordpress.com). Violeta lives in Pennsylvania with her husband and three children, all three of whom are Guatemalan-born.

ALISA GORDANEER lives and writes on an urban homestead in Victoria, B.C., Canada, with her husband and two small kids. She is currently working on a novel, a poetry collection, and a collection of essays. Her work has appeared in anthology publications including *My Wedding Dress*, *Three-Ring Circus*, *Women Who Eat*, *Breeder*, *Love and Pomegranates*, and *Threshold: Six Women, Six Poets*, as well as in a variety of periodicals. She has written several career guides and won numerous awards for her journalism and poetry, including the 2005 Dorothy Sargent Rosenberg Award and the 2005 Nuclear Age Peace Foundation's Barbara Mandigo Kelly Award.

ONA GRITZ'S second book for children, *Tangerines and Tea: My Grandparents and Me,* was named Best Alphabet Book of 2005 by *Nick Jr. Family Magazine* and one of the six best children's books of the year by *Scholastic Parent & Child* magazine. Her poetry has been published in numerous online and print literary journals. In 2007, she won the Inglis House poetry contest and the Late Blooms Poetry Postcard competition, and was nominated for two Pushcart Prizes. Her chapbook of poems, *Left Standing,* was released by Finishing Line Press in 2005. A columnist for *Literary Mama,* Ona's essays have also appeared in the anthology *It's a Boy: Women Writers on Raising Sons, Philly Mama, Stone Table Review,* and the forthcoming anthology *A Cup of Comfort for Single Moms.* Ona lives in Hoboken, New Jersey, with her eleven-year-old son.

JENNIFER GRAF GRONEBERG is a wife, a mother, and a writer. Her most recent book, *Road Map to Holland,* is about being a mother to Avery. She maintains a blog, "Pinwheels," for parents of children with Down syndrome, and you can read more about her and her family at www.jennifergrafgroneberg.com.

KRIS MALONE GROSSMAN studied at UC Berkeley and Sarah Lawrence College and really does hang her diplomas in the laundry room. She makes her home in southwestern Connecticut with her husband and three sons.

JANE HAMMONS lives with her two sons in the San Francisco Bay Area and teaches writing at UC Berkeley, where she is the recipient of a Distinguished Teaching Award. She is the senior editor for *Mom Writer's Literary Magazine* and has published both fiction and non-fiction in *Alaska Quarterly Review, Brain, Child: The Magazine for Thinking Mothers, Natural Bridge, Rhino, River Walk Journal, Slow Trains, taint,* and *Word Riot.* Her writing has twice been nominated for Pushcart Prizes.

MARRIT INGMAN is the author of *Inconsolable: How I Threw My Mental Health Out with the Diapers* and a regular contributor to *The Austin Chronicle.* Her writing has also appeared in *Brain, Child, Isthmus, The Coast Weekly,* AlterNet, *Clamor,* the *Anchorage Press, Charleston City Paper, Venus, Mamalicious,* and other publications. She has contributed to various anthologies, including *Mamaphonic: Mothering and Other Creative Acts,* from Soft Skull Press; *Secrets and Confidences: The Complicated Truth About Women's Friendships,* from Seal Press; and *The Risks of Sunbathing Topless and Other Funny Stories from the Road,* also from Seal Press. She has taught at Boston University, Springfield College, and Southwestern University.

SUSAN ITO, creative nonfiction coeditor at *Literary Mama,* lives in Oakland with her husband, two daughters, and mother. She is the coeditor of *A Ghost at Heart's Edge: Stories & Poems of Adoption.* She has been awarded fellowships and residencies at MacDowell, Blue Mountain Center, and Hedgebrook. Her essays and fiction have appeared widely, including in *Growing Up Asian American, Hip Mama, Making More Waves,* the *Bellevue Literary Review,* and most recently, the anthologies *CHOICE* and *For Keeps.* She writes a monthly column at *Literary Mama,* "Life in the Sandwich," and maintains a weblog, "ReadingWritingLiving" (http://readingwriting living.wordpress.com).

AMY L. JENKINS holds an MFA in literature and writing from Bennington College. Her recent publishing credits include *Wisconsin Academy Review, Flint Hills Review, The Florida Review, Literal Latte, Rosebud,* and *Earth Island Journal.* She serves as editor for AnthologiesOnline.com and teaches writing at Carroll College.

BARBARA KINGSOLVER is the author of numerous literary works, including *The Bean Trees, Animal Dreams, Pigs in Heaven, The Poisonwood Bible, Small Wonder,* and *Animal, Vegetable, Miracle.* She established The Bellwether Prize, which recognizes novels that serve as tools of social change. She and her family live on a farm in southwestern Virginia.

ANNE LAMOTT is the best-selling author of such books as *Traveling Mercies: Some Thoughts on Faith, Plan B: Further Thoughts on Faith, Grace (Eventually): Thoughts on Faith, Bird by Bird: Some Instructions on Writing and Life,* and *Operating Instructions: A Journal of My Son's First Year.* A past recipient of a Guggenheim Fellowship and a former columnist for *Salon* magazine, she lives in the San Francisco Bay Area.

VERA LANDRY writes about mothering and race for Anti-Racist Parent (www.antiracistparent.com). She is a former attorney and social worker who lives with her partner and their two sons in Berkeley, California. This essay was originally published in *Brain, Child* magazine.

STEPHANIE LOSEE is the coauthor (with Helaine Olen) of *Office Mate: The Employee Handbook for Finding—and Managing—Romance on the Job.* Her work has appeared in several anthologies as well as in *Fortune,* the *Los Angeles Times,* the *San Francisco Chronicle Magazine,* the *New York Post,* The Huffington Post, and *Child,* among others, and she is a frequent commentator on Northern California public radio.

JENNIFER MARGULIS is a freelance writer, consultant, parent educator, and former Fulbright scholar in Niger. She is the editor and coauthor of *Toddler: Real-Life Stories of Those Fickle, Irrational, Urgent, Tiny People We Love,* which won the Independent Publishers Book Association Award, and the author of *Why Babies Do That: Baffling Baby Behavior Explained.* Her writing has been published in *Ms.* magazine, *Pregnancy, Newsday, Mothering* magazine, *Brain, Child, World Pulse,* and dozens of other national and local magazines and newspapers. She lives in Ashland, Oregon, with her husband and three children. Find out more about her at www.toddlertrue stories.com.

SARAH MASTERSON is a writer, communications consultant, and mother based in Washington, D.C. She is the author of *D.C. Baby,* a resource handbook for Washington's expectant and new parents.

MARGARET MCCONNELL is a West Coast writer whose stories have appeared in publications such as *Hip Mama, Nervy Girl, Thereby Hangs a Tale,* and the travel anthology *A Woman Alone: Travel Tales from Around the Globe.*

KAREN MAEZEN MILLER is a wife, mother, Zen Buddhist priest, and author of *Momma Zen: Walking the Crooked Path of*

Motherhood. She lives in Sierra Madre, California, and can always be found at www.mommazen.com.

JENNIFER NIESSLEIN is the cofounder of *Brain, Child* magazine and the author of *Practically Perfect in Every Way: My Misadventures Through the World of Self-Help—and Back.* Her work has appeared in *The Nation,* on NPR's *Morning Edition,* on AlterNet, and elsewhere. She lives with her family in Charlottesville, Virginia.

HELAINE OLEN is the coauthor (with Stephanie Losee) of *Office Mate: The Employee Handbook for Finding—and Managing—Romance on the Job.* Her work in parenting, personal finance, and books has appeared in numerous print and online publications, including *The New York Times,* the *Los Angeles Times, The Wall Street Journal,* Salon.com, *The Washington Post,* and Babble.com. She is also the profiles and reviews associate editor at *Literary Mama* magazine, and is the mother of two boys. You can find her website at www.helaineolen.com.

BETH OSNES is one of the four founders of Mothers Acting Up. She holds a PhD in theater and teaches undergraduate courses and graduate seminars at the University of Colorado in Boulder. She was a Fulbright scholar in Malaysia, where she conducted field research on the shadow puppet theater. She is the author of *Acting: An International Encyclopedia* and *Twice Alive: A Spiritual Guide to Mothering Through Pregnancy and the Child's First Year,* and numerous articles on both theater and mothering. A book she is coediting, *The Theatrical Portrayal of Mothers,* will be published by Mellen Press in 2007. She created an educational video entitled *Cambodia: The People and the Performing Arts.* She and her husband, J.P., live in Boulder, Colorado, with their three children. For more information on Mothers Acting Up, visit www.mothersactingup.org.

NANCY PELOSI is the first woman to serve as the Speaker of the United States House of Representatives, a position that put her second in the line of presidential succession, after Vice President Dick Cheney. When she took office, she became the highest-ranking woman in the history of the U.S. government, bringing her closer in line to the U.S. presidency than any woman had come before. She is the mother of five and a grandmother.

ANNA QUINDLEN is the bestselling author of four novels (*Blessings, Black and Blue, One True Thing,* and *Object Lessons*) and four nonfiction books (*A Short Guide to a Happy Life, Living Out Loud, Thinking Out Loud,* and *How Reading Changed My Life*). She has also written two children's books (*The Tree That Came to Stay* and *Happily Ever After*). Her *New York Times* opinion column, "Public and Private," won the Pulitzer Prize in 1992. She and her family live in New York City.

GIGI ROSENBERG is a writer, teacher, and occasional performer of edgy, comic monologues on motherhood, relationships, and the existential nature of being. Her essays and how-to articles have been published in *Writer's Digest, The Oregonian,* the *Jewish Review, Cycle California! Magazine,* and *Parenting* (forthcoming). *The Hanukkah Bush,* her radio commentary, was featured on Oregon Public Broadcasting. Please find her at www.gigirosenberg.com.

DENISE ROY is the author of *Momfulness: Mothering with Mindfulness, Compassion, and Grace* and *My Monastery Is a Minivan,* named one of the best spiritual books of 2001 by *Spirituality*

& Health magazine. She is also in private practice as a licensed marriage and family therapist. She and her husband have three grown sons, a grade school–age daughter, and a foster daughter from Iran. Visit her website at www.deniseroy.com.

CINDY SHEEHAN is an antiwar activist, a founding member of Gold Star Families for Peace, founder of the former antiwar protest encampment Camp Casey, and the author of *Peace Mom: A Mother's Journey Through Heartache to Activism.* "Good Riddance, Attention Whore" was written in early 2007 to announce her decision to step down as the face of the peace movement and find other ways to work for political change. In 2007, she decided to run as an independent candidate against Nancy Pelosi for the U.S. House seat representing San Francisco in California's 8th congressional district.

TRACY THOMPSON is the author of *The Ghost in the House: Motherhood, Raising Children, and Struggling with Depression* and *The Beast: A Reckoning with Depression.* Her work has also appeared in a number of magazines, including *O, The Oprah Magazine* and *Civil War Times,* as well as in two other anthologies: *The Healing Circle,* published in 1998 by Plume Books, and *Out of Her Mind: Women Writing on Madness,* published in 2000 by Random House. In 1999, she was honored by the National Alliance for the Mentally Ill for her "lasting contribution to mental health issues." A former reporter for *The Washington Post* and the *Atlanta Journal-Constitution,* she lives in Maryland with her husband and their two daughters.

JUDITH STADTMAN TUCKER is a writer and activist. She is the founder and editor of the Mothers Movement Online, and has also worked on advocacy projects with Mothers & More, the National

Association of Mothers' Centers, Take Back Your Time, and the National Organization for Women's Mothers and Caregivers Economic Rights committee. She lives in Portsmouth, New Hampshire, with her husband and sons.

VALERIE WEAVER-ZERCHER is a writer and editor, and the mother of three young sons in Mechanicsburg, Pennsylvania. Her essays, reviews, and features have been published or are forthcoming in *Sojourners, Christian Century, Christianity Today, Brain, Child, Mothering,* and *The Other Side.*

STEPHANIE WILKINSON is the cofounder and coeditor of *Brain, Child: The Magazine for Thinking Mothers.* She lives with her husband and two children in Virginia.

MARION WINIK is the author of *Above Us Only Sky, Telling, First Comes Love, The Lunch-Box Chronicles: Notes from the Parenting Underground,* and *Rules for the Unruly: Living an Unconventional Life.* She has been a regular commentator on NPR's *All Things Considered* since 1991, and her articles and essays have appeared in *Redbook, Self, Cosmopolitan,* and numerous other publications. She lives in Pennsylvania with her husband and children. For more information, visit www.marionwinik.com.

ABOUT THE EDITOR

© Craig Strong

SHARI MACDONALD STRONG is a senior editor, political columnist, and former spirituality columnist at *Literary Mama* (www.literarymama.com). Her essay "On Wanting a Girl" appeared in the Seal Press anthology *It's a Girl: Women Writers on Raising Daughters* (edited by Andrea J. Buchanan). Her work has appeared in such places as *Mamazine* (www. mamazine.com), *Geez* magazine, and *Austin Mama,* and she has been a guest blogger for Leslie Morgan Steiner's "On Balance" blog at *The Washington Post* online. She is the mother of three children—twin boys born via gestational surrogacy, and a daughter adopted from Russia—all of whom were exceedingly pumped up about a potential John Kerry win in 2004, and all of whom joined the family via acts that were highly personal, maternal, and political in nature. Shari lives with her husband, photojournalist Craig Strong, and children in Portland, Oregon. You can visit her website at www.sharimac donaldstrong.com. For more information, and for bookclub/discussion questions, visit www.thematernalispolitical.com.